Ladies' Legs & Lemonade

Also by Kym Bonython

Modern Australian Painting and Sculpture
Modern Australian Painting 1960–70
Modern Australian Painting 1970–1975

In preparation:—

Modern Australian Painting 1975–1980

Ladies' Legs & Lemonade

KYM BONYTHON

RIGBY

GRAFFITI

I used to think I was indecisive . . . but now I'm not sure . . .

National Library of Australia
Cataloguing-in-Publication entry:

Bonython, Kym
 Ladies' Legs and Lemonade

 Index
 ISBN 0 7270 1191 x

 1. Bonython, Kym. I. Title.

700'.924

RIGBY LIMITED • ADELAIDE • SYDNEY
MELBOURNE • BRISBANE
First published 1979
Copyright © H. R. Bonython, 1979
All rights reserved.
Typeset by ProComp Productions, Adelaide
Photographs reproduced by Lasercolor, Adelaide
Printed in Australia by Griffin Press Limited, Netley

Contents

List of Illustrations

1

Beginnings

M Y FIRST 'at home' was 15 September 1920, the day I was born at 329 Wakefield Street, Adelaide, a broad thoroughfare lined with massive Moreton Bay fig trees. I became the almost classic example of the Virgoan, inheriting some of the virtues and almost all the faults of that astrological sign.

In 1978 Bryan Westwood, a talented artist whose work I have exhibited in my galleries for ten years, told me 'Virgo people have to do more than one thing at a time or they tend to go a little mad. Figuratively speaking, they cut the candle in two and then try to burn all four ends.'

Christmas must have been a busy time in the Bonython family. Father was born on September 10 and my brother Warren on September 11. Father was John Lavington Bonython, eldest son of John Langdon Bonython and Berlin-born Marie Louise Frederica Balthasar. The Bonythons are of Cornish stock, from the south-west corner of England. One, Stephen Bonython, was on record from the year 1277. From the somewhat later days of Symon, who died in 1398, there exists an unbroken ancestral line to the present day.

I am named after Hugh Reskymer Bonython, Sheriff of Cornwall in the 1620s, who lies buried in the Cury Church near Helston. The name by which I am known is the middle syllable of his second name. At the time of my birth the Rudyard Kipling book *Kim* was popular, and the combination of the two explains the unusual spelling of my nickname.

Among the few surviving family portraits is one of an eighteenth-century lawyer, Richard Bonython. Richard was something of a gambler. After losing most of the family properties, he hanged himself by tying a sheet around his neck and jumping off the balcony of Gray's Inn. He looked a little like me, too!

In the 1820s a Thomas Bonython decided to migrate to Canada. He lived for ten years on Prince Edward Island, where a son, George Langdon Bonython, was born. Thomas sent young George back to England to study as an architect, before he himself returned to England and sailed for South

1

Australia in 1840. George followed in 1854, bringing his six-year-old son John Langdon Bonython, and set up as a master builder in Adelaide.

In 1864 Langdon started as a junior reporter with Adelaide's morning paper, the *Advertiser*. By diligence and hard work he became a junior partner in 1879 and co-proprietor in 1884. In that year he also became Editor, a position he held for the next forty-five years. In 1893 he bought out his partner, Frederic Burden. In 1901 he was elected one of the original members of the first Commonwealth Parliament.

Langdon Bonython had eight children of whom my father Lavington was the eldest. He also joined the *Advertiser*, and played a leading part in its development, but his real interest lay in municipal affairs. At twenty-five he stood for election to the Adelaide City Council, and he was making an election speech when one of his audience, scornful of his apparent immaturity, shouted 'Does your mother know you're out?' To which Father replied 'Yes she does—and tomorrow I'll be in!' And he was, and there he remained as Councillor, Alderman, and Lord Mayor for the next forty-three years. No one has ever matched his record of long and faithful service.

In 1935, twenty-five years before his death, Father gave Adelaide its Town Hall clock. It stands high in the tower of the building where he spent so large a portion of his life, and by some coincidence it stopped almost exactly at the moment of his death. 'An electrical fault' was the official explanation of this incident.

Father's first wife was Blanche Ada, daughter of Sir John Cox Bray, K.C.M.G., Premier of South Australia 1881–84. They had three children: John (whom we call Jack), Betty, and Ada. Blanche Ada died in 1908, shortly after the birth of her namesake.

Constance Jean Warren, my mother, was born in 1891, daughter of Charles Herbert Warren and Alice Downer. She must have inherited her incredible energy from my maternal grandmother. On Gran's ninetieth birthday she planted no less than 3,000 anemones, but soon after that she broke a hip and lingered on painfully for several years until her death in 1960.

Mother had just turned twenty-one when she married Lavington in December 1912. She became known as the 'Baby Mayoress'. There were three children by this marriage: Warren born 1916, Katherine born 1918, and myself.

On one side of our Wakefield Street house lived the family physician, Dr John Gunson, and on the other side a German family named Langhans. Next to them were three unmarried Bowen sisters: Mabel, Leila, and Lois. Lois was my special friend and she spoiled me constantly. She was forever making gingerbread men, biscuits, and many other delicacies. They set the pattern for my outlandish tastes in food that earned me the nickname 'Clutterguts' in the second World War.

Down the road was the Adelaide Fire Station. Whitehaired and moustachioed Bob Morris, fireman-in-charge of the huge grey horses that drew the massive engines, came by our house each day while exercising his charges. He often took me for a ride on the engine or on the back of one of these enormous animals.

A double tramline ran down Wakefield Street. Among my earlier pleasures was the placement of some phosphorescent concoction upon the steel lines. It exploded with an ear-splitting bang when the vehicle passed over it, while we watched gleefully from behind the wooden fence facing the street.

My first contact with formal 'education' came in 1924 when one of my sisters took me to her school, Girton. In the 1970s Girton combined with King's College to become a co-educational school named Pembroke. I did not care much for the experience and spent the morning crying. Fifty-three years later, when I entered my youngest son Michael as a student at Pembroke, a question on the nomination form asked 'Have you or your family had any prior association with this school?' I could answer 'Yes, I attended as a pupil for one half day in 1924.'

In 1925 I joined the kindergarten section of another girls school, Creveen, in North Adelaide. In that year the family befriended a notable American concert singer, Arthur Jordan. When he returned to America he sent me an elaborate cowboy suit with real tigerskin on the chaps. I was so enamoured of this rigout that for several days I would not remove it and wore it to school—and to bed, I suspect. A photograph of me in this outfit was used on the invitations to my fiftieth birthday party, with the caption 'Forty-five years later—and still a lair!'

Among the things I remember about Creveen is the morning roll-call. The children sat on the floor in a circle, and the teacher gently touched our foreheads with a peacock feather as she called each name. My other most vivid recollection is of the furtive 'poppy shows' behind a hedge at the back of the school. Here curious students learned the fascinating difference between boys and girls through lifted skirts and lowered trousers.

One of our teachers was Kath Mellor, who became one of Australia's foremost kindergarten teachers and administrators. In 1977 we met again, less than a year before her death, and she recalled my mishap with a tiny bead I was playing with. I put it in my ear. And I pulled it out again. And I put it in my ear. And I pulled it out again. And I put it in my ear. And I could not get it out again. And the harder I tried, the further into my ear the bead went.

The Adelaide Children's Hospital stood just down the hill from Creveen. Miss Mellor told me that, after the doctor on duty had tried unsuccessfully to remove the object, I quavered 'I think I'll go and sit by the window. Maybe I might see a lucky black cat!'

Mother came to the school and took me to a doctor's surgery in the city where, under a general anaesthetic, the elusive bead was removed. After-

3

wards, as a special treat, she took me to Marshall's department store (later Myer's) and there allowed me to buy my very first gramophone record. It was an orchestral piece entitled *Over the Waves*, a twelve-inch recording with a bright green label that I can still visualise.

At Creveen I was asked to nominate 'the three greatest men the world has ever known'. I promptly answered 'Major Henry Seagrave, Jesus Christ and Dr Gunson.' Even at that point I had decided my priorities— Seagrave being the speed king of the generation!

My little world was snug and secure. Many good friends and several relations lived near Wakefield Street. Alfred Corbin, manager of the Adelaide Steamship Company, was a loving godfather. He lived just around the corner, on East Terrace, and his sweet wife Florence always had cold lemonade and hot buttered scones waiting every Sunday morning when I went there to play their pianola.

Next to the Corbins lived Dean Hay, a contemporary of my brother Jack. He was to introduce me to jazz in the very early 1930s. Close by, my Uncle Peter (Angas Parsons, later to become Chief Justice of South Australia) resided with his wife Elsie, my father's eldest sister. On the other side, nearer the city, lived Dr Letcher, whose stepdaughter Peggy was one of my first 'flames'. Years later, on my fourteenth birthday, Peggy raced up to me as I sat on my gaudily painted pushbike, gave me a brief peck on the cheek, and then rushed back into the house, a mass of blushing confusion.

The Brays, my Uncle Harry and Aunt Gertrude, were around the corner in Hutt Street. Harry was the brother of my father's first wife. Their eldest son, John, is one of South Australia's most distinguished scholars and served as Chief Justice of this State until 1978.

A hundred yards further west lived the Manning family. Richard Manning was one of my greatest friends in the pre-war days. His sister Eileen married Walter Janzow and through them, in 1932, I met young Clement Semmler. A brilliant student and schoolteacher, he became Assistant Manager of the Australian Broadcasting Commission and a champion of the cause of jazz music throughout his career with the A.B.C.

Also in Hutt Street was one of the town's dandies, Dr Harry Nott. He was always impeccably dressed and ever the possessor of the most exotic sports car in town. He and his equally glamorous wife had a daughter, Dorothy. She married the air hero Hughie Edwards, V.C., later the Governor of Western Australia.

Occasionally the even tenor of our existence was interrupted. In the mid-1920s our house was terrorised by a particularly sinister intruder. Several times the girls awoke to perceive this eerie figure standing over them. Once he had pulled back the bedclothes and was actually caressing the sleeping child. When the girls screamed he ran swift and silent from the room on sandshoed feet, at one time hurdling my cot to make his getaway through an open window.

4

One night Mother heard a noise in the cellar and awoke Father. He descended the stairs carrying a peculiar torch, with a light generated by the constant activation of a 'trigger' which produced a rather chilling, whistling sound. The beam soon picked up the crouching figure of the intruder. Immediately they came to grips.

I can still hear the weird noise of Dad's torch before he and the intruder battled in the cellar and then up the staircase, and recall my shock at hearing him call the prowler all kinds of obscene names. Probably we all understood such words but they were never used in polite families in those days, and they were certainly foreign to Father's strict yet gentle and religious nature.

Mother joined the fray, but the prowler broke free and escaped again. Some time later we discovered that he was an intimate and athletic friend of one of our domestics. He would often shin up and down the drainpipes to visit her bedroom during the night.

About this time, our family friend and relation Mollie Paxton (later Mrs Tim Hallam) asked me to tell her the things that I liked most in life. I quickly nominated 'Ladies' legs and lemonade' (although I pronounced this 'Yadies' yegs and yemonade'). These are still among my favourite objects— although I have raised my sights slightly since then.

By then, my brother Jack had gone to Cambridge to study Law. Apart from captaining Cambridge at lacrosse, perhaps his greatest international distinction during those years was to be named 'champion spitter of Cambridge'. He was able to attain a greater height on a certain university wall than any of his contemporaries.

In fields of more general acceptability he was an excellent tennis player and golfer and, until the achievements of my eldest son Christopher in the 1970s, he was the only sportsman of note in the entire family. Jack was the only Bonython who managed to break a leg in two different sports: once when playing Australian Rules football, and again while skiing in Switzerland.

My sister Betty, perhaps the most serious of the trio, accepted much of the responsibility of bringing up her younger half-brothers and sister. Ada was a 'flapper' who had a great crush on the heart-throb of the day, Rudolph Valentino. Upon the death of her idol, in 1927, Ada wore black stockings to school each day for two weeks— an unheard-of liberty for those days.

While we were at Wakefield Street I had my first experience of sex, at the grimy hands of our local dustman. His horse and cart plied the back lanes of our neighbourhood each week, and on the pretext of taking me for a ride on his creaky rattling dray he would soon be excitedly undoing my trouser fly. I do not believe I suffered any ill-effects.

2

Palmy Days at Eurilla

MOTHER LED a busy social life and very often we young children were left in the charge of our aged aunt, Min Warren. She was a spinster who had spent some time in China. One night, as she sat before her lonely fireplace in an Adelaide suburb, a piece of burning timber exploded. Apparently a piece of gelignite used to blast out tree stumps had remained within a mallee root, and the shattering bang made her almost completely deaf for the rest of her life. My enduring memory of dear Aunt Min is of her moving from room to room 'breaking wind' as she went. Her deafness obviously deluded her into believing that these emissions were silent, whereas the reverse was very much the case—to the amusement of we three children.

In my Creveen school report for 1925 is the comment 'He does not sing much.' This is still true, and my concept of purgatory is of spending eternity in a tourist bus forever travelling between Adelaide and Alice Springs, with the inevitable community singing all the way. My reluctance to break into song made it hard for me to credit Mother's comments about my 'angelic voice' after occasional ventures into 'The Rosary' or some similar ballad during my less self-conscious years.

We followed a nostalgic family ritual each Christmas Eve. All the children, led by Father and Grandfather Langdon Bonython, walked through the Adelaide streets crowded with people taking advantage of late-night shopping. We gaped at the tempting shop windows, while our elders dropped into stores and offices to wish 'A Merry Christmas' to friends and business associates. One of these worked in the clock department of Harris Scarfe's, and he sticks in my memory because he always wore a brown felt hat as he stood behind the counter. Adelaide was a more individualistic place in those days.

The smell of the Australian native pine trees tied to the verandah posts all along King William Street, the happy bustle of sightseers who good-naturedly jostled one another on the crowded footpaths, were in marked

6

contrast to our over-commercialised and frantic Christmas Eves that we endure nowadays.

Immediately after Christmas we would move up to our summer house, Eurilla, at Mount Lofty, east of the city and ten road miles from Adelaide. Eurilla (an Aboriginal word meaning 'mountain top') is a lovely old sandstone mansion built in 1884 for Sir William Milne and bought by Father in 1917.

Adjoining us to the north was Grandfather's property, Carminow, named after an old Bonython estate in Cornwall. The Carminow at Mount Lofty was built at about the same time as Eurilla. To the south was Mount Lofty House, a fascinating place filled with Oriental treasures by its owner, Mr J. W. Richardson, who had lived in Burma for fifteen years before he settled in the house in 1925.

I learned to ride a pushbike on the sloping driveways of Eurilla and Mount Lofty House. In those serene surroundings, I first fell in love with speed. I rigged a bent piece of cardboard around the bike's back wheel frame, with a length of string running to the springs of the bike seat. When I pulled the string the cardboard struck the spokes with a racket like the engine of a two-stroke motor cycle.

With so many children around, the house was full of gaiety and laughter. Mother was a renowned hostess and her parties were legendary. Games such as Charades, Sardines, and Seances were regular occurrences during those happy summer months.

To play Sardines we turned out every light and one person hid somewhere on the four levels of the building. Each of the rest of us had to locate the 'target', whether he or she was under a bed, in a wardrobe, or beneath the stairs of the tower. As each searcher found the hidden one he inserted himself into the hiding place. Soon we were crushed together, becoming more and more tightly packed as the searchers one by one discovered the heaving, giggling mass of humanity and jammed themselves amongst it.

Mother had 'a touch' with the ouija board and often got some quite prophetic answers from the upturned glass that glided across the polished table from letter to letter, spelling out its message. When she asked 'Will Kym marry?' the answer was 'Madly—at an early age!' Too true!

Our gardener and caretaker, Mr Mallyon, lived in the Lodge at the top of the Eurilla drive. He owned a quite ancient Indian motor cycle and side-car, and thereby hangs a tale.

Snakeskin accessories were in fashion, and I decided to make Mother a glamorous pair of snakeskin shoes. But first catch your snake!

Soon, on the Summit Road alongside Eurilla, I spotted a very dead sleepy lizard that had been run over by countless motor cars. I took this flattened corpse to our stables, where I realised that my first chore was to remove the creature's insides. After some thought an idea struck me: I would pump them out!

7

I cut off the extreme tip of the tail of the long-deceased reptile, then took Mr Mallyon's motor-cycle tyre pump from his machine and inserted the nozzle into the lizard's mouth. After a couple of vigorous strokes, my nostrils were assailed with a ghastly stench as black ooze bubbled from the lizard's rear end—and my enthusiasm for shoemaking promptly disappeared.

Neighbouring Carminow was one of the showplaces of the Adelaide Hills. I may not agree with my cousin Eric's belief that it was 'the most beautiful property in South Australia' but it certainly was magnificent, especially in those pre-war days. The odd thing is that Grandfather never, in my recollection, stayed a night in the house. He simply made regular Saturday-afternoon visits in his chauffeur-driven open Packard Tourer, with its hood folded neatly back.

Yet he employed a full-time head gardener, a Cornishman named Norman Triggs, and several under-gardeners. They kept the garden immaculate, with not one piece of gravel out of place. Exotic trees, shrubs, plants, and bulbs, many brought back from the old Bonython estates in Cornwall, grew in profusion in those long-gone days. A delicious aroma of ripening fruit hung heavily around the picturesque Apple House, half-way between the gates and the house overlooking beautiful Piccadilly Valley.

Unlike the garden, the white stone 'castle' of Carminow was a strangely forbidding building that seemed to have little of the charm and warmth of adjoining Eurilla—but maybe I was biased. An interesting feature was an ancient granite stone in the southern face of the building. Grandfather had imported it from Cornwall, and it had a strange history which, by the 1970s, had grown to legendary proportions.

When my wife and I returned to Adelaide in 1976, a young married girl worked part time for us. She had been brought up in the Mount Lofty area, and she told my wife that she had been told that the entire castle had been brought out from England, stone by stone. According to the story, the stones had been carried in three separate ships, which were caught in a mighty storm en route. Two sank, with great loss of life, but the survivor made it to Adelaide.

The facts were, as we laughingly enlightened her, that Carminow was built of South Australian stone, but Grandfather had imported three separate stones, each with the Bonython coat-of-arms engraved upon one surface. When the shipment reached Port Adelaide the crate containing the stones was dropped on the wharf and two of the three were shattered beyond repair. The remaining stone was carefully taken to its new home, where a careless tradesman inserted it with the undoubtedly weathered and worn family crest to the inside! How rumours do grow!

In the cow paddock at Eurilla we fashioned a dirt cricket pitch and used the trunk of a gum tree as a wicket. Warren and I, together with any friends who were staying with us, as well as the two Triggs boys, competed in a

TOP LEFT: Kym Bonython (*right*) with his mother, brother Warren and sister Katherine. TOP RIGHT: The Mount Lofty cowboy, 1925. BOTTOM: Christmas Day 1920, Carclew, North Adelaide. *Back row* Eric Bonython, Phil Angas Parsons, Jack Bonython, Lavington Bonython (Father) Herbert (Peter) Angas Parsons, Clive Bonython. *Middle row* Edith Bonython, Lady Bonython, Sir Langdon Bonython, Elsie Angas Parsons, Jean Bonython (Mother) nursing Kym, Barton Bonython. *Front row* Katherine, Ada, Betty and Warren Bonython, Geoffrey Angas Parsons (*Loaned by Warren Bonython*)

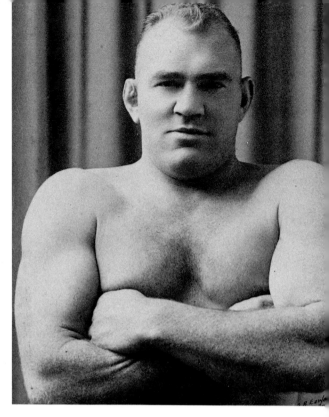
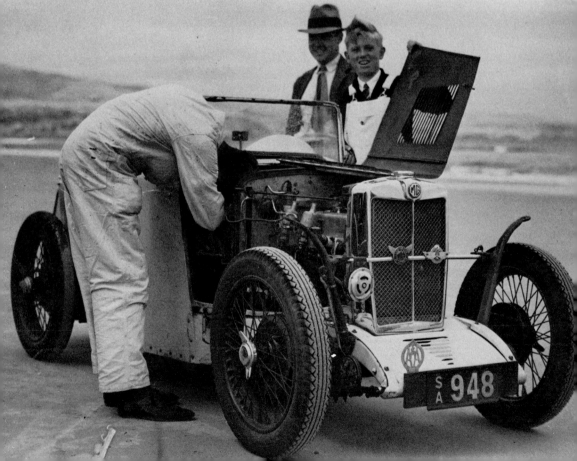

different Test Match each day. By 1978 the girth of that gum tree had grown until it was about five times the size it had been in 1930.

Apart from cricket, I passed the summer holidays at Eurilla by reading the books I had been given for Christmas, such as *Chums*, *Champion*, and *Boys Own* annuals: inventing tunes on the old Ronisch grand piano in the sitting-room; or playing hide-and-seek in the Carminow garden. At a younger age we kids explored the virgin bush running down the Mount Lofty slopes towards Piccadilly Valley. The discovery of large shell-like beetle wings, of many colours, indicated to us the recent presence there of fairies and gnomes.

The mains water supply does not run up to Eurilla and we had to rely on rainwater catchment from the roofs of the house. There was never much surplus for such luxuries as lawns, but we had one small patch where we played badminton, and where I pitched my Indian tent. One day a friend and I were indulging in a playful wrestling match on this grassed area when I felt the painful bites of 'jumper ants', so called because, when disturbed, they move in a series of miniature but aggressive leaps. We were rolling around on top of the ant nest.

My friend couldn't understand what I was yelling about, but I wrenched away from him and raced for the house. The ants were all over me and inside my clothes. Strewing garments as I ran, I made for the bathroom and leaped into the bath. The rainwater tanks were low and the shower gave only a pitiful trickle as I tried to wash the mass of infuriated creatures from my inflamed body. One jumper ant bite was painful enough, but I must have had over a hundred. It was a situation I have no wish to repeat!

Amidst life's uncertainties, there is only one thing of which I can be sure. I will not die an alcoholic. I have learned to tolerate champagne if I can disguise its taste with equal quantities of some sickening soft drink, but I have never developed a liking for grog. Perhaps subconsciously I have tried to live by a 'thought for the week' that I noticed outside a suburban Adelaide church at a very early age: 'It is better to be neat and tidy than tight and needy.'

Most of our side of the family inherited Father's almost paranoiac dislike of alcohol, a characteristic passed down from his own father. Mother had an occasional 'spot' but never very much. With this background I felt a profound shock at one Christmas dinner when Warren spoke authoritatively on the various brands and vintages of wines. However, I suspect that his interest in this field was accelerated by adherence to another family characteristic: a firm belief in the motto 'Waste not, want not.' Warren bought Romalo House, the former home of his father-in-law, Frank Young, which adjoined the famed Romalo Vineyards in the Adelaide foothills at Magill. The house included a sizeable and well-stocked cellar which I feel sure Warren could not allow to go to waste.

Thereafter, a feature of our family Christmas dinners was for Warren,

TOP LEFT: Kym Bonython walking back through the jungle to Koepang, February 1942. TOP RIGHT: New Zealand wrestler Bob King, 1935. BOTTOM: Kym Bonython (*right*) at Sellicks Beach Speed Trials 1935, with brothers Warren (*left*) and Jack. (*News and Mail photo*)

indulging his fanatical love of bushwalking, to bring the red wine in a haversack upon his back all the way from Adelaide. By the time he reached Eurilla, the wine was at just the right temperature.

Father was a very religious man who, for instance, would never allow us to play any games until after three p.m. on such holy days as Good Friday. Although the most considerate of men, he was conservative and shy, unlike my much more extrovert mother who, though equally kind, was renowned as the possessor of a wicked sense of humour.

She was quite a talented writer of verse, and in 1922 a small volume was published in a private edition. The following was not included, however:

> *A lady by name Jean Bonython*
> *Had good manners you could bet your life on.*
> *At Government House, she'd eat like a mouse*
> *But at home she'd stuff like a python.*

Almost until the end of her life she wrote a new verse on each of her birthdays. In 1928 she wrote:

> *My years have mounted to thirty-seven.*
> *But still I'm a long, long way from Heaven.*
> *If I'll ever get there, it's hard to tell*
> *But I'll make things hum if I go to Hell.*

She must have known something when she wrote the following lines when I was two:

> *When I behold your sleeping face*
> *Within your little cot*
> *I gaze upon its innocence*
> *And think of what you're not!*

Father was neither a violent man nor a disciplinarian. Apart from an occasional 'Slap him across the mouth, Jean!' he rarely laid a hand on his children. I was undoubtedly the most uncontrollable, and on one occasion, when I had been particularly wicked, he grabbed me, laid me across his knee, and started to smack my bottom. After the first stroke I cried 'You bwute!' After the second stroke 'You bwuddy bwute!' And on the third stroke 'You bwuddy bwugger!' At which point the entire family, including Father, collapsed into laughter and thereafter (my sister Betty claimed) never again did Father give me the treatment I regularly deserved.

Katherine tells a story of a family visit to Adelaide's Botanic Garden. While feeding bread to the ducks I overbalanced and fell into the lake. Katherine was wearing an overcoat, and so Mother had her take off her dress which I donned for the journey home. Despite this experience, dressing up in women's clothes has never become one of my fetishes.

Of Father's six children, Katherine showed most promise in the art and craft departments. She inherited Mother's gift for arranging flowers and was always quite skilled at knitting and making Barbola ware which she gave away to friends and relations at Christmas time. In later years she turned to weaving and to breeding black sheep. The fleeces supplied her looms. Her eldest daughter, Margaret, surpassed us all by becoming a weaver of national reputation. She has exhibited with success in both my Sydney and Adelaide galleries and had her work purchased by the National Gallery in Canberra.

A quest for money was an obsession from my earliest days. Quite often I would journey down Wakefield Street with a small tray slung around my neck, selling such trinkets as Mother may have brought back from dances on the Floating Palais. This was moored to the banks of the River Torrens which flows through the city. She gave me balloons, party caps, and coloured cottonwool balls, and I 'flogged' them to our indulgent neighbours. To add diversion I once distributed a sheaf of Father's unpaid bills into the letter-boxes of surrounding streets, to the embarrassment of my parents.

Once I positioned myself under the parental bed at Eurilla and with my feet pushing rhythmically upwards against the springs I chanted with maddening monotony 'Money, money, money, money, money' until my harassed parents got up and got rid of me with a few small coins. There are strange parallels in this story with the behaviour of my son Timothy which I shall recount later on.

One of my most lovable and colourful relatives was Uncle Frank Downer, brother of my grandmother. Uncle Frank was quite a ladies' man and one of the country's leading horsemen. A former Master of Hounds, he was the first person to jump the steeplechase hurdles on Adelaide's Morphett-ville Racecourse in 1885. At seventy-two he was also the last, immediately prior to their removal in 1935.

One of the characters of the town was Miss Nora Stewart, an austere martinet who for over forty years conducted *the* dance school of the city, which all aspiring young ladies and gentlemen must attend. Robert Helpmann was undoubtedly her star pupil. Mollie Paxton and Charles Lovett were two of her instructors. Mollie tells the story of Miss Stewart admonishing her innocent and blushing young things that under no circumstances were they *ever* to go out on the balcony with 'that Mr Downer' between dances at any function they might attend. In answer to their breathless and persistent demands for elaboration, Miss Stewart replied regally 'My dears! You'll learn later on, I'm sure!'

Once at a dinner Miss Stewart found herself seated next to Uncle Frank. As was his wont he spent the evening with his hand on her thigh, unclipping and clipping her stocking suspender. Eventually she said 'Mr Downer, if you persist in playing with my suspenders, when I get up from this table you are going to be just as embarrassed as I!' From what I've heard about Uncle Frank, I doubt it!

In 1928 we left Wakefield Street and moved to a large house on East Terrace, facing Victoria Park Racecourse and literally just a stone's throw from Mother's childhood home. Father named this house St Corantyn after an old church in Cornwall frequented by earlier generations of the family.

Jack had married, and on his return from Cambridge he moved into our old Wakefield Street home. Not long thereafter, both Ada and Betty took the plunge. Ada became engaged to Denis Heath from Birmingam, England, a member of a big brass fabricating business in that city. Victoria Reynolds, then the gossip writer for *Truth* newspaper, headlined the announcement with 'More Brass For Bonython Family'.

My eldest step-sister, Betty, was courted by a young lawyer and aspiring politician, Keith Cameron Wilson (later Senator Sir Keith Wilson), whom most of his friends called 'K.C.'. On the day that 'K.C.' fronted up to Father to seek his permission for the marriage, Betty was waiting nervously in the library. With typical obnoxious cynicism, I said 'I know what K.C.'s doing. He's asking Dad for yer hand in marriage!'

Consent was given, but it was decided that no announcement would be made for the present. Too late! I was already up and down Wakefield Street and East Terrace on my pushbike broadcasting the news!

So both girls were married within a month of each other in 1930, and only the children of the second family now lived in the parental home.

3

Masters and Motors

FROM CREVEEN SCHOOL I had gone to Queens College, North Adelaide, which I left in 1929 to enter St Peter's College. The Headmaster of the Preparatory School was 'Benny' Brooks. One of his sons, David, was my contemporary throughout my school life, and his slightly older brother, Phil, was to be a fellow flyer in 2 Squadron in Darwin during the black months of early 1942. In fact I saw poor Phil shot down by the Japanese in a daylight raid we made on Ambon.

St Peter's boasted a number of noteworthy and often colourful teachers. Our music master, George Gardener, had, shall we say, something of a drink problem. We began each morning with a brief service in the school chapel, and George played the pipe organ accompaniment for the hymns. Almost without fail, discordant notes would emanate from the instrument, causing George to tug his imaginary beard, scowl furiously, and soon disappear, ostensibly to make some adjustment at the rear of the organ. In fact he had a bottle of whisky secreted in the 'works'. He refreshed himself while the sniggering boys sang on unaccompanied.

My favourite teachers included Tim Wall, the famous Australian fast bowler; 'Cappo' Steel, who had been a captain in the 1st A.I.F; 'Rangi' Ware, named after a line of domestic brushware; the Reverend Pat McLaren; 'Balbas' MacIntosh of the beetling eyebrows, and Andrew Young. The latter was to leave school in disgrace for an aberration now seemingly of little public concern.

Andy Dyer, my geography teacher, is a remarkable man. Now over ninety, he seems as alert and sprightly as I recall him in 1930. I was never sure whether 'Andy' was an abbreviation of Andrew, or whether he was nicknamed after Andy Byer, a well-known character at the seaside resort of Victor Harbor. Andy Byer ran a small business selling fishing tackle, bait, and confectionery. One day I was in his rather seedy establishment when a hopeful fisherman asked for 'Six penn'oth of gentles, please, Andy.'

Andy's hand delved into the glass jar containing this mass of writhing

13

larvae mixed with sawdust. The maggots were served in a paper bag, and he turned to his next customer. 'Six penn'oth of boiled lollies, please, Andy.' In went the same hand to an adjoining jar of brightly-coloured sweets, and away went another satisfied and easy-to-please customer.

Felix Barton was a master who did much to involve the boys in outside activities. At one time he tried to build us a holiday camp on Summit Road, not far down from Eurilla. One necessary chore was to excavate a dam for water supply, and Felix always called for volunteers to dig what he called the 'bother', so as not to upset our delicate sensibilities.

'Snurbs' Thompson, our science master, took some outrageous ribbing from a procession of students over his many years at St Peter's. His attempts to coerce some unsuspecting student into taking one of his daughters to the dancing class became a regular Friday ritual.

One day some wag brought a piece of quartz featuring a large seam of gold for assessment by Mr Thompson. Snurbs, trying not to look too interested, murmured 'Hmm . . . and where did you get this rock, my boy?'

'Just off Summit Road, sir—a bit north of Bonython's house Eurilla.'

That was on a Friday. The next day a group of boys rode their pushbikes up to Mount Lofty and hid in the bush. Sure enough, Snurbs turned up in his ancient car together with two of his sons, with shovels, picks, and buckets. They made a predictably fruitless search, because the wag had taken the sample from Snurbs' own mineral display case in the school classroom.

Another character was Hubert Simpkins, who must have been one of the most likeably eccentric staff members in the history of the College. He was an Englishman (ex-army) and was once asked, in view of his oft-expressed low opinion of the place, just why he had come to Australia. He drawled 'Well, you know, the missionary spirit and all that, old boy!'

Simmo held court in a galvanised-iron classroom known as the Tin Tabernacle, built upon stilts at the eastern extremity of the school grounds. One day a freak hurricane lifted the entire building, complete with master and pupils, off the ground, and moved it several feet from its foundations. The bookcase behind Simmo's desk toppled forward, grazing his forehead, and he staggered into the adjoining more substantial building where Snurbs was conducting his class. Snurbs saw the trickle of blood on his associate's brow, and exclaimed 'Mr Simpkins, sir—you're hurt!'

'Only a flesh wound!' Simmo replied with fine bravado.

Sometimes Simmo rode to school on his horse, which he tethered outside the Tin Tabernacle. He gave some lucky boy the chore of feeding and grooming the animal, thus freeing him from the classroom for the rest of the lesson.

At other times he arrived on an ancient pushbike, on which he had to negotiate the sea of tall summer-dry grass that waved between the boundary fence and his classroom. Only Simmo knew, from experience, the meander-

14

ing track from gate to door. Occasionally some sadistic student placed a rock on his faintly defined path, and the class watched through the windows as the benighted teacher took the inevitable tumble.

Simmo lived in a world of his own. More than once the class gathered in his room while Simmo, slumped at his desk and gazing into space, seemed supremely ignorant of our presence despite the cacophony of noise. After ten minutes or more he would look up and say 'Good heavens—you boys here! How long have you been here?'

At one of the St Peter's fundraising fêtes a large glass jar was filled with dried peas and a leg of ham was offered as the prize for guessing the number of peas in the jar. Simmo applied all the logic of his scholarly skill by estimating the diameter of each pea and dividing that into the cubic capacity of the jar, and he never quite forgave me when my answer proved more nearly correct than that indicated by his calculations. My guess was a stab in the dark, but he came to within five of the correct number by his scientific calculations.

My favourite story about Simmo is of the day when, in a solicitous moment, he asked my classmate Geoff Larkins what he intended to do when he left school.

'I'm going on the land, sir!'

Simmo enquired 'What—as *manure?*'

Simmo died in Sydney in 1978.

Richard Holtham, the French master, lived in the Adelaide Hills and drove to town each day in a venerable Capitol-model Chev. I got on very well with Dickie, although his greatest admiration was reserved for boys with greater intellectual ability than I, alas, possessed—or at least had bothered to develop.

A freeway now runs over the spot where he used to live. Since his retirement he has spent most Australian winters in his beloved French Midi, returning to a tiny cottage in a town some distance from Adelaide. In 1978, exactly forty years after I left school, I visited him for the first time since my teens. In his late eighties, he still possessed the quick wit I remember so well. He told me that when such bright scholars as Don Dunstan, later Q.C. and Premier of South Australia, or David Hogarth (later Judge) were due to attend his class, he felt it necessary to do a little revision in case he was asked awkward questions. 'Of course, in *your* case, that was not necessary, dear boy!'

The annual fête was a big event on the school calendar. One of Dickie's pupils asked him if he would be attending, as he would like to introduce his mother and father to him. Dickie indicated that he would meet 'daddies' and '*perhaps* rich uncles' but '*not* mummies'.

Dunstan, who lived with his aunt, his parents being overseas, asked whether he might present her. A horrified Dickie replied 'Yoicks—aunties are even worse than mummies!'

15

Later in 1978 I was distressed to hear that he was in hospital. I sent him a 'Get Well' card. He replied 'My trouble is not ill health but just sheer old age. It will pass!'

Maybe I was too interested in outside activities such as motor racing and music, but I certainly was not a brilliant scholar except in 1935. Grandfather, in a rash moment (although by my past performance one could safely have taken bets), promised that if I topped my class he would give me whatever I wanted.

Somehow I achieved this rare result for each of the three terms. By a vast miscarriage of justice I even won the Scripture Prize, an incongruity of classic proportions. When the final results were announced Grandfather sent for me to come to his home in North Adelaide as he wished to give me 'a watch'. I did not intend to let him off so lightly, but I arrived expecting at least a gold watch on a gold chain. I bravely masked my disappointment when he presented me with a five-shilling stainless steel Big Ben pocket watch, suspended on a black bootlace, and kept my sights firmly fixed on 'whatever I wanted'. I knew exactly what *that* was.

Some years earlier, I had had my first motor cycle ride on an old Levis owned by Tom Power, boyfriend of Ida, one of our domestics. They married later and enjoyed a successful life in the hotel business. One unforgettable Saturday afternoon Tom took me up to Eurilla on the back of his motor bike, and I was hooked for life.

And so, just before Christmas 1935, I used threats of reprisals against my well-intentioned grandfather to blackmail Father into giving me my first motor cycle: a 175 cc XL model Triumph. A new way of life opened up for me.

Bob 'Bubbles' Richardson, from nearby Mount Lofty House, also was the proud owner of a Triumph, of slightly larger engine capacity. Between us we made the old Summit Road fairly buzz, but it wasn't long before I had my first and only accident. Riding down the gravelled Greenhill Road, then an alternative route from Mount Lofty to the city, I lost control rounding a curve of Mount Bonython and struck a fence post. The impact wrecked the front of the bike and threw me into the middle of the road.

My leg was badly cut and bruised but miraculously unbroken, and I was 'rescued' by our local milkman who loaded me onto the tray of his van and took me home. The bike suffered more damage than I did, and that fence post still has a slight list to starboard as a memento of my close encounter of the worst kind. The post has lasted longer than the motor cycle, but whether it will pre-decease the rider is anyone's guess.

From memory, that machine cost Father £69 10s. I expected it to perform like a much more powerful and expensive bike, but it was a good introduction to what I believe is one of the greatest pleasures available to man. Since December 1935 I have always owned a motor bike of some kind, and I remember each of them with special affection. After the Triumph briefly came a Royal Enfield, followed by one of my favourites: a Zundapp from Czechoslovakia. I still owned it when I joined the Air Force. Immediately after the war I bought an army disposals BSA and then, in fairly quick succession, two Vincent HRDs, a Bella scooter, a Honda, a Yamaha, and finally my present bike, a 1966 MV Agusta, acclaimed as the 'Rolls Royce of motor cycles'.

I ranged far and wide on my beloved bikes. In 1936 I rode alone to Melbourne and back, taking a day each way. That's nothing to brag about nowadays, but in 1936 long stretches of roads were merely sandy tracks, so treacherous that you had to 'paddle' your feet each side of the bike merely to maintain balance.

But I have never owned any machine for as long as the MV. While I was thinking about buying one I read a eulogistic road test in an American trade magazine, and I was captivated by the opening paragraph. It stated 'The MV Agusta's exhaust note can only be likened to the unique sound produced by the tearing of rich silk!' I repeated this to my friend Ross Luck, who remarked 'Christ—every time you ride the bloody thing you'll think you're raping someone!'

As a dedicated motorcyclist I abhor the legislation which forces one to wear a crash helmet. To an old enthusiast like me, half the joy of motor-cycling lies in the exhilaration and freedom so much reduced by the clamping confines of a helmet.

This legislation has been a contentious issue all over the world. In America it is enforced in some States but not all, and in one of the former a rider was halted by a police car and asked why he was not wearing a helmet.

'I am—I'm wearing it on my knee,' he said.

'That's no good—the law says you gotta wear it on your head.'

Reluctantly the bikie transferred the helmet to his head. A few miles further on he had an accident—and hurt his knee!

Another story tells that, during the long-haired, unisex era of the 1960s, a scruffy-looking pair was quizzed by a patronising 'wrinkly' who asked 'Which one of you has the menstrual cycle?'

'Oh no—we've got a Honda.'

Speed was top-fashion with young blades of the 1930s. By the time I turned thirteen, my brother Warren had taken delivery of one of the first MG sports cars, a Midget J2. In this car he successfully contested hill climbs, reliability trials, road races, and speed attempts. In February 1935, under the auspices of the Sporting Car Club of South Australia, he and his MG were among three cars to make attempts on Australian speed records at Sellicks Beach, south of Adelaide. This is a long stretch of sand where, many years earlier, an unlimited Australian record had been established.

The other entrants were John Dutton, of a noted South Australian country family, with his 30/98 Vauxhall, and another scion of a pastoral family, Peter Hawker, with his specially built twin-engined Essex.

Alas, Hawker's car blew a hole in a piston shortly after crossing the starting line at well over 120 m.p.h. John Dutton achieved a two-way speed of 92·34 m.p.h. Warren's figure of 76·49 m.p.h. incredibly stands, even in 1978, for this particular engine class.

My friend Bryan Monkton had flown down from Adelaide in his antique DH9 biplane and landed on the beach. I took a movie film of this machine with its four cockpits, one behind the other, flying along the course while the Essex Special flashed beneath it at what looked to be twice the speed of the aircraft. Unfortunately that film and all my motor racing reels disappeared mysteriously while I was on war service. They would be invaluable historical records today.

The trip home to Adelaide lingers in my memory. It was a protracted and increasingly hair-raising pub crawl. The contestants, together with numerous fans, made their first stop at the Sellicks Hill Hotel. Thereafter it was the survival of the fittest through the various pubs en route to the city.

Among the entourage was John Dutton's brother Dick, who possessed one of the most beautiful cars ever seen in South Australia: a 1934 Packard V12 drophead coupé. He and the other drivers, infected by the speed trials, tried to set some records of their own on the way home.

At about 100 m.p.h. the convoy of cars rounded a bend to enter the township of Aldinga, and encountered an elderly woman driver taking lessons in reversing on a normally lonely stretch of road. Her car stalled diagonally across the road, and some of us screamed past to the left, others to the right of the distraught learner.

Shortly thereafter, on a series of switchbacks that I still have trouble in identifying, the road took a sudden ninety-degree right turn immediately over the brow of a steep hill. Dick Dutton, by then well-lubricated, hit the turn at just under the 'ton', and for months after that the broad black skid marks of the noble Packard remained as mute evidence of the powerful braking system of the American juggernaut.

For most of the trip home I rode as passenger with Warren, who at that time was still a teetotaller. On other legs I travelled with some of the less inhibited members of the party. It was a nerve-racking experience, but we all made it back to Adelaide without accidents or arrests to mar the historic occasion.

Only five days later Warren won the fifty-mile handicap race on the beach at Buckland Park, north of Adelaide. The press of the day wrote 'A feature of his win was the system carried out in conjunction with his younger brother in the pits. His brother signalled to him at each lap the impression he had made upon the rest of the field and the number of laps traversed.' Big deal! In fact, Warren attributes his success to the sign 'GO FASTER!' which I held up each time he passed the pits.

Another feature of the meeting was a race between the Dutton Packard and Barr Smith's Rolls. The latter won by a chromed bumper.

18

My first competitive appearance was at a Sporting Car Club hill climb just out of Victor Harbor. A section of the road alongside the Bluff and up Waitpinga Hill was closed for the occasion. I was permitted to make a run on my hard-done-by Triumph.

With silencer removed, I was waiting at the start line wearing a tightly fitting T-shirt. My moment of glory was eclipsed by a repulsive child who came up and shouted 'Are you a little boy or a little girl?' My subsequent run did nothing for the record books, either.

Grandfather owned one of the first cars in Adelaide. It was perhaps from him that the story came about a well-known Adelaide doctor who owned another vehicle. Like many early cars it had a peculiarity: in this case that you had to press down hard on the clutch pedal to engage reverse gear. He knocked down a pedestrian and in his anxiety pushed the clutch pedal down too hard. The car promptly went into reverse and ran over the victim again.

The pace setter in the Bonython family was my maiden aunt Ada. The youngest of my grandfather's family, she had a mad passion for cars. Some ten years before her death she had already owned well over thirty vehicles — one for only half a day! An incredible record for those days.

Ada, like her younger namesake in our family, was full of life. Besides being a car freak, she hero-worshipped Napoleon Bonaparte, and she was also quite a poet.

One of Ada's cars was a racing Baby Austin with a clutch so fierce that I do not think she ever tamed it. The first few yards of every journey were a remarkable series of leaps and bounds, with Ada hanging desperately to the wheel.

She and her older sister Edith were spinsters, though they had been great beauties in their youth. Many times I wondered why neither had married — perhaps Grandfather had frightened off would-be suitors. Ada was the more worldly of the two, and Edith became almost a recluse in her later years. She hated the sunlight. Her father's house, Carclew, was a dark place at the best of times but Edith always had the heavy velvet curtains drawn and the electric light on, even in the middle of the day.

She also wore black veils to protect her eyes against the light. Her only outings were regular daily runs in one of Grandfather's cars, driven by Mr Wood the chauffeur, usually along the same uninteresting route with all the car blinds drawn and her face obscured behind her veils. A chrome handrail ran along the back of the front seat and she had it wrapped in black cloth to eliminate its glare.

Both daughters lived for their father, and they must have had a lonely life when he died in 1939. Edith died in 1956 but Ada survived until 1965.

Their isolation from society kept the sisters ignorant of many worldly matters. For instance, I believe that neither of them ever rode on public transport.

Cousin Clive was their main confidant. He recalls an occasion when Edith telephoned him at his office with a curious story. She had received a strange phone call in which an anonymous voice asked 'Is that Miss Bonython? Miss Edith Bonython?'

'Yes.'

'I'm sending you a gross of French letters.'

'Oh — that's *terribly* nice of you!'

The caller cut off and she rang Clive to ask the meaning of these 'French letters' that she was so kindly being sent.

As a child I spent many a Sunday evening at Carclew, reading to the aunts funny stories from newspapers and asking them riddles I had read in 'Possum's Page' of the Adelaide *Sunday Mail*; playing the latest Clapham and Dwyer, Jack Hulbert or Harry Tate comedy records; and then moving into the room where Grandfather's pianola was located, to amuse myself for hours while Dad kept Grandfather company in his gloomy library.

Grandfather kept up his newspaper routine, of not retiring until two or three a.m., until the end of his long life. Even in mid-winter he never had a fire in his study, his only concession being a woollen rug around his legs.

Carclew is situated on the best piece of real estate in Adelaide, on the crest of Montefiore Hill, overlooking the city and the Oval. It is a monstrous piece of architecture, looking rather like a set from an Alfred Hitchcock movie. When Ada died the family put the property on the market and it was purchased by the Adelaide City Council as the site for the proposed Festival Concert Hall. After much controversy, mainly centring around Carclew's inaccessibility to public transport and the fact that it is directly beneath the flight path to Adelaide Airport, another site was chosen near the Adelaide Railway Station and the Festival complex was built there.

The decision against Carclew sparked off a great discussion as to what should be done with this valuable piece of land, and the *Sunday Mail* canvassed a number of local identities for their comments. My cousin Eric, who had been brought up in Carclew following the premature death of his parents, and whose taste in art and furniture was very much nineteenth-century, was anxious for the building to be used as an annexe of the State Art Gallery and as a home for a display of Victoriana.

I was uncharitable enough to let myself be quoted as saying 'The only reason the building should be preserved is that it is a prime example of the world's worst period of architecture' and Eric never forgave me. In retrospect, and perhaps with the mellowing of years, I now believe it is an historic building that tells something of an important period of our civilisation. But it certainly is not a house I would care to live in.

The State Government bought the property from the Council and turned it into a children's recreation centre. In the 1970s, during the financial recession, far more than the original value of the property was spent in restoring it to a condition unmatched since the 1880s.

4

Of Ovals, Reels, and Rings

As A SPORTSMAN, I never set the world on fire. Participation in all sports was compulsory at St Peter's College, but my only glimmering of ability was as a sprinter. I won a few medals, and a tiny cup about thrice the size of a thimble, when I ran a close second to Philip Game in the Junior School 100 yards Championship in 1932.

I was pretty hopeless at football and finished my scholastic years in the 5th eighteen. This was about as low as one could sink, but I was a little better as a cricketer. I played regularly in the school Thirds, and for a little while, as a result of a blazing 125-not-out innings against St Peter's arch-rival Prince Alfred College (during which I smashed three school windows) I was elevated into the Seconds.

Alas, I never repeated that apparently freakish performance. As with some other things during my life I was inclined impetuously to lash out at every ball. On the rare occasions when I 'had my eye in' I acquitted myself reasonably well, but such innings were few and far between.

But I remained a keen follower of cricket and I've often found great relaxation in just lying on the grassy mounds at the Adelaide Oval, one of the most beautiful playing fields in the world, and watching the often lethargic action unfold on the green spaces before me.

I was there on that memorable day in 1933 when the English Captain, Douglas Jardine, directed his fast bowler Harold Larwood to bowl the infamous 'bodyline' at the Australian team under Bill Woodfull. When one of Larwood's lethal deliveries felled Woodfull with a blow over the heart, South Australians probably came nearer to vaulting the picket fence and tearing the Poms apart than they ever have before or since.

In those days, before the start of the day's play, it was a ritual to purchase one's 'box lunch' from the long-gone Okeh Café in King William Street just near the Town Hall. This enforced an early start from Mount Lofty, and then, box lunch in hand, I had to join the great queues lined up outside the Oval gates awaiting admission.

21

During one Test Series the entry was so slow that I made the un-characteristic gesture of bursting into song with 'If I had the wings of an angel, Then over these walls I would fly', much to the amusement of the equally frustrated multitude surrounding us.

Katherine and I once attended a Test with our older sisters' friend, Roma Woolcock. Our seats were half-way along a tightly-packed row of benches, and with monotonous regularity we forced our way past the other unfortunates seated between us and the aisle in order to purchase soft drinks, or another meat pie, or to go to the lavatory. As we approached one couple for the tenth time, the man said resignedly 'Here come the Mitchells' (Mitchells being a well-known Adelaide furniture remover whose slogan was 'keep moving').

Those were great days for cricket fanatics and I was fortunate to see some of the outstanding performers at the very peak of their careers: such sportsmen as Donald Bradman, Len Hutton, Bill Ponsford, Herbert Sutcliffe, and Clarrie Grimmett.

I grew up in the age of the moving picture, and I well recall going to the Wondergraph Theatre in Hindley Street in 1929 to see the world's first talking picture, *Sonny Boy* with Al Jolson.

Being something of a loner I sat in the back row of the dress circle, but I soon made friends with the usherettes. I still see a few of them to this day. One of my favourites was Betsy Rosengarten. Another, employed at the York Theatre in Rundle Street, was a young Swedish girl then living in Adelaide. She was Mai Zetterling. Years after her return to Europe she became one of the leading film directors of the 'new wave' with her then startling production, a film version of her book *Night Games*.

On Saturday mornings I went to the Regent Theatre for the children's matinées. Among the variety of cartoons and short films presented for the entertainment of the young there was an on-stage quiz, the main prize being either a garish mantel radio or a ghastly three-piece moquette lounge suite. Fortunately for Mother I was never able to scoop the pool.

The release of the African adventure movie *Trader Horn* at the Majestic was a red-letter day for Adelaide's youngsters. I remember going to the theatre for the eleven a.m. session on its first Saturday morning and remaining there until the evening session concluded at eleven p.m. Modern adolescents, inured to every kind of blood and violence on the screen, probably would find the film pretty naive, but in those days its presentation of a group of whites braving danger from savage tribes was enough to make young hair stand on end.

Jackie Coogan, Wallace Beery, Harold Lloyd, Tom Mix, Charlie Chaplin, Buster Keaton, Our Gang, The Collegians, and Laurel and Hardy were among my favourites. In the silent-screen era, movies had a glamour which seems to have faded. We certainly didn't notice the lack of sound. An orchestra, or at least a piano, played appropriate music or provided sound effects for each scene. During the first World War epic *Hell's Angels* a motor cycle was set up in the orchestra pit, and during the exciting dog fights on the screen the bike was fired up and the throttle 'blipped' to coincide with the diving and rolling war planes above.

Wests Theatre, in Hindley Street, was a huge movie house that boasted a large live orchestra. Directed by an English saxophonist, Howard Jacobs, it played a bracket of tunes prior to the show, and another during the intermission before the main film. Since those days another theatre has been constructed upon the old site, and even that disappeared in 1978 to make way for a large Chinese restaurant.

By masterly persuasion, I convinced Father that if he purchased a movie projector there would be less demand by me for money to go to the theatres each Saturday. In 1932 he bought a Kodascope Model C and a 16-mm camera. In the cellar beneath our East Terrace house I set up the 'Theatre du Roi' with a 'sixpence admission' sign prominently displayed as one descended the stairs. My homemade movies may not have been expert but they are certainly fascinating reminders of a time long past.

In the early 1930s Mother took me to Melbourne and we stayed at the Menzies Hotel. She enjoyed breakfast in bed, something I have never learned to tolerate. So, while she was eating in her room, I was seated in solitary splendour in the palatial hotel dining-room. After about four days I was curious enough to ask the waiter why the white-hatted gentleman was peering around the kitchen door in my direction. He said 'The chef wants to see the person who orders sausages, ice cream, and ginger ale for breakfast each morning!' It will not surprise my friends to learn that, if I had my choice, this would be my breakfast menu today.

Another early pleasure was attending the wrestling and boxing matches presented during the winter months in the empty pool area of the Adelaide City Baths, then located on the present site of the Festival Theatre. The manager of the Baths was Charlie Bastard who, naturally enough, insisted upon verbal emphasis on the second syllable of his name.

I don't think the action was quite as deliberately fixed in those days as it seems to be now. The grunts of effort and yells of pain seemed to be more genuine.

Billy Meeske, Tiger Higgins, Hughie Whitman, and Big Chief Little Wolf were some of the big names of the day. Meeske and Higgins in particular were arch-rivals, and I remember when Meeske picked up from the corner of the ring a sawdust-filled enamel bowl into which contestants expectorated between rounds, and crashed it on the head of his seemingly unsuspecting opponent with such force that the noise echoed through the cavernous space of the Baths.

During another bout, when Hughie Whitman was officiating as referee, Meeske ripped the white cricket pants from Hughie's body to reveal a considerably motheaten pair of woollen trunks beneath. If he'd worn them

23

on a metropolitan beach he probably would have been prosecuted, even nowadays.

My favourite was a Greek-American, Leo Demetral. Like most wrestlers he was a huge man and he sported two magnificent cauliflower ears. I had the pleasure of personal acquaintance with him, made through a gymnasium I was attending, and I found him an extremely pleasant person. Occasionally, on Sunday mornings, I went with him to another gym, on Hindley Street, where he worked out with local hopefuls.

I remember him perched precariously on the flimsy pillion seat of my diminutive motor cycle while I took him to Adelaide's airport at Parafield. We watched Keith Litchfield, whom I knew and admired for his prowess as a speedway rider, trying to coax his underpowered, two-cylinder homemade *Flying Flea* into the air.

Demetral's *bête noire* was a New Zealand-born wrestler, Bob King, whose speciality was the 'flying tackle'. He bounced from one side of the ring to the other, ostensibly to confuse his opponent. When the other man was sufficiently confused, King lowered his head like a fighting bull, butted him in the midriff, lifted the dazed adversary above his head, and crashed him to the canvas to achieve a 'fall' upon the mandatory count of three.

Perhaps some of Bob King's weatherbeaten looks could be attributed to an incident in New Zealand. The ring was set up on the stage of an Auckland theatre and at the climax of the bout Bob went into his famous flying tackle routine, culminating in his head-down charge. But at the last moment his opponent took unscheduled avoiding action. The human missile shot past its target, flew head-first between the ropes, and then, with a resounding crash of timber and chords, through the lid of the grand piano standing several feet below in the orchestra pit.

Occasionally I came suddenly face-to-face with King's fierce countenance in the streets of Adelaide. He, knowing my allegiance to his rival Demetral, lunged snarling towards me and caused my youthful heart to miss several beats. Nearly forty years later I bumped into him once again, in Sydney's Kings Cross. By then he was a Jack-of-all-trades, doing odd jobs around the apartment of the celebrated Australian artist, Russell Drysdale. The stage mannerisms of the 1930s had disappeared and he was a gentle and kindly character for whom nothing was ever too much trouble . . . perhaps the genuine personality of a man who had been acting a part twenty-four hours a day.

Over the years, during my time as a gallery owner in Sydney, I had occasion to use Bob's services more than once, notably when I went to the apartment of a long-term debtor to retrieve a valuable work of art for which I had not been paid. Bob King's countenance may have struck fear into the heart of the miscreant, but he still did not pay!

In the 1930s I went with my brother Jack to the Exhibition Building on North Terrace, long ago torn down, to witness a demonstration boxing

Top: 2 Squadron Lockheed Hudson, flown by Flight Lieutenant Simon Fraser, near Darwin 1942. (*Author's photo*). Bottom: 2 Squadron Hudson afire at R.A.A.F. base Darwin, 1942. In foreground is wreck of U.S.A.F. Kittyhawk destroyed while taking off during the first Japanese raid on Darwin.

display by a fighter regarded as a potential champion of the world. This coffee-coloured Adonis was Young Stribling. Never before had I seen such a magnificent physical specimen nor such a classic boxer. Unfortunately he was killed in an automobile accident not long after his Australian tour. The promise evident even to my untrained eye was never to be realised.

During the height of the wrestling boom, rival promoters occasionally staged a series of matches in the Exhibition Building in competition with the City Baths management. Victoria Reynolds, the society writer for *Truth*, was quite a regular patron at these displays. Once she was sitting behind me during a tense moment when both fighters were silently grappling with each other on the mat. 'Bite him in the bread basket!' exhorted Miss Reynolds viciously.

Despite her rather awesome appearance and acid tongue Victoria Reynolds had a heart of gold, and I recall Mother's admiration of the many good deeds she did for others behind the scenes. Her platinum-blonde daughter, Tanya, was one of the genuine beauties of Adelaide in those pre-war days.

Tim, the eldest son of my second family, became equally enthusiastic about wrestling during the early 1970s. 'World Championship Wrestling', as it was by then titled, was successfully promoted in Australia by a real showman, Jim Barnett. I often met Jim, an American, on domestic airliners travelling between the Australian cities and we became quite friendly. He had an apartment in Sydney and another in Paris, but he called Atlanta, Georgia, his home. He was a great art fancier and his various residences, he said, were decorated with some of the greatest names in art of the twentieth century.

To my perhaps jaundiced eye, wrestling had by the 1970s become rather a farce. A contestant could send his opponent into paroxysms of pain from blows or kicks that obviously missed their mark.

Each Sunday morning local TV stations screened highlights from the previous week's matches, interspersed with plugs for coming attractions from contestants due to appear the following week. Among the most entertaining of these latter-day malevolent mat men were two Germans, the Von Steiger Brothers. They dressed in black leather jackets, black leather pants, black leather boots, and black polo-neck sweaters. Each carried a leather jockey's whip with which he cracked his leggings to emphasise a point during interviews. Each sported a polished bald head.

I remember one particular 'come on' which went 'My brother and I come from Hamburg, the toughest city in all of Europe. We come from the toughest street in all Hamburg. The further down the street you go, the tougher it gets. We — lived — in — the — LAST — house!'

The last time I met Jim Barnett was on a flight between Adelaide and Sydney. The previous night I had taken my boys to the wrestling. A feature of that entertainment had been the appearance of two sets of dwarfs whose

TOP: Flight Lieutenant Rob Burns Cuming, Ambon 1941, on the site where the Japanese massacred a number of Australian servicemen four months later. BOTTOM: Wing Commander Frank Headlam, C.O. 2 Squadron, with Flight Lieutenant Jim Hepburn and the daughter of an American missionary, Ambon 1941. (*Author's photos*)

nimble antics had the crowd on its feet, open-mouthed in amazement at their speed and timing.

During the flight two of these little fellows came up to Barnett like the proverbial cats, with their faces wreathed in smiles. Later, he confided in me that the boys were feeling particularly relaxed and happy because an Adelaide schoolmistress had come to their hotel after the contest and 'taken care' of each of them in succession!

As my father used to remark 'As the old woman said when she kissed the cow: "There's no accounting for tastes."'

There could have been some concerned parents if they'd known of the nocturnal pastimes of their children's teacher, but maybe she was a teacher at one of Adelaide's new Colleges of Advanced Education.

5

Four Wheels of My Own

As a TEENAGER, to use a then-unknown word, I counted the days until I was old enough to drive a car of my own. In South Australia you are not permitted to drive a car on public roads until the age of sixteen, but I had in fact practised on several occasions with my brother-in-law, K.C. Wilson. Every few weeks he drove his tiny red Baby Austin about fifty miles from Adelaide to Victor Harbor in the course of his legal practice and sometimes I went with him. He would allow me to take the wheel briefly on the homeward journey along straight stretches of road.

In those days there was no such thing as a driving test. You merely went to the Motor Vehicles Department, filled out a form, paid your ten shillings, and the necessary licence was issued. You could legally obtain a motor-cycle licence at fourteen and this included the right to ride a motor cycle and side-car—a three-wheeled vehicle. Three-wheeled cars were considered to be in the same category as motor cycles, so that you could even drive these at the lower age.

The Morgan three-wheeler was a well-known English vehicle at that time but I had no hope of persuading Father to buy one for me. Nor did I succeed in my vain efforts to have Alec Winter, a midget car driver at the speedway, build me such a machine. So I had to wait until I reached the magic age of sixteen. One of Warren's friends was a mechanic and used car dealer named McCallum, who had his garage almost in the centre of the city in Pirie Street. Mac occasionally worked on Warren's MG. Knowing my passion for cars, particularly racing cars, he offered me an Amilcar Grand Sports for the princely sum of £10.

It was the identical model used in that hilarious French comedy film *Monsieur Hulot's Holiday*, and this particular car had been owned by one Pompey Pederson. In it, years before, he had set the speed record between Adelaide and Victor Harbor, and by the time I laid eyes on it it was even more quaint than the specimen driven by Jacques Tati.

The bonnet was flattened aluminium, held in place by two crossed

27

leather straps. The crude tail section was three-ply wood. The seats were lumps of sponge rubber. The headlights were attached to a flimsy bar that hung precariously between the two front mudguards. In the centre of this bar was an antique but strident motor horn. I loved it all on sight.

I cannot remember how I raised the £10 — what I sold or whom I blackmailed. But I bought it, and I imagine it cost my poor father about £20 per week to keep it on the road thereafter.

I picked it up at five o'clock one night and proceeded to drive it home through rush hour traffic. It was my first solo in a motor car inside or outside the city, and when I'd driven about 500 yards from the garage I had to negotiate my first niney-degree turn to the right, into Hutt Street. Either I was going too fast or the tyres were under-inflated, but by the time I straightened up both rear tyres had come completely adrift from their rims. The tubes on each side were protruding, ominously blown up, and stretched almost to bursting point like two giant gumboils.

I hot-footed it back to Mac who came out in the fading light and replaced the tyres. I then crept home in a much more conservative way until I reached East Terrace.

My *affaire* with the Amilcar absorbed most of my waking hours. At least once per week I painted that pointed tail section in a different hue, and after a couple of months one could chip off a piece of paint resembling the then-popular rainbow 'all-day suckers', sold in the local shop for a penny each.

The car had no hood. If it rained I carried an umbrella, which considerably reduced my progress. In the vibrating timber floor there happened to be a cunningly concealed hole. A speed of 37 m.p.h. created a blast of air guaranteed to raise the skirt of any unsuspecting girl who ventured into the cramped cockpit, and blow it over her head. This certainly proved to be a good ice breaker!

In the early hours of one morning, when I should have been home in bed, I had just dropped the 'girl of the month' at her parents' home when for no apparent reason the confounded horn started to blow continuously. It was well past her curfew also, and this sudden raucous noise promised future restrictions on our clandestine outings. I was never much of a mechanic, and I could think only of one way to stop its raucous yawping. I grasped the electrical wire that led to the horn, gave it a tremendous tug, and the entire bracket on which the horn and headlights were attached came off in my hand — and the horn kept blowing — and the lights kept blazing! At this point 'Dad' arrived on the scene. Exit another 'flame'.

During the 1936 Christmas holidays, the Sporting Car Club promoted a carnival of road racing on a section of public highway in the Port Elliot–Victor Harbor area. Most of the big names of the day came from interstate to compete in the events.

When it came to preparing the course, necessity was the mother of invention. One of the Club members, Freddie Le Messurier, perched precariously upon the tail section of a diminutive Austin, marking the white track lines by pouring paint onto the rear tyre of the vehicle as it moved cautiously around the circuit.

Among the interstate visitors was Geoffrey Derham, a new acquaintance from Melbourne and a member of a well-known stockbroking firm in that city. When the meeting was over, I was keen to drive my Amilcar back to Melbourne in convoy with Geoff and his smart Vauxhall Sports, but Father refused to finance the trip. But he rarely questioned the running repairs bills that he paid for me, from another Adelaide workshop owned by Jack MacDonald. I knew that Father would not receive the account until the following month and so I had Jack build me a huge petrol tank holding nearly twenty gallons—almost enough to get me to Melbourne. The only place to fit the tank was on a bracket beneath the bonnet extending half-way over the top of the engine.

We went to Melbourne by way of Mount Gambier, which involved about 150 miles of rough gravel roadway, particularly through South Australia's Coorong. By the time we reached our first stop, Geoff could hardly drive for laughing. He was following me in his much more sophisticated vehicle at a safe distance, and he said my flimsy Amilcar resembled a mud crab scuttling from one side of the road to another as I bounced my way over the corrugations.

Alas, the bumps sprang some leaks in the newly-soldered seams of the petrol tank. Fuel was dripping ominously close to the spark plugs of the ancient engine as we limped into our stopover for the night. Next day an intrepid and somewhat foolhardy Mount Gambier mechanic endeavoured to re-weld the seams. Petrol vapour in the tank exploded perilously close to his face, but eventually I was back on the road. However, the rough section of the previous day also had bent the tail shaft. Anything over about 20 m.p.h. caused such severe vibration that I felt my teeth would drop out.

Eventually I crept into Warrnambool, Victoria, where I left the Amilcar at a local garage for repairs and went on to Melbourne in Geoff's vehicle.

Geoff's parents invited me to stay in their nineteenth-century two-storey mansion in the Melbourne suburb of Kew. His father was a jovial but conservative man, rather like a smaller version of my grandfather John Langdon Bonython. A fanatic about table manners, he admonished me to 'Sit up, Bonitie!' when I slumped into a slovenly position at the dining-table: a phrase I used on each of my own children in much later years.

When he heard the story of the Amilcar he called Father, who sent me £10 to have it shipped home from Melbourne by coastal freighter. There was no hope of driving it home. Mercifully, perhaps, I forget what Father had to say about the whole matter.

My next car also was an Amilcar, but a model with a bigger engine and comparatively huge body. It had a vast space between the back of the driver's seat and the rear passenger seat. One Saturday morning, driving down busy Rundle Street with Bryan Monkton, I turned to say something to him and found he was busily putting a golf ball around the floor between the seats.

Bryan, then a keen amateur pilot, flew at the Royal Aero Club at Parafield, Adelaide's only airport in the 1930s. He was building his own aircraft in his back yard and he was the proud owner of a magnificent Isotta Fraschini, imported to South Australia years before by Jack Hume, one of the pioneers of broadcasting in this State. One weekend Bryan decided to modify his Isotta. He took to it with an axe and chopped the conservative-looking hood right down to door-level. After this sacrilegious act he performed a splendid job converting the Isotta, using beautifully-polished timbers, into one of the most handsome touring cars on South Australian roads. If only the Isotta had survived it would be worth an absolute fortune now that veteran cars are so valuable.

That same weekend I decided to do a paint job on my 'new' Amilcar, and thought I would make a real job of it by using a solution of caustic soda to strip the old paintwork right down to the solid steel body. But my abilities as a painter were about on a par with my qualifications as a mechanic, and after a few hours the Amilcar looked as though it had some dreadful disease. Raw patches of metal were interspersed with cancerous areas of paint.

I didn't want my parents to see the mess I'd made and so I parked the apparition around the corner until my aeroplane-building, car-converting friend could help me make it more presentable.

Now that I had 'wings' my pursuit of the opposite sex was speeded up. My first girlfriend, in a pretty one-sided affair, was Mary Ellis, a glorious creature from the seaside suburb of Glenelg. Competition for her favours was intense and soon her other suitors drove me off with a barrage of stones. I retired dejectedly to potentially greener pastures.

On Saturday morning visits to the Pirie Street roller-skating rink I became enamoured of Alannah Wallman, sister of one of my schoolfriends. But all I picked up was a huge splinter from the creaking floorboards. I still have the scar in my hand forty-five years later.

My first real love was Irene MacIntosh, daughter of the Harbour Master at Port Adelaide. She lived at another seaside suburb, Largs Bay. She wasn't allowed to ride on my motor cycle and so I would walk to the railway station with her after she'd finished work in a city store, ride the bike eight miles down to Largs Bay, and meet her at the other end.

Her brother Ron, a medical student at Adelaide University, was a more than capable pianist. Once, with Alan Pilgrim on bass and me on the drums, we performed on stage at the annual Varsity Revue. Today, Ron is one of Adelaide's leading gynaecologists and Alan is the Warden of the Anglican church at Crafers, not far from Mount Lofty. Ron delivered all three children of my second family.

During the 1930s formal dances played a leading part in the social scene. I really hated them. The only steps I had managed to master at dancing class were those which had fallen out of fashion, such as the Pride of Erin or the Schottische. Probably I was more interested in playing drums than in learning the intricacies of the waltz, tango, fox trot, or valeta.

As soon as we arrived at a dance we were given little programmes with pencils attached, and we were expected to fill them up as soon as possible. But apart from being a terrible dancer I was painfully shy. I dared not ask strange girls to dance and inflict my clumsiness on them. I managed to take the floor with Adrienne Tolley, Roma Woods, and Buzzie Brooks, for whom I had 'mad passions', and a few girls with whom I had more platonic relationships, such as Juliet O'Dea, Marjorie 'Spookie' Johnson, Joan Beauchamp, Midge Mitchell, and Joan Rust. They were always very good to me and tolerated my stumbling steps. Otherwise I would be walking around outside or talking to the band musicians.

Buzzie Brooks, the youngest of three children of a noted pastoral family, lived at Buckland Park, a big property about twenty-five miles north of Adelaide. Hector, her oldest brother, once scared the daylights out of me by threatening that his father would 'take the horsewhip to me' if I got too free with Buzzie. Perish the thought!

Hector and his wife Joan lived in a cottage a few hundred yards from the main homestead, and Joan and I shared a private joke that, when things got too hot for me at the main house, I could always retire to the safety of the cottage behind an imaginary Siegfried Line between the two residences.

There were always guests galore at Buckland Park and my mother used to tell the story of a time when one of Hector's friends went to thank Mrs Brooks for her hospitality. She was getting dressed, but she went to her bedroom door to talk to him and held a garment in front of her. But she forgot there was a full-length mirror behind her, and Mother composed a poem to mark the occasion:

> Mrs Brooks, in but a singlet clad
> Was caught, to her confusion, by a lad.
> So hoping this shortcoming to disguise
> Dangled a petticoat before his eyes,
> And, like an ostrich with its head concealed,
> Imagined nothing else was thus revealed.
>
> But to be quite sure, when in natural state you're
> Not, alas! holding a mirror up to nature!
> She did not realise that, by fate unkind,
> A mirror was reflecting her behind!

Although I was shy in some ways I was precocious in others. If I was speechless in the drawing-rooms and 'coming-out' parties of Adelaide society I was quite able to express myself by beating out a rhythm on the drums or speeding along on two or four wheels. As the song says nowadays 'Music was my mistress', and I could listen to it for hours.

Mother was renowned as a flower arranger and in Adelaide's Centenary Year, 1936, she was given the task of organising a huge floral pageant as part of the celebrations. It was Adelaide's first Flower Day, an annual event thereafter, and she planned the great floral designs covering the lawns of North Terrace. A large number of motorised floats drove as a pageant from the Torrens Parade Ground up past the Town Hall, where I had stationed myself to make a movie record of the occasion. My 16-mm camera contained one of the first reels of colour film ever released for amateur use.

Of all the beautiful subjects I photographed that day one of the most striking was an auburn-haired young lady watching the procession from the Town Hall balcony. Alan King, a contemporary from Prince's College, was with me, and with masculine egotism we made a bet as to who could talk this unknown damsel into a date. I found that she worked in the City Engineer's Office, and although she was a few years older than I was I managed to make her acquaintance and, through sheer persistence, beat Alan to the post less than a week later. The lady, now one of Adelaide's 'upper-crust', may not care to remember thus being 'chatted up'.

Alan was one of my numerous boyhood friends who did not survive the second World War. He was lost at sea in the cruiser H.M.A.S. *Sydney*.

My numerous city acquaintances included one of the characters of Adelaide, Keith Minchin, who ran the long-gone Koala Farm in the parklands of North Adelaide just opposite the Memorial Hospital.

Keith was crippled by polio at an early age but he never let his infirmity damp his spirits. He drove around town in a tiny Ford that barely contained his huge frame plus a collapsible wheelchair and two smelly Australian terriers. The somewhat rancid car, like his house in nearby Medindie, always was in a terrible mess.

The Koala Farm, with its koalas, kangaroos, and other Australian animals, together with a performing seal and a miniature train drawn by a motorised locomotive, was a great favourite with Adelaide children. In earlier years it was known as the Snake Farm, and was a constant source of fascination to my mother. She was enamoured of snakes in general, and despite Father's protestations she often persuaded the keeper, Mr French, to let her go into the cages and handle the reptiles. I haven't inherited this fascination, and the mere thought of snakes gives me nightmares.

After one session with the snakes, Mother took a tramcar back to the city and soon noticed the other passengers edging apprehensively away from her. They were all staring at her hat, and when she reached exploringly upwards she found a snake which had wrapped itself round the brim and gone to sleep. Much to the relief of the other travellers, she got off at the next stop and took the reptile back to the Snake Farm.

Eventually a tiger snake bit Mr French and he died at the Royal

Adelaide Hospital. Father put his foot down and forbade Mother to make further calls on her beloved but deadly creatures.

Keith Minchin's office always seemed to contain one or two beautiful damsels. I don't know where they came from, but they were never far away from jovial Keith. I made unsuccessful attempts to court one of them just before the war, and when I was stationed at R.A.A.F. Laverton, near Melbourne, in 1941, I spotted her in a restaurant escorted by a greyhaired gentleman very much her senior. I blundered over to their table, full of pleasure at seeing her again, and gave her a cheerful greeting. My face fell when she said coldly and purposefully 'I think your friends are wanting you back at your table!'

Keith shared my passion for home movies. His infirmity did not prevent him from travelling the world, and on a trip to Cape Town he determined to photograph the scenic drive that winds behind the city across the foot of Table Mountain. He hired a motor bike and sidecar with a black African driver, and rigged up a complicated tripod for his camera. The resultant production would have done credit to Andy Warhol and the underground cinema movement. He had miscalculated the angle of the camera, and the thirty-minute film showed nothing but a close-up of the twisting road surface. Occasionally a heap of cow or horse manure flashed across the screen to break the monotony.

Keith, a son of a former Director of the Adelaide Zoo, had great rapport with animals, and Mother told me an amusing story about this. One night he was driving his little Ford down Frome Road, which was ill-lit in those days, towards the Zoo. Suddenly he collided with a dark bulk that turned out to be an elephant. Naturally he thought it had strayed from the Zoo, and he used his car to shepherd it gently back into the grounds. As he reported the incident to a disbelieving nightwatchman the elephant quenched its thirst by sucking up the contents of a goldfish tank, and when Keith drove back to it the pachyderm greeted him by vomiting up all the goldfish.

It transpired that the elephant did not come from the Zoo at all. It had strayed from a circus camped in the parklands, and when Keith located the circus owner he gave Keith a torrent of abuse and threats of legal action for allegedly poisoning the elephant with goldfish. Not to be outdone, Keith threatened a counter-action for damage to his disreputable car, which had survived far more severe traumas than a mere collision with an elephant. Apparently this threat subdued the circus owner and the matter was allowed to rest.

The Koala Farm closed in 1970 when the area was reclaimed for parklands, and the indomitable Minchin is now no more.

For almost as long as I can remember the domestic staff at our East Terrace home consisted of the cook, Tillie Parkinson; a maid, Ina Parham; and a gardener-cum-chauffeur, Charlie Slattery. Alcohol was Charlie's downfall in more ways than one. Once, he fell when cleaning a second-storey window, but his fall was broken by a convenient camellia bush. After years of warnings, Father dispensed with his services after one particularly hair-raising drive.

I believe Slattery never overcame his problem. For years thereafter this poor soul came knocking at our door whenever his affairs reached a low ebb, seeking money or a meal — or both. Mother always gave them to him, and a tearful Slattery uttered his sorrowful catch cry 'You're an angel from heaven, Lady Bonython!' I seriously considered using this phrase on the spot where the remains of my dear mother lie in her beloved Eurilla garden.

Mother never learned to drive a car and Father was far from expert, especially in his later years. Machinery, including such newfangled gadgets as TV, tended to baffle him. But he drove very carefully, apart from one nerve-shattering habit. On his weekly drive from Adelaide to the family farm in the hills he had to cross the railway line just past Mount Barker. It passed over a fairly long straight stretch of road, and as he approached the line he accelerated steadily with constant nervous glances left and right, always repeating 'The trouble with train-crossings — is — that — very often — the car stalls — *on the line!*'

At that moment, with the car doing about seventy, we would hit the tracks. It leapt into the air with a bone-shaking crash while Father, like some aged Evel Knievel, gripped the wheel with a look of fanatical determination.

My addiction to cars and motor bikes tended to intensify my 'loner's' attitude to life but still I made many friends. All too many of them perished during the war: such men as Richard Harding-Browne, Bunny Richards, Rex Whitington, and John Goodfellow. Other friends of my formative years now are pillars of the Establishment. Richard Blackburn, son of the V.C. hero of two World Wars, is now a judge. So is Bill Forster, whose high scholastic abilities made his destiny clear from an early age. But when I stayed at his Largs Bay home during one school holiday, and we tried devoutly to invent a new swear word uniquely our own, the best we could come up with was 'Thut!'

Jock Gosse, head prefect during my last year at St Peter's in 1938, is now a 'captain of industry'. One of his older brothers, Jim, was what one might call nowadays 'a real tearaway'. He worked for his father and was in charge of the wine and spirits department of a large family company — a fateful combination and the equivalent of making me the manager of a sweetshop. Early one morning, when he and a friend were returning from a convivial party, they decided to make some use of a ·22 rifle belonging to one of them. The lights of North Terrace, Adelaide's boulevard of culture, proved irresistible targets and they drove up and down the terrace on the right and wrong sides of the road taking pot-shots at the street lights.

Adelaide was a much smaller and friendlier place in those days. When a strong arm of the law finally appeared he merely said kindly 'Now, now, Mr Gosse: it's time you and your friend went home and slept it off!'

Jim tended to be late for work in the mornings. One day his father snapped 'Where have you been? You should have been here at nine!'

Jim asked politely 'Why? What happened?'

One of my good friends was Don Millager, known as 'Slug' because of his bulk and his pasty complexion. His father, an American, was an executive in the Australian branch of General Motors, and Don was the first American youth of my acquaintance. Like the rest of us he yearned ardently for a car of his own but his parents didn't agree. He saved his pocket money, worked odd jobs, and bought a huge and dilapidated old hearse which he parked outside the family mansion on fashionable Strangways Terrace, North Adelaide. The ploy worked very well and his father came good with a brand new car.

Don eventually became a sports car dealer in Garden City, a suburb of New York. Twenty years later, one of the people to whom he introduced me was an American speedway promoter, Duke Donaldson. I'll have more to say about him later.

The son of another American executive with G.M. was Ray Denny. I believe that in a roundabout way he saved my life, and I'll be telling the story during those of my war experiences.

It relates to the fact that, on his way back to America, Ray sent me a gaudy Hawaiian shirt from Honolulu. Adelaide had never seen anything like it in those days, and in my enthusiasm to cut a dash I put it on and strutted forth immediately I took it from the parcel. I should have had it washed first, because the dyes inflicted an outbreak of dermatitis which spread quickly over my whole body. It has recurred ever since.

Other friends included Arthur Porter, Don McMichael, Jack Kenny, Ross Truscott, Bryn Thomas, Ron Bickford, Murray Elliott, and Tassie Aitken. Some were with me in the Cadet Corps at St Peter's, in which I was a lowly private until I rose to what I regarded as my true *métier*, Corporal commanding the Drum Corps.

I believe in military training for young males. Every citizen has an obligation to prepare to defend his country, so that it may not be faced with the hopeless task of scratching together an army when the enemy is at the gates. When I left school I joined the Adelaide Rifles (10th Battalion, Militia), in which my brother Jack also was a private. We attended Monday drill nights at the Torrens Parade Ground and regular camps and manoeuvres at the Woodside Army Camp in the hills east of Adelaide. Neither of us was General Staff material.

A plumber's mate, Normie Myers, was the N.C.O. whose task was to instil some military discipline into my platoon. He began invariably by barking 'All right, youse cunts! On yer feet!'

Today I meet Norman quite frequently, the pillar of respectability as a bookseller's representative, and recall those earlier encounters with amusement.

Like most youngsters I had no real idea as to what I wanted to do when I left school—apart from being a jazz drummer. My wise brother Jack advised me that whatever career I settled on I'd be thankful for a knowledge of bookkeeping, and his brother-in-law, Bill Harcus, found me a job as junior with the firm of chartered accountants in which he was a partner: J. F. Key, Reid & Co. Also I took a Hemingway Robertson correspondence course in accountancy and sought further knowledge through private lessons with Norman Paynter, then a tutor at St Mark's University College. In later years Norman took orders and he is now Archdeacon of Adelaide.

If history had rolled placidly on I might have become a chartered accountant. But on 3 September 1939, a month before the death of Grandfather at the age of ninety-one, my future together with that of millions of other young men was settled by the outbreak of the second World War.

6

Up, Up, and Away

E ARLY IN THE second World War there was a joke which ran: 'What did you do in the Great War, Daddy?' The answer was 'I was on the waiting list for the Empire Air Training Scheme.'.

Everyone knew that war was coming, but precious little was done about preparing for it. I resigned from my job, volunteered for the R.A.A.F., and expected to be called up at any moment. But the machinery simply did not exist for training the eager volunteers. I had an old two-seater Chev roadster in those days, and to pass some time I drove it to Sydney to visit Bryan Monkton. On the way I saw a car pulled up by the roadside with a puncture. The woman driver hailed me for assistance, and while I was changing her tyre she told me she was a gypsy. 'If you cross my palm with silver I'll read your fortune,' she said.

I did so, and after reading my palm she said 'Yes . . . I can see it clearly . . . you'll be killed in an air crash in the month of March.'

With that cheerful forecast I continued on my way. Needless to say I haven't perished in an air crash so far, but I'm always relieved when another April comes around.

In Sydney, Bryan suggested that on my way back to Adelaide I should call at R.A.A.F. headquarters in Melbourne and talk to a Squadron Leader Davis, the officer supervising the intake of air crew.

When I asked Davis how long I'd have to wait for my call-up he said 'About three months.' But then a thought struck him and he said 'Just a minute' and left the room. Returning, he asked 'Can you be in Sydney by tomorrow morning?'

Rather bewildered, I said 'Yes.' Apparently a draft of recruits was en route to Sydney but one of the volunteers had not turned up. I was given his place, and a few minutes later I was driving back to Sydney.

The gypsy's warning was rather strongly in my mind as I drove along, and during the next few years there were plenty of chances for her prophesy to come true. With a little less luck, it would have done.

I went through the usual basic training, and my first flight as Cadet Bonython was at Mascot Aerodrome, Sydney, on 8 March 1940. I was posted to B Flight of No. 4 Elementary Flying Training School, whose chief instructor was a civilian pilot, Alan Clancy. B Flight operated out of the old Kingsford Smith Flying School, and A Flight, instructed by Bryan Monkton, used the hangars of the Royal Aero Club of New South Wales. They had Tiger Moths and we had the somewhat older DH60s.

Flying the open-cockpit DH60 was an exhilarating experience, especially since we had no parachutes. The influx of would-be pilots had far outstripped such luxuries. We used to practise aerobatics and forced landings over the empty sandhills of Cronulla or the vast expanses of open country between Mascot and the ocean, now occupied by the Bonnie Doone and Lakes Golf Clubs.

But for a while it seemed that my destiny did not lie in the air, and I feared I might end up 'flying a desk' in the administration section of the R.A.A.F. Luckily I soon established a rapport with Alan Clancy and I think he took something of a fatherly liking to me. After a month's training I had to undergo a special test, with Flying Officer Bill Barker, chief flight check pilot of the R.A.A.F., in the instructor's cockpit. Obviously my potential as a pilot was very much in doubt, and I think Alan had much to do with keeping me in the course.

Clancy and his wife were very good to me and we went out on the town occasionally. He was a superb pilot, a friend and contemporary of Charles Kingsford Smith, but there is a sad postscript to his story. After the war he flew again as a commercial pilot, but in 1957, landing at the coastal town of Evans Head in the dark and in bad weather, his aircraft crashed and was destroyed.

He was grounded by the Department of Civil Aviation, which ordered a test on his instrument-flying abilities. Two examiners, in a DC3 aircraft, gave him the usual searching test. On an approach to Camden Airport, west of Sydney, he was instructed to abort the landing and 'go round again', and as he obeyed one of the examiners 'pulled' an engine. Soon after this the DC3 crashed into trees at one end of the airfield, and caught fire. Clancy, with a broken leg and other injuries, was pinned in the wreckage and had a very narrow escape.

He sued the D.C.A. for £10,000 damages. The noted barrister John Kerr, later Sir John and Governor-General, acted for him but the action was only partially successful. Clancy was awarded £3,000, but his flying career was over.

Jobs were scarce for ex-pilots in those days but he found one as a security guard at Sydney University. Three years later, aged only fifty-two, he died of a heart attack. Perhaps I'd be accused of sentimentality if I called it a broken heart.

But that lay in the future when, after ten hours' instruction, Clancy said I was ready to solo. Every pilot has vivid memories of his first solo and I am no exception, especially since Mascot in those days was only an undulating grassy paddock with no marked runways. Even so it was Sydney's main commercial airport, and trainees had to keep an eye open for civilian aircraft. But I got the DH60 off the ground and, even more important, landed it again in one piece.

I'd got through my first March in defiance of the gypsy's warning but the dangers of flying were rubbed home by a tragic incident when a member of the course was doing aerobatic training over the Sydney suburb of Randwick. Apparently the instructor, Lennie Bayliss, forgot to fasten his safety harness. When the pilot rolled the aircraft Bayliss fell to his death in the main street of Randwick, and the shaken pupil, who had yet to fly solo, had to land the aircraft unaided.

But with the solo under my belt I felt I could spread my wings. Bryan Monkton and I hired a Puss Moth from the Aero Club in order to fly home to Adelaide for the Easter Break, and we hedge-hopped all the way. That was the way to fly! A mighty contrast to the Visual Flight Rules and Instrument Flight Rules one must accept in today's comparatively over-crowded skies.

The barracks at Mascot were still being built, and so we were billeted at the nearby Brighton-le-Sands Hotel and ferried to the airfield by bus. I thought I'd learned a little about life in Adelaide but this association with a bunch of roistering young bucks really opened my innocent eyes. Any of the hotel staff who wore skirts were far from safe with my fellow cadets—and I'm not sure they wanted to be.

Two of the chief 'villains' of the course were cadets Pat Osborne and Laurie Brown, who seemed always to be in hazardous situations on the ground or in the air. The climax came when they went to Tom Ugly's Club, a few miles from the hotel. Emboldened by a few drinks they made a play for an attractive girl, but it turned out that she was accompanied by her regular boyfriend, who just happened to be the professional light heavyweight champion of the State.

Before long, Pat and Laurie were invited to 'Come outside for a moment.' Unsuspectingly they walked out into a side lane, where a group of thugs gave them a savage beating. Laurie wore the scars of that encounter for many years.

It was a strange period. Most of us were in our late teens or very early twenties and in civil life none would have been trusted with more than a lowly office job. Quickly we reverted to schoolboy high spirits and there were some pretty wild ragging raids between members of the two courses when we moved into barracks towards the end of our training period.

Faces from those days pass through my mind, such as Jim Bullmore, stepson of the newspaper magnate Frank Packer, whose portrait by William Dobell was used as the jacket illustration of a book on the R.A.A.F. called

Valiant Youth. Poor Jim died in action soon after that. And there were Mick Grace, later to be Managing Director of the great Sydney department store Grace Brothers, Paul Flack from a well-known Melbourne accountancy firm, Bob Russell of Pioneer Sugar, and many others.

Most of us had nicknames. Ken Peters, for some forgotten reason, was known as 'Tugboat'. There was Bill 'Invisible Man' Stewart, Sid 'Tittybags' Brasier, Peter 'Pot' Ash, Pat 'Stoker' Osborne, Bill 'Boozer' Watt, Roger 'The Lodger' Blanchard, Bob 'Old Man' Russell, Ted 'Smiler' Jones, Aub 'Strawberry' Oates, John 'Swede' Darnton, Reggie 'Rabbit' Norris, Stuart 'Prof' Hermes, Graham 'Ace' Pace, Bob 'Blob' Donovan, Phil 'Dillybag' Ashton, Roy 'Oaf' Sayer, and Norm Lamb, who naturally enough was called 'Lambie Pie'.

The limited training facilities meant that our elementary course lasted a full four months, which involved fifty hours of dual flying, fifty hours solo, and classroom instruction. When the course ended the Chief Flying Instructor noted in my logbook 'Side slipping approaches dangerous.' But I passed, and I was sent on to Victoria to continue training at Point Cook.

At Point Cook, potential fighter pilots trained in Hawker Demons, while those considered to be more suitable for bombing or reconnaissance were allocated to Avro Ansons. I was among the latter.

There were a few relics of earlier days among the Demons and Ansons, including the venerable Wapiti. Its characteristics included an amazingly slow propeller idling speed, but even so the aircraftsman who actually walked through the revolving prop without noticing must have been one of the luckiest people on the planet.

A feature of the Anson was a very long radio aerial wrapped around a drum, rather in the manner of a garden hose. When you were airborne you unreeled the aerial and it trailed below the aircraft, kept reasonably steady by a couple of dozen small lead weights.

Unfortunately one of our course forgot about the aerial when he decided to 'shoot up' a company of soldiers out on manoeuvres. It was a great dummy attack but it had rather serious consequences, because the aerial weights injured several soldiers. The pilot was demoted from Cadet to Sergeant Pilot, and perhaps was lucky that his punishment was not more severe.

I managed to improve my flying assessment to 'above average' but only four days later, on 13 August 1940, I blotted my record. On a cross-country exercise to Deniliquin I tried to land down-wind and crashed into a barbed wire fence. The aircraft was slightly damaged but I completed a go-around circuit with a post and several lengths of barbed wire trailing dangerously in my slipstream.

On the same day a Lockheed Hudson of my future 2 Squadron crashed on landing at Canberra and killed its passenger load of cabinet ministers and high-ranking officers.

Top: Three Beaufort bombers drop their torpedoes in a practice attack at Jervis Bay, 1943 (*Author's photo*).   Bottom: The U.S. Navy Torpedo Maintenance Unit, Jervis Bay, 1943. (*R.A.A.F. photo*)

The second stage of my training ended with an 'above average' rating in navigation but 'below average' in gunnery and bombing. I was transferred to 2 (General Reconnaissance) Squadron at nearby Laverton and had my first taste of its Lockheed Hudson twin-engine reconnaissance bombers. For a long time the Hudsons were Jacks-of-all-trades in the R.A.A.F.

The schoolboy days of training were over, and as a Pilot Officer I was low man on the totem pole among men of whom the majority were vastly more experienced than I was. Some were hard nuts and many distinguished themselves on active service in various theatres of war.

As second pilot, I flew mostly with Bob Dalkin, Mick Cowan, or Neville Hemsworth. Neville was a member of a distinguished flying family and his brother, Gough, first sighted the Japanese invasion fleet in the Coral Sea. Ordered to 'Shadow the enemy until further notice' he obeyed and was never seen again.

Our C.O. was Wing Commander Freddie Thomas, later a Lord Mayor of Melbourne. The Adjutant, an old roúe named Wally 'Caesar' Baird, had a classic Roman profile and a great appetite for the good things of life.

Flight Lieutenant Rob Burns Cuming, flight commander of A Flight, was a fellow-Adelaidean. He had been a university boxing champion and before the war gained some notoriety by knocking down the famous tenor Richard Tauber. Tauber had come to Adelaide on a concert tour, accompanied by his beautiful film-star wife Diana Napier. Rob made a pass at her in the lounge of the conservative South Australian Hotel. Quite naturally, Tauber remonstrated vigorously and Rob responded by flattening him with a right to the jaw.

B Flight was commanded by John Ryland, later the General Manager of Trans-Australia Airlines; and Squadron Leader Allen Love, a well-known Melbourne architect, commanded C Flight.

Our main operational function was to give air cover to the troopships sailing westwards with 2nd A.I.F. men for the Middle East. No. 6 Squadron, based at Richmond near Sydney, gave coverage from north of Sydney down to Mallacoota on the south-eastern tip of Australia. We took over from there and patrolled almost as far west as Adelaide, watching for lurking U-boats or minelayers.

While on these duties, Neville Hemsworth and I achieved the possibly unique distinction of losing the *Queen Mary*.

The giant liner was embarking troops in Hobart, and because of her high speed she did not have a naval escort. She could outrun any submarine of that era. But we were to escort her from Hobart out into the open sea, and we flew our Hudson there on the evening before her sailing-day. We had to put up at a hotel for the night, and the only one handy to the airfield was a pretty seedy caravanserai.

In those days Australian suburban and country hotels were notorious for their brutish inhospitality. This one was no exception and Neville and I

TOP LEFT: Kym Bonython (*left*) with Flying Officer Keith Roget, in front of a Mosquito of 87 Squadron, Coomallie Creek, Darwin, 1945. TOP RIGHT: Squadron Leader 'Bluey' Truscott, C.O. 76 Squadron (*centre*), with Wing Commander Sam Balmer, C.O. 100 Squadron (*left*) and Squadron Leader Les Jackson, C.O. 75 Squadron, at Milne Bay October 1942. (*Australian War Memorial negative No. 26642*). BOTTOM: U.S.A.F. Lockheed Lodestar transport takes off from Milne Bay under usual difficult conditions (*Author's photo*)

spent a memorable night in a double bed apparently stuffed with coconuts and swarming with a vicious population of bed bugs.

Still scratching, we took off in the dark and made our rendezvous with the liner as she steamed down the Derwent estuary. But once in the open sea the weather deteriorated rapidly into low cloud and rain. We were flying a patterned search ahead of the *Queen Mary*, seeking for signs of U-boat activity, but in the thick weather we soon lost sight of the liner and despite intensive searching we could not find her again. Of course this was in the days before airborne radar. Finally we had to give up and return shamefacedly to base.

A somewhat more hair-raising incident occurred when I was flying as second pilot with Mick Cowan. We had been patrolling off the southern coast and were to spend the night at Mount Gambier. As darkness fell, so did the rain. It felt as though we were flying through the ocean instead of above it but we groped our way to the little country airport.

Eight or nine other aircraft were trying to land and for a while we all milled around in the same patch of cloud. The airstrip was under inches of water and chaos reigned supreme. Someone fired off red Very lights from one end of the strip while another hopeful flashed a green Aldis lamp from the other end.

Mick lined up the strip and began his approach, and soon ordered me to 'Lower fifteen degrees flap.' I depressed the lever and the flaps began to run out, just as I glimpsed a tall radio mast looming directly ahead through the rain and murk.

Frantically I shouted at Mick to make a quick turn. He did so, but in the excitement I forgot the flaps. By that time they were fully extended and we were dangerously close to the ground. To retract them at that instant would have caused a sudden and fatal loss of altitude and so all Mick could do was pour on the power.

The aircraft wallowed ahead just above stalling speed, and we went in over the fence at a most peculiar attitude: nose down and tail up. We literally 'splashed down' into the mud and water of the airstrip. We could hardly believe we were safely down and it took some moments for us to recover enough nervous strength to taxi onto the tarmac.

While 2 Squadron was based at Laverton I had a renewed burst of film-making enthusiasm and decided to make a documentary showing squadron activities in those halcyon days before Japan erupted into the war. I called this masterpiece *Guardians of the Trade Routes*.

I used all kinds of tricky effects to obtain action shots. I took my movie camera into Melbourne theatres and surreptitiously filmed sequences from British newsreels. I had a special titler which enabled me to flash graphic descriptions on the screen, and to obtain an extra dramatic effect when the squadron was allegedly going into action I set fire to the paper title. As it went up in flames it revealed a bathing beauty on a magazine cover lying on a couch behind the titling device, which somewhat spoiled the effect.

Since we were technically on active service, such camera work was strictly illegal. The axe fell on me when some of my forbidden films were intercepted on their way back from a clandestine processor.

A nasty bit of work on the staff of Southern Area Command had me dragged before the Area Officer commanding Southern Area, Air Commodore Adrian Cole. Cole ordered a 'severe reprimand' to be logged against my record, for photographing such forbidden objects as the Hudson cockpit, with a silhouette of our far-from-secret bombsight, and some incredibly bad take-offs and landings at our advanced operational bases at Bairnsdale, Sale, and Mallacoota.

Luckily the powers-that-be never viewed a film still with the processor. It showed a troop convoy of the *Queen Mary*, *Queen Elizabeth*, and *Ile de France* escorted by H.M.A.S. *Sydney* and several other Australian warships.

The other illicit films were confiscated and another stage in my movie-making career came to an end. Fortunately the films later came under the jurisdiction of our then Commanding Officer, Freddie Thomas, who spirited them back to me. They are precious examples of some of the worst films ever made during those carefree days.

Thirty years later I was named the first Chairman of the Experimental Film and Television Fund of the Australian Council for the Arts. I thought there might be some resentment of my appointment to such a position, and used to disarm criticism by pointing out that I was not without experience in film-making, and telling the story of *Guardians of the Trade Routes*.

Sometimes I think my reprimand would have been much more severe if it had not been for the fact that a Group Captain, a Wing Commander, and two Squadron Leaders played leading parts in the epic!

There is a tailpiece to the story. Later in the war I was showing some flying films at Townsville Air Base when a voice from the back of the room said 'Well—I see you're still at it, Bonython!' It was the same officer who had 'dobbed me in' to Southern Area Command.

The new 'epic', little better in quality than my first effort, actually was quite legal. It showed aerial torpedo training techniques then being taught at Nowra and I made it with the blessing of the R.A.A.F. But I still felt some embarrassment as I explained this to my superior officer, and I don't think he quite believed me.

With rather malicious satisfaction I heard soon afterwards that the same officer, while landing a DC3 at Canberra, forgot the elementary procedure of releasing the wheel brakes and stood the aircraft on its nose.

I flew a lot with Neville Hemsworth, and I'm glad to say that, together with Mick Cowan and Bob Dalkin, he survived the war. Neville married one of the most beautiful girls I've ever known. In late 1941 they produced a daughter, Sue, and I was asked to be godfather.

For months after Sue was born Neville would give me a wicked grin and ask 'Are you *sure* there's never been anything between you and Joan? The more I look at Sue, the more I think she looks like you!' Alas, I could never claim anything more than a platonic friendship with Joan Hemsworth although understandably I was infatuated with her. Sue grew up into a marvellous girl and now runs a holiday camp for riding enthusiasts near Camden, New South Wales.

The Women's Auxiliary Air Force was formed in February 1941 and an influx of W.A.A.F.s added some spice to the previously all-male life at Laverton. My favourite was a pretty girl named Betty, and what went on in the Duty Control Officers' tower above the hangar at night was not strictly according to Air Force Orders.

The Spencer Tracy version of the film *Dr Jekyll and Mr Hyde* showed in Melbourne at that time. Whenever Hyde began his dirty work he whistled 'You Should See Me Dance the Polka', and I whistled the same tune whenever I came up behind Betty as she walked along one of the roads round the base. It was poignantly amusing to see her feelings betrayed by the flush rising up her neck.

We did plenty of walking because petrol rationing was enforced, though I had fitted my Chev roadster with one of the newfangled gas producers. This monster had to be filled with dusty coal, which was then heated up by lighting a kerosene-soaked asbestos wick. When the coal began to generate gas, I started the engine with petrol and then switched over to gas power. To drive more than about twenty miles I had to carry another sack of coal in the boot, together with a long dustcoat and heavy leather gloves.

Refuelling en route was a hazardous operation. Donning coat and gloves, I gingerly opened the lid of the generator and leapt backwards a second before the well-heated apparatus erupted like a miniature atom bomb, spraying dust and sparks. When it cooled down a little I emptied another sackful into the hopper and took off again—almost literally full steam ahead.

Guest nights in the Laverton officers' mess became hectic affairs and I did not envy the stewards who had to clean up broken glass, wrecked furniture, emptied fire extinguishers, and torn carpets. The cost of the damage was added to our mess bills.

As usual I was one of the few teetotallers on the scene, but such hard livers as Bill White seemed to be able to keep on drinking until the early hours, refresh themselves with about ninety minutes' sleep, and appear on deck hale and hearty while those of us who had gone to bed early were blinking blearily at our breakfasts.

On one memorable occasion Bill chose to ignore the flare path on a pitch-black early morning take-off. He made his own course at about forty-five degrees angle to the flares, and narrowly escaped disaster when his still retracting undercarriage struck and dislodged some of the sandbags stacked around one of the airfield bomb dumps.

Neville Hemsworth tried hard to find an alcoholic beverage to my liking and we spent one Saturday morning in Melbourne's Hotel Australia while he ordered drink after drink for me to sample. I took one sip and disgustedly pushed each glass away. For economy's sake Neville felt obliged to consume the remainder, and by lunch-time he was forced to abandon the attempt to educate me. I took him with me to visit my good friends the Robert Lanes in Toorak, and we had not gone far before he felt an overpowering need to relieve himself. The only facilities I could offer were a couple of empty bottles and he conducted a shuttle service, filling one while he emptied the other through the car window among the all-unconscious homegoing traffic on Toorak Road.

I celebrated my twenty-first birthday in Melbourne. Mother, who could not attend, hired a private dining-room in the Menzies for a dozen of my squadron mates, with their wives or girl friends, to give me a dinner-party. They presented me with a gold pen and pencil set, and a highlight of the evening was when Flying Officer David Campbell, now the noted Australian poet, read out the instructions accompanying the set, headed 'How to renew the lead in your pencil.' I wish I had a tape-recording of his straightfaced but suggestive rendering . . . and it would be nice if I could remember his advice today!

I think we all knew that our cheerful and comparatively untroubled Laverton days could not last very long but we made the most of them and it seemed there always was something to laugh about.

One incident concerned a well-known Melbourne businessman, who had made the melancholy request that his ashes should be scattered over the waters of Port Phillip Bay. Apparently the influence of his relatives extended into the R.A.A.F. and in due course a pilot of our squadron was deputed for this task.

Hudson aircraft were fitted with chutes for dropping 'drift markers'. These burst on contact with the water and left a large silver patch used by the navigator to estimate bearings of wind force and direction. The idea was that the ashes should be discharged through this same chute.

The pilot put the urn in place and pulled the lever. Theoretically, the ashes should have spilled from the urn as it fell. Instead, the wind blast tore the lid from the urn while it was still in the chute and the ashes gushed back into the cabin. The unfortunate pilot was almost choked by the blizzard of human ashes which filled his mouth, nose, and eyes and smothered the inside of the cabin. He finally managed to grope his way in to a landing. It was decided that the bereaved relatives had better not know the fate of their beloved's remains.

Another legend concerned the squadron Lothario. The story goes that he took his current girlfriend home one night and, in passionate desperation, was giving her 'the treatment' standing up on the front porch.

In the midst of this frenzied activity the front door opened to reveal a very irate father. It seems that every time the girl's bottom went into reverse thrust it rang the door bell. Lothario decided that discretion was the better part of valour and vanished into the darkness.

One day I noticed that the officers' mess staff included a cook whose features were indubitably Chinese. This seemed like an answer to a prayer, because the records I had been collecting ever since I was a teenager included a genuine Chinese recording. My cousin Eric Bonython had brought it back from Darwin on one of his trips into the Northern Territory.

The only writing on the label was in Chinese. The recording seemed to be of a Chinese opera, clamorous with cymbals, gongs, wood blocks rattling, and nasal voices wailing weird and unintelligible sounds. But one of its charms was that, if you listened intently to the very end, you could hear a background voice saying 'All right, Mick—you can turn it off now. They've finished!'

I'd always wanted to know what the record was all about. Abrim with anticipation I took my gramophone into the kitchen, placed it on the Aga cooker, and told the cook 'Just listen to this!'

He listened inscrutably, and when the record ended I asked expectantly 'Now, what was that all about?'

In a broad Aussie accent he said 'How the bloody hell should I know? I've never been out of bloody Melbourne in me bloody life!'

We were still granted the occasional weekend leave, from which we had to report back at nine a.m. on the Monday. I risked one or two trips home to Adelaide, even though this meant I'd be thirty minutes late because the train didn't arrive back in Melbourne until nine. But on one of these trips a derailment on the line delayed the train. It was diverted via Geelong and I was biting my nails as the delay dragged out until I was four-and-a-half hours late. At last the train steamed right past the airfield, slowing to about 15 m.p.h. as it approached Laverton railway station. I thought the 'express' would not stop at this station and so I flung out my suitcase and leapt into space, rolling over and over as I hit the ground. As I picked myself up and dusted myself off I saw the train stop about 100 yards further on, to disgorge several leering airmen.

7

Dangerous Days

THE WAR SEEMED to come a little nearer to 2 Squadron in September 1941. We were sent on a familiarisation flight to Darwin and the Netherland East Indies, the area in which we were to serve when the Japanese onslaught erupted.

Life in the tropics was still fairly leisurely and Darwin was full of unusual characters. Commanding Officer of the R.A.A.F. base was Group Captain 'Moth' Eaton, whose idiosyncrasies included keeping two pet crocodiles in a pool outside the officers' mess. These inoffensive creatures met their fate when a disgruntled officer who had gone a little 'troppo', as it was called in those days, despatched them with his revolver.

Another troppo pilot, of 13 Squadron, kept a huge python in a basket under his bed. One night he reeled from the mess to the wooden stairs leading up to his quarters, and almost tripped over a snake coiled at the foot of the stairs. Thinking that his friends were playing their usual practical jokes he growled 'Irresponsible bastards,' lifted the snake and wrapped it round his neck, and staggered up the steps. Crooning reassuringly to the snake he bent down to place it in the basket, only to meet the beady stare of his own python already comfortably ensconced.

In those days Indonesia was still the Netherlands East Indies and Dutch merchants and officials lived in lethargic colonial style on the islands to the north of Australia. I fear that a good many of them perished when the Japanese swarmed over the islands.

We visited Koepang, Ambon, and Namlea, which was later to become a penal settlement for political prisoners of various Indonesian regimes. The familiarisation flight seemed almost like a holiday as we flew above the mountainous jungle-clad islands and landed at one or another of the airstrips carved out of the forest. I took the opportunity to make my second documentary film, entitled, with some lack of originality, *Tropical Paradise*. To stretch the film out a little I spliced some clips of the Fitzroy Gardens, Melbourne, or other Australian scenery, among the equatorial scenes.

When I was filming on the island of Amboina I shot one sequence on a beautiful promontory. I could not know that within a few months the Japanese would massacre a number of Australian servicemen on that very spot, including some of my squadron mates.

During our few days at Ambon we picked up a few words of the local language, including 'ini perampuan' (this girl). In those days, *Esquire* magazine was the equivalent of the modern *Playboy* and was much sought after for its Petty girls and other scantily-clad and generously-endowed young ladies. With characteristic schoolboy humour we showed these to the Indonesian mess-boys and taught them to say 'Ini perampuan good fuck.'

We flew to Melbourne in October 1941 and I was posted to 1 Squadron, stationed by Kota Bahru in what was then Malaya. But, perhaps because of my brief visit to the tropics, my old problem of dermatitis had flared up again. It was a recurrent nuisance, and the R.A.A.F. doctors already had given me ray treatment at Randwick Army Hospital in an effort to keep it under control. This time, it was to save my life.

When I was medically examined for the overseas posting, the doctors at Laverton rejected me. They said the angry rash would be aggravated by a spell in a tropical climate. Ron Siggins of Adelaide was posted in my place as second pilot to Flight Lieutenant Jones. Jones and his crew were the first Australian fliers to be shot down, with no survivors, when the first waves of Japanese aircraft swept across Malaya. Inevitably I would have sat beside Jones if the doctors had not forbidden my posting.

Despite the dermatitis, I accompanied 2 Squadron when we were transferred to Darwin in the early hours of 8 December 1941. By that time our C.O. was the admirable Wing Commander Frank Headlam, who was to finish his career as Air Vice-Marshal and Deputy Chief of Air Staff before his death in 1977. Neville Hemsworth had at last managed to get me off solo in a Hudson, but I was still second pilot when we took off for Darwin.

After five hours and fifteen minutes in the air we landed at Oodnadatta, to be greeted with the news that the Japanese had bombed Pearl Harbor. Our orders were changed and we flew to Koepang, on Timor Island, via Alice Springs and Darwin.

Our recent 'holiday' in the islands seemed to fade into the very distant past. Together with elements of 13 Squadron, from Darwin, we flew out of Koepang, Ambon, and Namlea. I was promoted to first pilot, and captain of my own aircraft. My second pilot was Pilot Officer Peter Thompson, from Albury, New South Wales. The crew included a very reluctant Warrant Officer, George Wiburd, who later won a D.F.M.

George had been switched from the crew of Rob Burns Cuming, who was considerably more experienced than I was. I did not blame George for his loudly-expressed apprehension at flying with a man who had only recently made his first solo in a Hudson, but, by one of the ironies of war, the transfer saved George's life.

Only a couple of weeks after George had joined my crew, Rob Cuming took off from Koepang with his aircraft crammed with ten people and a load of stores. They were destined for our advance base at Namlea, but Rob Cuming crashed on take-off. Everyone died in the overloaded aircraft.

Only a few minutes after the crash I returned from sea patrol. I had to make my landing approach directly over the still-blazing wreckage on the airstrip, and after landing I unwisely succumbed to my feelings of curiosity and went over to have a look. It was the first time I had ever been close to a recent wreck and the experience was so shocking that I vowed I would never do it again. The sight of smouldering, grotesquely-distorted bodies, and the stench of their burning, are still vivid in my memory.

Poor Rob Cuming was not the only one to perish in those early days. My schoolfriend, Flying Officer John Goodfellow from Port Pirie, was lost soon after take-off from Koepang. One by one my squadron buddies were eliminated as the Japanese thrust relentlessly closer to Australia.

The Hudson was designed for bombing and reconnaissance but because of the shortage of aircraft we used them for everything from transports to strafing attacks. The Japanese with their faster and better-armed aircraft had virtual control of the air and there was not much chance for a Hudson which encountered them. One day, when Australian aerial losses were becoming depressingly formidable, Neville Hemsworth held his service revolver against my arm and asked 'Shall I pull the trigger now or will you take what's coming to you within the next few months?'

I decided that he'd better pull the trigger, but as it turned out I would have been the loser on that deal. I came through physically unscathed, but Hemmy was not so lucky. A few months later when he was flying his Hudson off the north coast of New Guinea, a trigger-happy American anti-aircraft gunner shot him down in flames. He managed to crash-land the blazing aircraft in shallow water and fight his way out of the inferno, but he left a good part of his throttle hand melted onto the controls and suffered ghastly burns to his face and chest. The scars are still visible.

On 12 January 1942 I was flying one of the regular sea patrols to the north-east of Timor when I spotted an unexpected flotilla of warships. There was absolutely no intelligence available on the movements of Allied shipping or aircraft in those waters, but I happened to be carrying a copy of Jane's *All the World's Fighting Ships*. I flipped through the pages, and more by good luck than good judgement I chanced on a silhouette which seemed to correspond with the leading ship of the flotilla.

Approaching dangerously close, I told the navigator to flash a message with the Aldis lamp: 'Are you the *Marblehead*?'

The United States cruiser replied promptly 'Yes. Keep away or we shoot you down!'

In those days of confusion no one trusted a strange ship or aircraft. We had a narrow escape on our way back to base. A Japanese fighter pounced on us but we managed to lose him in a convenient cloud.

The invaders were moving so fast that they soon began to launch attacks on Koepang airfield, which consisted of two wide unsealed strips coming together in a vast open space of gleaming white coral. As a target it was unmistakeable and unmissable, especially since the Japanese soon learned that our 'defences' consisted only of a few army machine-guns. They were sited in pill-boxes with such narrow slits that the guns had only a ten degree elevation.

There were no Allied fighter aircraft in the area, and the Japanese attacked on a regular schedule each day. The Hudsons were no match for the Zero fighters escorting the Japanese bombers. As the fateful hour approached, the men who were not flying could only get out of the way and watch from vantage points around the airfield.

The enemy became increasingly pugnacious. One pilot even showed his contempt for us by an audacious display of aerobatics. He made an approach onto the runway and ran his wheels along the ground, then made a wide 'ground loop' with his tail up and machine-guns firing before taking off again in the original direction of his approach.

Our squadron Meteorological Officer, Bryan Rofe, who was another Adelaide man, often met me after the war and he reminded me of an occasion when the Japanese seemed to appear out of nowhere with machine-guns belching. He saw me bolt for cover over a bank and took a flying leap after me. While still in mid-air he realised that the creek into which he was jumping was about twelve feet beneath him.

Poor Bryan survived the experience, and some months in the jungle after Japanese occupation, only to die untimely young from a heart attack after the war.

The fierce tropical heat of Koepang kept us sweating continuously and tested my teetotalism to the full. Once when I returned from patrol I found that the only drinking water, which had to be boiled for safety's sake, was still almost at boiling-point. My squadron mates were enjoying frosted bottles of beer with dewy condensation drops trickling down their chilled exteriors. The sight was so tempting that I took a gulp—and promptly spat it out again. Even with my mouth and body crying out for moisture I couldn't tolerate the taste, which reminded me of the smell of dead mice decaying under wooden floorboards.

My greatest joy was the occasional arrival of a large Thermos of Amscol icecream straight from Adelaide. Mother sent it packed in a new product known as 'dry ice', and even though the icecream was mostly froth by the time it arrived in Timor there was always a cold and reasonably firm centre. I was so eager to consume this delicacy that often the first two mouthfuls did not even make it down my throat. I certainly didn't share too much of it with the other pilots, as I did Mother's tins of her famous homemade shortbread. These goodies kept arriving until the Japanese were almost on our doorstep, because our friend Captain John Chapman, Chief Pilot of the now-defunct Guinea Airways, carried them on his regular flights from Adelaide to Darwin. From there they came by R.A.A.F. flights.

Even the steadily increasing menace of the Japanese did not prevent us from enjoying some tastes of civilised life. A staff of Timorese, including some very young boys, looked after our domestic wants, and these kids knew me as 'Tuan Lagi Makan' (Mr More Food) or 'Tuan Music' because of my ever-present gramophone.

I was developing my love for classical music, and the sounds of Debussy's *Poissons d'Or* or *La Jeune Fille aux Cheveux de Lin*, or the music of Delius and Ravel, sounded exactly right as they floated across the moonlit valleys near our quarters.

Aircraft servicing facilities were very limited and we had to fly to Darwin for maintenance work. On 28 January 1942 I was returning to Koepang after one such flight when base radioed that the airfield was under heavy air attack. I must land at an emergency field known as Mena River, in the south-west corner of the island. We had flown over this area and it looked to be a nice big open space, but no one had ever landed there. As I approached I saw what looked like soft green grass, and made what I expected to be a perfect landing. Unfortunately the grass was six feet high and I was misled into trying to land on top of it. It felt as though the bottom had dropped out of the Hudson when we actually hit the ground.

However, we had landed on the one spot where the ground under the grass was comparatively smooth — not that it made much difference in the long run. When we explored a little we found numerous muddy pools where water buffalo had wallowed.

We set about camouflaging the Hudson with branches, but regulations forced us to keep in regular touch with base by radio. I am certain that the enemy obtained a fix on these radio signals, because a flight of Zeros swooped down next morning and shot up the aircraft. She burst into flames as they roared away, and a few moments later we heard more gunfire from the nearby ocean. We learned afterwards that the British Imperial Airways flying-boat *Corio* had been shot down, with heavy loss of life.

I had removed my precious gramophone and records from the Hudson before the attack, but 'casualties' included a tin of Mother's shortbread. I photographed the blackened remnants by way of a souvenir.

We could do nothing but camp until we were rescued. It was the wet season and it rained torrentially every day. Although we were ankle-deep in mud, we built a crude grass hut which kept off the worst of the downpours.

The place was a hell-hole and the Timorese had more sense than to live there. The nearest village was about twelve miles away, in the much healthier foothills. Innumerable mosquitoes made our lives a misery, and we were also plagued by insects we named 'armoured cars' because their grey shells were so tough that it was almost impossible to crush them between

51

the fingers. They inflicted scores of painful bites.

But we dared not move from the spot. Every couple of days, a message was dropped from the air advising us to stay where we were and that we would be picked up 'very shortly'. If we wandered away we might lose all hope of rescue.

After six days, a message was dropped saying that the U.S. destroyer *Peary*, which already had been damaged by misdirected R.A.A.F. bombs, would arrive off a nearby beach on the following night. The *Peary* carried drums of aviation fuel and oil for the long-awaited Kittyhawk fighters of the U.S. Air Force—which never arrived—and we were to help unload the drums and stack them on the beach.

We plodded some miles through the swamp to the seashore. The *Peary* hove in sight at dusk, and the crew tossed overboard the 44-gallon drums lashed together in groups of four. To guide them to the beach, the destroyer launched a small row boat manned by five seamen clad only in underpants and gob caps.

We watched the little boat eagerly as it rose and fell on the surf, but just as it neared the shore it slewed around and was swamped by one of the breakers. The five men struggled ashore and joined our disconsolate group.

Fortunately we had rescued enough tinned food from the Hudson to keep us all going, and we shared around our remaining garments. There was nothing to do but lead the sailors back to our grass hut and try to make the best of things.

The tough long-service bo'sun who led the Yank party made two of the most memorable comments I heard during the war. One night, as we sat dejectedly in the water that trickled across the muddy floor of our grass hut, he drawled 'I know now what that guy meant when he said "It could be worse."'

Then, as we beat off the incessant attacks of ravenous mosquitoes, he said 'Maybe you think these here mosquitoes are big, but man! Up in the Philippines them mosquitoes are so big they can stand on their flat feet and fuck a turkey!'

The *Peary* had vanished and we seemed to be forgotten, but we sat it out until the day when one of the American sailors began fooling around with a revolver and managed to blow off his thumb. We had no way of dealing with the ugly wound, and as the senior officer present I decided to override our previous orders and lead the party back to base.

We trudged through the thick bush to the nearest village. The villagers provided us with several tiny Timor ponies, and I loaded one of them with my precious gramophone and records. We set off through sixty miles of bush, through rivers and up and down mountain tracks, to the base at Koepang.

It was a tough trek with some memorable sights, including a snake at least twenty feet long hanging from a tree, and a gigantic spider whose body, apart from its legs, was almost as big as a football.

On the first night we stopped at a mountain village, where the locals shared their meal of tough chicken cooked in egg yolk. After days of bully beef it tasted delicious. I unpacked the gramophone and played them some records, and they were so taken with Gene Krupa's drumming in Benny Goodman's *Sing, Sing, Sing* that they assembled their gamelan band and reciprocated with an impromptu concert.

To their surprise and delight I took over one of the drums and played along with them. One of the old men present asked in halting Malay, that even I could understand, 'What tribe you from?'

Thirty-six hours later we reached another village. This one had telephone contact with Koepang and we were able to get a message through to the airfield. They sent a truck to pick us up and we arrived about four p.m.

In the blackness of the next morning I was among those ordered to board a flying-boat for Darwin. We were the lucky ones.

At dawn, hundreds of Japanese paratroops landed near the airfield and occupied the area. Those of us who remained, including Peter Thompson who was left in charge of fuel supplies, escaped to join Sparrowforce of the A.I.F. This hardy group of fighting men carried on a guerrilla war against the Japanese for several months until the remnants were taken off by a U.S. submarine, but Peter had succumbed to dysentery and I never saw him again.

North of Koepang, few of 2 Squadron remained. The Japanese had overrun Ambon, but Bill White won a D.F.C. for his gallant attempts to fight against impossible odds. His aircraft, by that time known as 'The Flying Colander', was badly damaged but he insisted on 'one more lash at the Japs'. It was the last, for after that his aircraft was too shot-up to fly any more and a few days later he was captured and beheaded by the Japanese.

Bob Law-Smith made aviation history by cramming an amazing twenty-three men into his Hudson. He used up the entire runway before struggling into the air for Darwin and safety.

In the Singapore area things were equally grim. My brother-in-law Colin Verco, a Hudson pilot in 1 Squadron, went through a series of hair-raising incidents before he escaped via Java with a plane-load of his mates. Their perilous flight to north-west Australia included mid-air refuelling from drums of aviation spirit.

After severe operational losses during the Japanese invasion the remnants of 2 and 13 Squadrons were combined under the joint command of Frank Headlam and John Ryland. Those who made it back to Australia included Neville Hemsworth, Bob Dalkin, Ivan Black, Clive Foreman, Mick Finlayson, Simon Fraser, Johnny Venn, Neil Badger, Arthur Sharp, Dick Overhue, and Ian Hay. Duncan McKenzie became my new second pilot, and Sergeant Wireless Air Gunners John Schofield and Trevor Menzies were posted to my crew.

Soon after reaching Darwin I developed dengue fever, probably incubated since my days at the Mena River. With a temperature of nearly 105 degrees I was ordered into the R.A.A.F. base hospital on Darwin airfield on 18 February 1942.

Next morning was beautifully sunny and clear. Neville Hemsworth dropped in to see me at about ten a.m. We had been chatting for about fifteen minutes when we heard the distant rumble of aircraft engines. Looking through the window we soon saw great formations of aircraft to the north-west, and despite my enfeebled condition we were jubilant at what we thought to be the long-awaited arrival of American aerial reinforcements.

Our joy was short-lived. Almost immediately we heard the familiar whistle of falling bombs. As usual, the Japanese precision bombing against no opposition was impeccable. A stick of bombs thundered right across the airfield, from one side of the perimeter to the other, without falling outside the fences.

Neville and I already had dashed out of the hospital ward, down the outside stairs, and into nearby slit trenches. We barely had time to get our heads down before the ward erupted under a direct hit, together with a number of other buildings on the base.

My gramophone bore its usual charmed life. It was in our living quarters, which were untouched.

As the first wave of bombers roared away, Neville and I raised cautious heads to survey the chaos. Only a few yards away there was a bomb-crater big enough to hold a truck. We heard aircraft taking off, and saw the newly-arrived Kittyhawk fighters of the U.S. Air Force struggling into the air.

Like everyone else, the American pilots were caught with their pants down. Swarms of Zero fighters began to strafe the airfield, and hit the Kittyhawks before they became airborne. I saw one after another of them shot down from twenty or thirty feet, with their undercarriages still not retracted, or set on fire while still on the ground.

Soon the next wave of bombers was overhead: twenty-seven of them striking at the wharves and township of Darwin. A gigantic explosion made me look towards the harbour, and I saw great baulks of timber spiralling slowly upwards against huge clouds of black smoke. The cargo ship *Neptuna*, hit by several bombs, had blown up when the flames reached ammunition still in her holds.

The luckless *Peary* was another victim. Most of her crew died and the submerged wreck is now a declared War Grave. There is a rumour that the destroyer carried gold bullion rescued from the East Indies, but the wreck remains inviolate.

In all 135 Japanese aircraft killed about 235 civilians and servicemen, and the attack was followed by a shameful panic. Apparently some quite high-ranking officers advised their troops simply to 'head south', and soldiers joined the fleeing civilians who expected a Japanese invasion.

The senior R.A.A.F. officer was Group Captain Frederick Scherger, later to become Chairman of T.A.A. He assembled all available ground staff and aircrew and told us that we must set an example to the rest of the people in the area by 'standing fast'. Another wave of bombers later in the morning completed the chaos, but by that afternoon we were reaching some kind of reorganisation.

Despite my high temperature I checked out of what was left of the hospital, feeling that the remaining beds would be better employed for those injured in the raids. After the second attack, surviving Hudson aircrews were placed on standby. We were to attack the Japanese aircraft carriers as soon as they could be spotted by our reconnaissance, but, thank God, the carriers were not located. Unescorted Hudsons wouldn't have had a prayer of surviving a low-level attack on these formidable targets with their attendant fighters.

At ten o'clock that night, those of us remaining on the base attended a macabre funeral service. By lantern light, the unfortunates who had been killed that day were wrapped in army blankets and rolled into hastily-dug graves on the edge of the airfield.

In my semi-delirious state the prospects of the morrow were not encouraging, and I believe most of us felt that the Japanese would be landing in Australia at dawn. But it was another of those classic occasions, like Hitler's failure to invade England after Dunkirk, when the victor failed to grab the spoils. It would have been a walk-over for the Japanese if they had landed in north-west Australia, and the course of the war might have altered if they had established a base there.

But the threat of invasion remained and the air raids continued. Consequently the squadron soon was withdrawn to Daly Waters, some 270 miles south of Darwin. From there we would stage into Darwin to carry out patrols to the north, returning to Daly Waters for fuel and engine servicing.

Daly Waters had to be seen to be believed. It was 'dispersal' to the nth degree. Our sleeping quarters were two miles from the airfield in one direction, and the mess was a mile from the airfield in the other direction. The ablution huts lay a mile-and-a-half away in yet another direction. There was no transport, and after a walk through the powdery dust from the mess to the ablution huts and back one might as well not have bothered with a shower.

A dominant feature was the huge latrines, containing two rows of thirty seats poised over trenches. An unlucky aircraftsman was given the job of 'burning out the latrines' but nobody told him he was supposed to empty powdered lime onto the foetid heaps of excreta. He followed the instruction literally, emptied a few cans of petrol into the latrines, and tossed in a lighted match. There was a gigantic explosion and an entire row of seats leapt several feet in the air, then collapsed like a bird with a broken wing. Fortunately no one was enthroned at that moment!

Daly Waters was so impracticable as an air base that the R.A.A.F. abandoned it before the end of 1942.

With makeshift crews, few if any parachutes, limited supplies of bombs and ammunition, machines often peppered with bullet-holes, and airstrips pocked with bomb craters, the squadrons continued their reconnaissance work. Furthermore, they launched a number of audacious raids against the Japanese bases in Timor and Amboina.

On one night raid Flight Lieutenant Dalkin earned a D.F.C. He flew over the airfield at Koepang, where we had been based until recently, and spotted a number of Japanese aircraft apparently practising night flying. Lowering his undercarriage he signalled to the control tower and flew low as though about to land. Then, at the last moment, he retracted the wheels and made a bombing and strafing run across the airfield, destroying a large number of aircraft parked wing-tip to wing-tip by the complacent Japs.

The American fighter squadrons intended for the defence of Darwin had been virtually annihilated and so the Japanese had little opposition to their continued raids other than some Australian anti-aircraft guns. Usually these were ineffectual but they had occasional successes.

As in Timor, the Japs came over with clockwork regularity to demonstrate their precision bombing techniques, and the R.A.A.F. airfield was a hot spot until a squadron of R.A.A.F. Spitfires arrived from the Middle East. These evened the odds and the attacks became much less frequent.

I was determined to preserve my beloved gramophone and records from harm and carried them wherever we went in the north-west. When the air raid sirens sounded I would sometimes have to make several quick trips between my quarters and the nearest slit trench until I had all the records safely below ground level. I was sure that I was more likely to perish from looking after my records, or from dashing to keep a date with some girl, than from direct confrontation with the enemy.

I kept my camera active, too. During one raid I took a photo of Johnny Venn, a West Australian, as he gazed upwards with hands on his tin helmet and said excitedly 'It's all right, boys — the bombs are going to overshoot us!' Next moment the world exploded as a great cluster of bombs burst all around our funk-hole.

Johnny was a real devil-may-care airman and one of the finest people I ever knew. Soon after this event he was forced to ditch his aircraft on the beach at Melville Island after a raid on Ambon. He was rescued, but two days later he was caught in the blast of his own bombs as they exploded on a Japanese ship in Ambon Bay. His aircraft disintegrated.

Our days were occupied with patrols over the Timor Sea, to the north and north-west of Darwin, to look for Japanese warships or carriers. On one patrol I had the most frightening experience of my life when I flew innocently into the heart of a tropical storm.

The aircraft leapt and bucked frantically in the battering up-draughts

TOP: 2 Squadron pilots at Mount Lofty, September 1941. *From left* Flying Officers Bill White, David Campbell, Neville Hemsworth, Flight Lieutenant Allen Love.   BOTTOM: Pilots of 100 Squadron at Milne Bay, September 1942. *From left* Flight Lieutenant Don Stumm, Squadron Leader L. A. (Smokey) Douglas, Squadron Leader Cliff Bernard, Wing Commander Sam Balmer. Only Douglas survived the war (*Author's photos*)

and down-draughts and seemed to do everything but turn completely on her back. It was impossible to control her and all I could do was set the automatic pilot and hope for the best.

The airspeed indicator needle revolved two or three times in one direction and then whizzed around the other way. The bank and turn indicators went completely crazy. Inside the solid-looking mass of cloud the light was an ominous dirty green, fading to yellow as coloured flashes of electrical discharge danced across the windscreen. But there was no way to get out of the storm and all I could do was hope the automatic pilot was a better flyer than I was — a fairly safe assumption!

After a spell of this battering we flew into the 'eye of the storm', a calm patch amidst the cyclonic winds, where we were able to wipe our sweating brows as we faced re-entry into the horrific turbulence. It was the only way to escape being carried along with the storm.

After that I always made a wide circuit around cloud formations that even looked as though they might be tropical storms.

On that day I formulated a philosophy which has served me well ever since: Don't lose your head. Stay calm. Think your way through. Quieten down, because panic follows loss of judgement, and panic means disaster and death.

TOP: Flight Lieutenant Neville Hemsworth, Flight Lieutenant Bryan Rofe the Squadron Meteorological Officer, and Pilot Officer Peter Thompson at Koepang, January 1942. BOTTOM: Wing Commander Sam Balmer watches one of his Beauforts take off at Milne Bay while a U.S.A.F. Aircobra fighter stands by (*Author's photos*)

8

Goodbye Darwin—Hello Milne Bay

BY APRIL 1942 I was the last pilot remaining in the Darwin area of those who had arrived on 8 December 1941. Although I felt I was a veteran, I had made plenty of mistakes. One of these was when, on a routine patrol, I spotted a small lugger anchored in a bay of the Trobriand Islands.

I had this information radioed back to base. No one knew for certain whether the enemy occupied the Trobriands at that time, but base believed they did. I was ordered to attack.

We carried four 250-pound bombs as well as our ·303 machine-guns, and my first attack was a bomb run. I swooped down to about 300 feet, pushed the release button, and four bombs whistled down onto the hapless vessel. They straddled the little ship, and on my next run I decided to use gunfire. I made several strafing runs, raking the decks with a hail of bullets, and with my eye pressed to the gunsight I did not notice the frantic activity aboard the lugger.

I certainly heard about it later. She carried a crew of desperate Dutchmen who were island-hopping just ahead of the Japs, and it seems that my bullets riddled the vessel and actually went right up the mast on which a crewman was trying to hoist a Dutch flag. The bombs landed close enough to cripple the steering gear, and our unfortunate Allies had to spend a perilous week at anchor while they repaired it. They expected the Japs to turn up at any moment.

When the battered craft finally limped into Darwin the crew made a beeline for the R.A.A.F. base, to express their opinion of the Aussie bastard who had nearly killed them all. Luckily I was alerted and spent the next couple of hours well away from squadron barracks, until the enraged group had departed.

By that time the U.S. Air Force B17s ('Flying Fortresses') were operating from the area, and on 26 March I acted as observer for a Captain Lewis. He was one of many pilots who claimed to have been General MacArthur's personal flyer.

The B17 crew thought I would be able to give expert first-hand advice on targets in western Timor. We took off in darkness, and dawn revealed almost ten-tenths cloud over Timor. Nothing showed but an occasional tall peak poking through the cloud, and when Lewis asked impatiently 'Where the hell are we?' I had to answer 'How the hell do I know?' The Yanks then dropped their bombs indiscriminately and we headed for home . . . but Captain Lewis and his navigator had great difficulty in finding the way.

The Americans were used to such facilities as radar and radio beacons, which did not exist in northern Australia at that time. We had flown without them, but the Yanks found it hard to accustom themselves to seat-of-the-pants flying and sometimes seemed almost helpless without these facilities.

One pilot, flying up through central Australia to Darwin, radioed base to 'turn on the air beacons'. This was impossible because they were non-existent, and the pilot and his crew were never heard of again.

Later, when I was instructing at Jervis Bay, a B25 (Mitchell) bomber landed at Moruya, about 200 miles south of Sydney. The pilot walked up to me and asked 'Say, is this Brisbane?'

Such errors help one to understand Captain Lewis' helplessness when he made a landfall on the lonely coast of north-west Australia. The utter desolation of that part of our continent can be appreciated only by those who have seen it, and as we glimpsed the coastline through heavy rain and low cloud I felt very far from home.

We were completely lost, and the featureless coastline gave us no guidance. The fuel gauges were registering empty tanks, and Lewis ordered all of us to don parachutes and stand by to bail out. It was a chilling prospect. The chances of our being found in such inhospitable country were less than remote.

Probably we were only moments away from 'hitting the silk' when the bomb-cratered landing strip at Wyndham loomed into sight. After a some-what scary landing the B17 rolled to a halt, and the sense of exhausted relief that swept over me reminded me of the dangerous landing at Mount Gambier in 1941. So much had happened since then that it seemed a lifetime ago.

I had had no recurrence of dengue fever but I began to suffer other tropical ailments such as severe stomach cramps from dehydration. The remedy was to eat bread and butter lavishly coated with salt, but there was no such easy cure for the prickly heat rash which smothered my skin. And, worst of all, I soon found I was allergic to the bites of Darwin sandflies during the wet season. The bites on my legs turned septic.

I'm extremely lucky that I wasn't punctured by anything more lethal than sandflies. Our Hudsons were carrying out many tasks for which they had not been designed, including the dive-bombing of enemy ships, but they could not fight the fast and manoeuvrable Zeros. When a Zero came dangerously close we were forced into violent evasive action, such as throwing the Hudson into a severe crablike manoeuvre. The enemy pilot would tend to miscalculate speed and direction and overshoot the target. But, alas, not often enough.

Whenever I was attacked by Zeros I was lucky in finding a nearby cloud to conceal me, and I escaped from several encounters with no more than a few holes in the metal skin of the aircraft.

On our raids over Ambon we flew close to the Trobriand Islands. Bob Dalkin told us that if he ever failed to return we should look for him on these islands. 'I shall be the Luluai of Saumlaki,' he said. Years later I saw one of the *Mondo Cane* films which revealed that the lustful ladies of the Trobriands literally chase their menfolk along the beaches to obtain gratification. If 2 Squadron had known this I'm sure we should all have found excuses to crash-land on the snow-white beaches!

Along with our airmen, many of the legendary Darwin traditions also were dying. War had become a serious business and the 'characters' of the outback were pushed aside by its consequences.

One of the stories about these old-timers concerned the rickety railway train that ran between Katherine and Darwin, pausing at all stops in between. The local roads were primitive to the point of non-existence and the railway was a principal method of transport. The stories about it were fantastic and colourful. According to the yarn I heard, a big landowner boarded the train at Katherine, bearing a large suitcase and impeccably dressed in a white suit. There is no snobbery in the outback, and the passenger took the first opportunity of lugging his suitcase along to the driver's platform. It was loaded with booze instead of clothing, and in due course the train arrived in Darwin with the 'cocky' at the controls. A search party had to go out after the driver and fireman, who had indulged too freely in the contents of the suitcase and fallen by the wayside.

My last operational flight out of Darwin was on 14 June 1942, and the Japs gave me a good send-off. Ignorant of the fact that an air raid was going on I returned to base and made a good landing approach. As we rolled along the runway we were ringed with explosions. One of them set fire to Clive Foreman's aircraft as he landed immediately behind me.

Since April we had been under command of Squadron Leader A. B. 'Titch' McFarlane, D.F.C., a fearless flyer who had been with the squadron in the East Indies. The unit had earned a formidable reputation for battling against heavy odds and had been awarded a U.S. Presidential Citation. Since 8 December 1941 I had logged nearly 700 hours of flying, mostly on operations, and I had had a charmed life. I was more than happy to be posted south, with two weeks' leave before reporting to Laverton as a pilot in 100 (Beaufort) Squadron. It was commanded by Wing Commander Sam Balmer, from the Western District of Victoria, who was later to lose his life in a night-bomber over Europe.

The Beaufort was a typical British aircraft: twin-engine, sturdy, and capable of taking almost unlimited punishment. I became very fond of the Beaufort, even to the point of over-confidence, despite her many little design quirks such as the location of the undercarriage lever. It removed most of the skin from your knuckles every time you used it.

After two hours of 'circuits and bumps' I went solo. Soon after that I was assigned Pilot Officer Doug Thomas, from my home town of Adelaide, as my radio operator and navigator. He flew with me for a long time.

After nearly a month of sea patrols along the Victorian coast we were ordered to Nowra, 100 miles south of Sydney, for a torpedo training course. Nowra then was commanded by an R.A.F. pilot, Wing Commander Green. The Chief Flying Instructor was another R.A.F. type, Squadron Leader Tony Gadd, D.F.C. He had much experience in aerial torpedo warfare in the European theatre.

We had to learn a whole new battle technique. The attack had to be flown at minimum altitude in extremely tight formation, so that the attackers would not be silhouetted against the sky. When within striking distance of the target, each flight would fan out, pull up to about 150 feet, and, with the aid of a newly-developed torpedo sight that involved calculations of the course and speed of the target vessel, drop the torpedo on a course that should intercept and sink the ship.

Immediately the torpedo was released, only a few hundred yards from the target and within point-blank gun range, the pilot had to take violent evasive action such as yawing the aircraft, making steep climbs and dives, and constantly changing height and direction. Hopefully, all this wild corkscrewing would distract the enemy gunners, who would of course be doing their best to shoot us down.

The very day we finished our course, each Beaufort was loaded with a live torpedo and we were sent to Milne Bay on the eastern tip of New Guinea. This area, defended by a meagre force of Australians and Americans, was the vital 'hinge' of the Japanese invasion force heading for Port Moresby. It was under round-the-clock assault by enemy land, sea, and air forces.

Milne Bay is one of the wettest places on earth and we landed in a downpour so heavy you could almost swim through it. The airstrip consisted only of an interlocking series of metal mesh sheets laid end to end over the mud. If you could keep your aircraft on these sheets they prevented it from sinking into the mud, but they were as slippery as ice. Several aircraft skidded out of control into the surrounding quagmire and sank axle-deep.

Soon after the sun went down the area was bombarded by enemy warships that sailed into the bay. Apparently this was a regular occurrence, and the Air Officer Commanding, Group Captain 'Bull' Garing, D.F.C., anticipated another visit on the following day. He ordered us to stand by to give the enemy an unpleasant surprise, as soon as they were sighted en route to the area for their next attack.

In mid-afternoon a Japanese cruiser with a destroyer escort was spotted in the approaches to Milne Bay. Our torpedo aircraft took off with an R.A.A.F. fighter cover of Kittyhawks led by one of the best-known of all Australian aces: 'Bluey' Truscott, the former Victorian football hero.

It was the kind of day you dream about for a holiday. Visibility was unlimited. The air was dead still. The sea was an oily mirror. For a torpedo attack it was not a dream but a nightmare.

The enemy began shooting at us when we were still ten miles away. By the time we were three miles away, barely skimming the surface, we were dodging through great fountains of water thrown up by everything the cruisers and destroyers could fling at us. When we reached dropping range, which was supposed to be 1,000 yards, we seemed to be flying through a solid mass of bursting shells, incendiary bullets and cannon shells, and foaming explosions.

By the time we had dropped our torpedoes and made frantic left-hand turns, we were almost over the enemy bows. We could hardly have got any closer but it seems that none of our torpedoes scored a hit. We were using American-type torpedoes at that time, and these were inclined to be unstable in the air before diving into the water. Since the war some American submariners have written scathingly about the failure of their torpedoes to run straight until they were improved. Maybe this was the reason for our lack of success.

But the Japanese Navy never tried to enter Milne Bay again. Perhaps we scared them off. They more or less abandoned their ground troops to their fate, and the planned attack on Port Moresby never eventuated.

The Japanese shooting (or projectiles) was better than ours during the attack. Most aircraft returned with a number of bullet or shrapnel holes.

A sidelight on the use of aerial torpedoes was the fact that they were powered by liquid alcohol. Members of our ground crew 'milked' some of this fuel from the torpedo motors, mixed it with raisins in a coconut shell, and buried it in the ground to ferment. This jungle juice was an explosive brew, and rumour has it that a couple of men went blind after drinking it.

No replacement torpedoes were available in New Guinea and so we had to fly back to Townsville after every drop to pick up fresh 'fish'. On one of these brief visits I met Aircraftswoman Jean Paine, a wireless operator at Area Headquarters, who was later to become my wife.

After Milne Bay, we began attacks on shipping in the Solomon Islands region. The system we used was to fly at night in such a way that any ships we sighted were silhouetted against the moon. Often the ships were at anchor, and there were plenty of them to be found. When we saw a ship we made an attacking run, without escort, and dropped the torpedo — often before we were spotted by the enemy crew.

On one of these attacks, in the Buin/Faisi area, I lost another good friend: Flight Lieutenant Don Stumm of Brisbane. He failed to return from a moonlight attack but we never knew whether he was shot down or whether he crashed into the sea by misjudging his altitude—always a possibility over the sea, especially at night.

On another trip to Townsville I met a U.S. Air Force captain, Fred Eaton, who was flying B17s over New Guinea and points north and east. He took part in an historic raid against Rabaul from Townsville, the first launched by the U.S.A.F. from east Australia against Japanese-occupied territory.

Rabaul was a hive of Japanese activity, and the six B17s in the raid met heavy opposition. Fred's plane was so badly damaged that he had to crash-land in the jungle on the north coast of New Guinea, but he and his whole crew managed to walk to safety.

In 1978 the aircraft was discovered in a remarkable state of preservation, and it is being salvaged for inclusion in the Papua Air Museum. Fred and the surviving members of his crew will be invited for the unveiling.

Fred, like me, is a great jazz fan. After the war we kept up our friendship and I frequently cite his career as demonstrating the benefits of free enterprise. He finished the war as a Colonel commanding a bomber group over Europe, went back to his home in Scarsdale, New York, and became a pilot for American Airlines.

When this palled he joined the staff of Sears Roebuck, the huge mail-order and department store combine. His talents sent him rapidly up the ladder of promotion. At the time I first visited him he was in charge of personnel in Chicago. When I next saw him he was in a similar position in New York. Soon he was transferred to Atlanta, Georgia, where he was head of personnel for the southern States. In 1977 he retired after seventeen years in charge of the Sears Roebuck operation in South America, based at Caracas, Venezuela.

Today he lives in retirement at Hilton Head Island, on the edge of the twelfth fairway of a golf course where the celebrated Heritage Classic Tournament is held each year. He still pilots his own aircraft.

It seems that my family has some links with the U.S.A. Langdon Bonython kept up a correspondence with a friend in Massachusetts concerning the American branch of the family. Richard Bonython landed in New England in 1630, only ten years after the Pilgrim Fathers, and on 12 February that year the Council of Plymouth granted him an area on the Saco River known today as Old Orchard. There is still a Bonython School (they pronounce it 'Bonny-thon') at Saco although we haven't traced any descendants from Richard's son John, whose tombstone bears the telling epitaph:

Here lies Bonython, the Sagamore of Saco
He lived a Rogue and died a Knave and
Went to Hobbo Wocko

When Langdon Bonython's correspondent wrote to Father in 1942 he named several young relations in the armed forces who might serve in Australia. One, Todd Dabney, was in the U.S.A.F., and pure instinct made me visit a squadron of Aircobra fighters based at Milne Bay. These fighters were said to be more heavily armoured for their size than a battleship, and certainly they had the glide path of a brick.

I went across the airstrip and asked the first Yank I saw 'Does anyone here know a Lieutenant Dabney?'

The answer was 'Sure—that's him over there.'

Thus I met Todd Dabney, who was to become godfather to my first child, Robyn. Todd had a distinguished war record and featured on the front cover of *Life* magazine. I have visited him in his picturesque hometown of Richmond, Virginia, on several occasions.

I made my third documentary movie during this tour of duty and titled it *These Eagles—Incognito*. Opening credits showed it was a 'Bullshit Pictures Production' with a trademark of a rather uncomfortable cow ringed with the slogan 'Per Ardua ad Terra Firma,' a variant on the R.A.F./R.A.A.F. motto 'Per Ardua ad Astra' (by hard work to the stars).

Some incredibly hairy landings and take-offs from the Milne Bay runway, where the aircraft literally vanished amidst clouds of mud and water, were high spots of the film. Also I captured one of 'Bluey' Truscott's typically outrageous landings. Truscott was a helluva shot but a terrible pilot, and it is ironical that after all his victories he died by crashing into the sea, off north-west Australia, through an apparently simple pilot error.

In December 1942, after twelve months spent mostly on operations, I was posted to the Torpedo Training School at Nowra. En route to this posting Jean and I were married in Sydney on 23 December, thus fulfilling the ouija board's prediction.

Wing Commander Owen 'Shorty' Dibbs, an amiable giant, had become C.O. of the unit, and the instructor pilots included Flight Lieutenant Jim Ryan of Perth. After years of safe flying, Ryan died tragically as a passenger in an aircraft accident only a few days after the war ended.

Jean and I set up house in a cottage we rented near Bomaderry, on the north side of the Shoalhaven River near Nowra. We had no telephone in the cottage but I had an easy way to advise her of my movements. The unit had a Wackett Trainer, a light Australian-built aircraft used for spotting torpedo drops from the Beauforts, and often I flew it home via Nowra from observation flights. I would circle the cottage until Jean came outside, throttle back the engine, bellow 'I won't be home for dinner!' and fly on to base when she waved acknowledgement.

Housekeeping was a new experience for both of us. Soon after our marriage we entertained a high-ranking officer to dinner and Jean whipped up a special toffee pudding from a magazine recipe. All went well until she served the pudding. Our guest took one mouthful and became strangely silent. After a few embarrassing moments he rose, still in silence, and left the room.

Jean and I looked at each other, wondering what was wrong, but our guest soon returned and rather shyly explained that he wore false teeth. One bite of toffee pudding had glued them together, so that he had literally to prise them apart.

Life was fairly hectic at Nowra. Each month a new course of trainee pilots would arrive for torpedo attack training. We instructors drilled them in low-altitude close-formation flying and then, with the old Sydney ferry *Burrabra* as a target, in the technique of aiming and dropping torpedoes.

Such attacks called for wild manoeuvres that were hard on the aircraft. Control cables needed constant tightening to compensate for the strain, and the sudden yaws and jerks could be equally hard on aircrew. One of my crew, Flying Officer Geoff Brokenshire, suffered a broken arm.

But we instructors had to drill the trainees into this vigorous but skilful manoeuvring and emphasise that by the time they dropped torpedoes they were in point-blank range of enemy gunners, so that they had to do everything possible to distract them.

The attacks were as spectacular as they were dangerous. We flew so low that the slipstreams threw up great rooster tails of water behind us. On 14 April 1943 we staged a special attack in Jervis Bay to be filmed by newsreel cameramen, and two aircraft were flown by instructors Dave Day and Ray 'Grassy' Green. One of them miscalculated and the two Beauforts touched, damaging the ailerons of one and the elevators of the other. One rolled to the left and crashed into the sea and the other shot vertically upwards, rolled over, and also crashed. The crews of both Beauforts perished.

In 1978, when I participated in an American Express credit card advertising campaign, I received a letter from a Mr Ernest Morgen asking whether I was the same Flight Lieutenant Bonython whom he remembered from Nowra.

Morgen had been an engineer officer with the Commonwealth Aircraft Corporation, then involved in the development of a new aerial torpedo sight. I took him up on a test flight for the sight, and he was somewhat shaken when I told him 'It's no use wearing a parachute because we never fly high enough to use it. And there's not much point in wearing a Mae West because there are so many sharks in Jervis Bay that you may as well drown quickly instead of floating around to be eaten gradually.'

But, as usual, the gypsy's warning that I would die in an air crash was postponed . . . although I had another narrow escape.

It happened when I took our dental officer, Flight Lieutenant Ken Robertson, for his first ride in an aircraft. He flew with me on an observation flight in the Wackett Trainer, and on our way back to base the engine developed a fuel block. We were actually within sight of Nowra airfield, a rather undulating strip carved out of the heavy surrounding timber, and with the engine stammering and stuttering I tried to stretch my glide to reach the eastern end of the runway.

This was a dangerous course at the best of times but the only alternative was to crash in the treetops. Luck wasn't with me and we crash-landed about 100 yards short of the runway. The timber had been knocked down for several hundred yards approaching the tarmac but the thick stumps still remained. More by good fortune than good management I hit one of these slightly to the side of the cockpit. Another foot to the right and I would have had the engine in my lap.

I suffered only a few bruises and scratches, and Ken also was able to walk away from the wreck. But, thirty-five years later, he still has certain back troubles which he attributes to the accident. He has been my dentist ever since the war and so I wonder whether he has been reaping a prolonged revenge.

As on most R.A.A.F. stations in those days the mess parties were fast and frequent. Ernest Morgen remembered one of them in his letter to me and said that when he flew with me on a mock attack next day my violent evasive manoeuvres after dropping the torpedo made him wish he was dead!

One of the 'hard cases' of the base was Lieutenant Dennis George, R.A.N. Reserve. During our farewell party for Tony Gadd, who was returning to England, he competed in one of those drinking contests to be won by the man who sank most drinks in the shortest time. I had the reputation of being the squadron's fastest drinker, though only of 'lolly water', and in this contest I drank eighteen lemon squashes in two minutes twenty-four seconds.

Someone else sank twelve gins in three minutes five seconds, and Dennis George topped the score with eighteen crèmes-de-menthe in three minutes twenty seconds.

Soon after that some bright spark exploded a smoke bomb in the mess. As perhaps the only sober man around I was concerned for Dennis' safety. The last time I had seen him he was sitting on the floor with his back to the wall, his open mouth and protruding tongue stained a bilious green from crème-de-menthe.

I fought my way into the billiards room and dragged him semi-conscious from under the table, ignored by two intrepid airmen who were playing snooker in gas-masks.

I heard that Dennis did not see out the war but died of liver trouble. This was perhaps not surprising but it deprived me of the pleasure of observing his promised entry into politics. He felt he was sure to win on the slogan 'Vote George, for Grog and Grummet.' ('Grummet' is navy slang for sex.)

As well as training young pilots to become torpedo bombers we were involved in the changeover from the fat stubby American torpedoes, with their unstable glide path from aircraft to water, to the longer and slimmer

British torpedoes which seemed more suitable to aerial work.

Also we aided in the development of the new aerial radar system and operated as a reconnaissance unit off the east coast. Several Japanese submarines had attacked shipping along the coast, and two-man submarines had even entered Sydney Harbour and shelled the waterside suburbs.

At one period we suffered a number of inexplicable fatal training accidents, and a close check of our aircraft revealed that a couple of them had control cables partially sawn through. Obviously there was a saboteur at work, and 'Shorty' Dibbs and I, unknown to each other, decided on some unofficial patrolling.

Revolvers in hand, we prowled around the base late one night. I heard a sound, and fired at a dark furtive form. Shorty did likewise. Fortunately we recognised each other's voices before continuing a possibly fatal shoot-out.

But maybe our activities had some effect. All aircraft were grounded, checked, and flight-tested, and we had no more problems after that, so perhaps the saboteur had been frightened off.

In September 1943 the unit moved from Nowra to Jervis Bay, where a new airfield had been completed near the township. The R.A.A.F. moved into the old R.A.N. station buildings and found themselves in an idyllic situation. It was a beautiful spot, with gleaming white sands and blue sea (which concealed numerous sharks) and it was a bachelor's paradise. Lonely office girls from Sydney flocked down for holidays at the well-known resort, and unattached members of our unit were inundated by bright young things hell-bent on having the time of their lives with handsome airmen—who were happy to oblige. Each Saturday our boys took station at the bus terminal to look over the 'new crop' arriving from the city, and neither sex wasted any time in striking up new acquaintance.

When we moved, our station commander was Wing Commander Frank Ell. For obvious reasons he was nicknamed 'Munger'. He seemed to be a rather strange bird but I had no problems with him until one 'dining in' night. These nights are a service tradition, with every officer expected to be present. In peacetime special dress uniforms are worn, and the ceremonial includes that of 'passing the port' in traditional style and the Royal Toast proposed by the youngest officer present.

After the formal dinner the mess president usually allows a certain amount of horseplay. Sometimes he imposes penalties for actual or imaginary misdeeds, and on one occasion Ell ordered me to drink three pints of beer.

As a teetotaller, I refused. He took this in bad humour and next morning had me paraded before him for 'failing to obey a lawful command'. But nothing came of it, and after the war I learned from Air Commodore Knox-Knight, who was Area Officer Commanding in 1943, that if I had chosen to take the case to higher authority then Ell would have 'got the rocket' instead of me.

Jean and I shared a house in Jervis Bay with Jim Ryan and his wife and small son. At that time I was so enraptured with air force life that I seriously considered transferring to the permanent R.A.A.F. after the war. I must have been mad!

It was here that the little daughter of a fellow-officer, unable to pronounce my surname, converted it into 'Kym the Night Man'. A dubious distinction if I ever heard one, because a 'night man' used to remove the 'night soil' from outdoor privies.

I was adopted by a black mongrel dog, to whom I gave the unoriginal name of Nigger. He followed me as I rode my R.A.A.F. Indian motor cycle from the house to the airfield, and pranced excitedly whenever I returned from a flight. On one occasion, as he leapt into the air, I heard a slight *ping*! and saw him shaking his head in a puzzled way. The top inch-and-a-half of one ear had been neatly clipped off by the still-turning propeller!

Training accidents continued to take the lives of some of our best men. Doug Thomas, who had become quite a radar expert and checked out trainee crews in its operation, perished in one of these. On 17 January 1944, while flying with Flight Sergeant Doepel from Brisbane, an exceptionally capable pilot, the aircraft suddenly and inexplicably dived steeply from about 2,500 feet into the sea. All aboard were killed.

In April 1944, No. 6 O.T.U. of Nowra and Jervis Bay ceased to exist, and for a month or so I filled in time with my old friend Neville Hemsworth, by that time Squadron Leader commanding 37 Transport Squadron. They carried supplies and personnel around a circuit from Laverton to Darwin and back via various Western Australian bases.

In May I took command of an odd little outfit called Torpedo Development Flight, Nowra. It consisted only of a Moth Minor and a Beaufort, and our function was to aid the development and launching of a wholly Australian torpedo. During three months I dropped forty-seven torpedoes, culminating with the first Australian Mark 15 model at the navy range on Pittwater near Sydney's Palm Beach on 19 July. But the whole operation seemed rather pointless because the R.A.A.F. had phased out torpedo-bomber operations. Before the war ended I was to laugh at hearing the story that R.A.A.F. torpedo development had only lasted so long because the Bonython family had supported it financially. The story said 'They liked them!'

9

Eye in the Sky

AFTER NEARLY eighteen months of rear echelon service I was considerably browned off, and I had the unit signwriter paint the slogan 'Don't Get Around Much Any More', illustrated by four disgruntled Dead End Kids, upon our office door. So, at the beginning of August, I was relieved to be transferred to 5 O.T.U., at Williamtown in New South Wales, for a conversion course on Mosquito (photo reconnaissance) aircraft.

The Mosquito was one of the glamour aircraft of the war, although it was not ideal for tropical conditions. Built of fabric-covered plywood, it was extremely light and a joy to fly, but in savage tropical rainstorms the fabric could start to peel away from leading surfaces, exposing the plywood, which also opened up until an entire wing disintegrated. This happened in several known cases.

As if this was not enough, some delivery pilots had a selfish habit of putting on a violent display of aerobatics before handing over a Mosquito to its operational unit. I recall at least one disaster caused by an unexplained wing collapse, and I suspect it could be traced to unnecessary stresses before delivery.

The Mosquito was a two-seater, with just enough room for a pilot and a radio operator/navigator to sit side by side. I was fortunate in my partner, Flying Officer Keith Roget of Melbourne. He flew with me for my last 350 hours in the R.A.A.F. and eventually was Mentioned in Despatches. He certainly deserved more than this. Whatever success I achieved was due to his support.

In September 1944, as Flight Commander of A Flight, 87 Photo Reconnaissance Squadron, I began my third operational tour. We were based at Coomallie Creek, about twenty miles south of Darwin. From Coomallie Creek we flew over Timor, the Celebes, and Ambon. For flights further west, over Java and even Borneo, we staged out through the airstrips at Broome or Drysdale River Mission Station.

Our aircraft was lightened for maximum speed and endurance. We carried no weapons and every inch of space available was filled with photo gear and extra fuel tanks. There was no automatic pilot. Flights lasting more than eight hours tested the endurance of the strongest pilot.

As we covered stretches of open sea our parachutes each incorporated an inflatable rubber dinghy. We had to sit on the dinghy air bottle and after a couple of hours in the air one became overwhelmingly conscious of the hard bottle under one's bottom. During the last two or three hours of a flight it became pure agony.

Whenever we operated out of Broome or Drysdale we had to take a mechanic with us from Coomallie, to refuel and service the Mosquito before we went on. These staging points were three hours from Darwin and there was nowhere for the mechanic to sit except on the floor, between the navigator's legs. It must have been an uncomfortable flight for the mechanic, who could not even see out of the aircraft. He had to await our return from the flight over enemy territory, and then make another uncomfortable journey back to Coomallie.

Our function was to cover enemy-occupied ports and airfields, watching for any build-up of activities on land, sea, or in the air. New airstrips were noted, the fighter strength on existing airstrips kept under observation, and all shipping movements recorded.

Our speed was our defence. Our flights were so regular that we always met anti-aircraft fire and our photographs showed fighters taking off to intercept us, but even on the couple of occasions when the fighters drew near I had simply to open the throttle to leave them miles behind.

With 87 Squadron I flew seventeen missions comprising 112 flying hours, including a flight to central Java that was the longest ever undertaken by the squadron.

Our C.O. was Squadron Leader Herbie Gamble of Melbourne, a lolly-water manufacturer in peacetime. Our aircraft included a lone Wirraway, used for communications, and a Lockheed Lightning fighter converted for photographic use. Of all wartime aircraft my great ambition was to fly a Lightning, but it was not to be. Shortly before I arrived at the squadron, Flying Officer John Rush was flying the Lightning when it crashed, exploded, and burned at Darwin. I'm glad that Rush survived the accident but I never really forgave him for depriving me of the opportunity to fly that most beautiful of wartime aircraft.

Wing Commander Stewart Jamieson (who became Australian Ambassador to Russia after the war) was the Area Intelligence Officer, with Squadron Leader Reg Rechner, of Adelaide, as his deputy. Reg had won a D.F.C. when flying Blenheims in the Middle East.

Later I discovered that Jamieson was a good judge of modern Australian art, but then I only knew he had some peculiar ideas about gleaning intelligence. One of these involved a build-up of warships and merchant ships in Surabaya harbour, already revealed by high-altitude photography.

Jamieson believed this shipping should be photographed again, from a very low level. His plan was for an aircraft to fly the whole length of the harbour below 200 feet, just above the eagerly expectant Japanese cruisers, destroyers, and protectively-armed merchant ships.

The uninitiated might think that this could be done at high speed, but no! At that altitude, to prevent gaps between the photographs, the pilot would have to make the run at half-throttle and at a maximum speed of about 160 m.p.h.

I was keenly interested in this operation because I had been chosen for it. My interest (and apprehension) heightened when Jamieson explained that a single run, in which I might hope to take the enemy by surprise, would not be enough. I must then make a 180 degree turn to photograph objects on the other side of the aircraft. Any Japanese gunner who missed me the first time certainly would be ready and waiting when I flew over him again.

In anticipation of this apparently suicidal mission I spent several days in the Mosquito practising low-level flying over water, using a reservoir just outside Darwin. I was about ready to go when I was delighted to hear that the operation was cancelled.

Later, I found Rechner had convinced Jamieson that the photographs could be taken as effectively from 20,000 as from 200 feet. Often since then I have publicly acknowledged that Rechner saved my life. Another lucky escape!

A point we discussed frequently was whether, if we were captured, we should claim our true ranks or pretend to be non-commissioned officers. Many believed that the higher the rank, the more likely one was to be tortured and executed.

Whenever we staged through Broome or Drysdale we were expected to bring back 'goodies' for our fellow officers. Drysdale was noted for its oysters (which I did not eat) and Broome provided cases of the celebrated Swan beer of Western Australia (which I did not drink). I did not bother to record how many oysters we managed to collect off the rocks, but my log book does note '4½ cases', '3 cases', etc. against flights from Broome back to Darwin.

I rather resented the time spent in collecting these delicacies because Broome has one of the most spectacular beaches in Australia and in those days was a unique township inhabited by Chinese, Aborigines, and various local 'characters', although a good many had departed after some savage Japanese air raids.

We used to be accommodated in the picturesque Broome Hotel. One of its features was a white cockatoo with a raucous and filthy vocabulary, gleaned no doubt from the rough and tough pearl fishermen who once congregated there. Whenever a woman walked into the lounge the cockatoo screamed 'Get outa here ya dirty whore!' and similar endearing phrases.

After the war, Russell Drysdale told me a memorable story about Broome. It concerned an Aboriginal prostitute known to the locals as 'No

Pants Nancy', who was about to deliver her sixth illegitimate child. A concerned white lady asked her 'Well, Nancy, who's the father this time?'

Nancy scratched her head and replied 'Well, missus, it's like this: when ya gits yer arm caught in a circular saw, it's 'ard to say which tooth cut ya!'

The Broome airstrip, of unsealed orange dust (or mud) was dangerously short. It was a nerve-racking ordeal to ease the Mosquito into the air, heavily laden with fuel for the long return flight to Java, before hitting the safety fence.

On one trip, the mechanic we brought from Darwin was the rather dim son of a noted Australian general. He wore thick glasses reminiscent of 'Dr Cyclops' and I believe his mates called him that.

The mechanic had to check the twin Mosquito engines before our take-off. One of his tasks was to refill the radiators with glycol coolant, but Cyclops apparently forgot to replace the glycol filler plugs on both engines. We took off at first light, and as we made it once more over the boundary fence I was horrified to see the engine temperature gauges rising so rapidly that the needles went right off the clock. Also I could see two white jets of escaping coolant streaming back over the wings.

Returning to an airfield when you have barely gained altitude is one of the most dangerous manoeuvres possible in flying. With my heart in my mouth I executed a slow turn and plonked the Mosquito down about twenty yards inside the fence, only moments before the engines would have seized up. Apparently Cyclops had forgotten to replace the plugs because he was suffering from a severe case of the 'trots', but I had no sympathy and tore a strip off him a yard wide.

It was yet another example of my well-proven theory that my narrowest escapes during the war came through the errors of 'friends' rather than from the efforts of the enemy. I had yet another example while at Coomallie.

As Flight Commander, one of my duties was to check out newly-arrived pilots. By that time they were arriving with far less experience than pilots earlier in the war, and sometimes they would not arrive in Darwin until two months after they had converted to Mosquitos. Pre-embarkation leave, and the long overland trip through Alice Springs, took up the time and made them more than a little 'rusty' before they joined the squadron.

The squadron had no dual-control Mosquitoes. On check-out flights I had to sit in the navigator's seat, which was considerably lower than the pilot's, and give verbal instructions to the new pilot. I had one or two rather hairy experiences at the hands of these youngsters, and the worst came only a few seconds after take-off with a new pilot.

Coomallie airstrip had a fairly steep tree-clad hill at the end of the north-south runway, and I saw at once that we were not going to clear it. Branches of the gum trees literally were brushing our wingtips and I saw that the hapless pilot had mistakenly pulled back on the propeller pitch controls instead of the throttle controls. He was reducing propeller pitch

Top left: Wackett Trainer bites the dust, Nowra 1943. Top right: Sweetening up Jumbo with some milk chocolate. Bottom: Squadron Leader O'Neill (*left*) instructs Kym Bonython on Mosquito aircraft at Williamtown, New South Wales, 1944 (*Sydney Morning Herald photo*)

with consequent loss of climbing power. I slammed all the levers forward with one hand and with the other knocked the youngster's hand from the control column and eased it back. By that time we were almost scraping our way up the hillside, but somehow we made it over the top.

Someone has said that 'War consists of long periods of intense boredom interrupted by brief periods of intense fear.' There was plenty of time to become bored at Coomallie, where there was little occupation between operational flights, but I managed to find things to do.

The unit had a big brute of an Indian twin-cylindered motor cycle, and so I was able to indulge in one of my favourite hobbies. I became quite proficient on the heavy machine and was adept at speeding it down the runway at about 50 m.p.h., gingerly climbing onto the rider's seat until I was standing erect and with arms outstretched, and then guiding the bike with movements of the body from left to right.

When I was not lairing it up in this manner I rode the Indian round the countryside, and discovered the army camps which were deserted now that the land war had moved into the islands. Past occupants had planted crops of delicious watermelons, and these enabled me to indulge my deprived sweet palate to the point of satiation.

Bryan Monkton was stationed at Darwin, flying one of the famous Catalina flying-boats. I seized the opportunity to go on short jaunts in one or another of the Cats, which were used for extremely long-range reconnaissance and minelaying operations. Sometimes they were in the air for nearly twenty-four hours at a time. I was amazed by the performance of these aircraft, which seemed to have but one speed: eighty knots. They took off, climbed, cruised, and landed again all at the same speed. A few Cats are still in service in various places around the world: a tribute to their great versatility.

Another relief from boredom came through my friend John Chapman of Guinea Airways. I'd been at Coomallie only a month when John allowed me to smuggle aboard his southbound Lockheed passenger aircraft for an illicit night in Adelaide. After that I made no less than four unofficial trips home and stayed up to five days at a time. God knows how I got away with it, although there was one occasion when R.A.A.F. Service Police came rattling at the door of the Lockheed just before take-off. The pilot refused to unlock it until they had departed.

The squadron naturally had its share of characters who kept life interesting: people like Gil Lundberg and Arthur Spurgin of Brisbane; Bill Sudlow and Arthur Phillips; Ron Langsford from Adelaide; Lennie Lobb who was Herbie Gamble's navigator; and Jim Gillespie who died in an air crash just before I finished my tour of duty at Coomallie. Our wireless expert, Flight Lieutenant Jack Dowling, later became a world expert in radar and settled in the U.S.A.

One of my favourite characters in the squadron was a wild man named

TOP: With Robyn, Christopher, and Jean Bonython and Gingerbread, Mount Pleasant 1951. BOTTOM: 'The Fairest of them All'. Haughty Belle of the Isle, imported Jersey cow, with the dairy in the background, Mount Pleasant 1952.

Alan Proctor, who for some reason that I have never discovered committed suicide when flying for Qantas after the war.

I shared a tent with the engineering officer, Flying Officer Roy Bradshaw, and he and Alan sometimes combined to torment me. Roy also was a 'wild man' in his own way, and I heard later that he had been taken off general duties and demoted from Wing Commander to Flying Officer after he had 'borrowed' a DC3 from Sale airfield and flown off to Tasmania with his current girlfriend for a naughty weekend. I don't know whether the constant playing of my gramophone or remorse for this regrettable incident drove him to the grog, but on most nights he came to bed very much the worse for wear.

One day an attractive American nurse visited our mess and spent the day from mid-morning onwards drinking with the boys at the bar. Poor Roy could keep pace in the grog department but stood little chance in this contest against his younger and more glamorous fellow officers. He managed to spend the afternoon plaintively stroking the fair lady's bottom but could reach no further, and by the time he came to bed he had an erection of gargantuan proportions. He draped his towel over it and with tears running down his face sobbed 'Hell, Kym — what am I going to do with this?'

As a non-drinker I usually went to bed earlier than my carousing mates, and one night I was woken from a deep sleep when Bradshaw staggered into the dark tent moaning thickly 'I think I'm going to be sick . . . yes, I *know* I'm going to be sick!'

He retched revoltingly and I heard the horrid splash of vomit onto the floor of our tent. He snored off to sleep but I spent a restless night almost overpowered by the stench — only to discover next morning that it had been a 'Proctor prank'. As Bradshaw made the appropriate noises Proctor, out of sight in the darkness, sloshed water from a bucket onto the floor. Such is the power of imagination!

All such diversions formed a mere background to the serious business of war — although sometimes it did not seem too serious. Some of my most enjoyable flights were to spy out the land for the so-called 'cloak and dagger boys': the commando units who engaged in sabotage and reconnaissance in enemy-occupied territory. We flew along the Bali and Lombok coastlines at less than treetop level to make sure the coast was clear, and Javanese fishermen and bare-breasted Balinese beauties waved cheerfully at us as we roared past. One could almost forget there was a war. Certainly I didn't dream that, thirty years later, I would be holidaying on the same beaches: living in the lap of luxury in five-star hotels set amidst the same palm trees, with Indonesian musicians playing Western-style jazz in the bars.

But there were still some hair-raising incidents. On one of these, only two days after scraping over the mountain in that check-out episode, we made a flight lasting seven hours and forty minutes to East Java and back.

We used a new Mosquito, just delivered from down south, and on the almost three-hour flight from Darwin to Broome I carried out fuel consumption checks because this was the Mosquito's first operational sortie. All seemed in order.

It was our practice to fly on inner tanks from take-off until we sighted the enemy coastline, and to make regular fuel checks during this part of the flight. When we crossed the coast we switched to outer tanks and discontinued engine checks until the return journey. We concentrated on watching for enemy interceptors instead.

When we had been over Java for about an hour, and were photographing our various targets, I happened to glance at the fuel gauges. I was startled by the low levels they indicated, and a quick calculation showed we were using fuel twice as fast as usual. I deduced that a serious leak had developed somewhere between the engines and the outer tanks.

We were about 1,000 miles from home. Everything in between was open sea or enemy-held territory. I decided immediately to abandon the mission, and made a steep turn for home. The time seemed to drag agonisingly as we flew south-eastwards. As usual, the radio and radar aids were worse than useless in helping us to fly straight home, but Keith's excellent navigation helped us to hit Broome right on the button. When we landed we had less than five minutes' fuel remaining.

By August 1945 the war had lasted for almost a quarter of my lifespan until that time. We talked about what we'd do 'after the war' but even though the war in Europe had ended it seemed there would be many more months of fighting before Japan surrendered. When the atom bombs brought hostilities to an abrupt conclusion they saved the lives of many Allied servicemen.

I was on leave in Adelaide when the war ended and had completed nearly five-and-a-half years' service in the R.A.A.F. I suppose I had become a 'fair enough' pilot, and certainly my side-slipping approaches had ceased to be so dangerous, but I was happy to hang up my helmet and goggles. I have never piloted an aircraft since my discharge.

I made — and lost — many dear friends during the war, and I am grateful for the opportunity it gave me to mix with such a broad spectrum of society. But, like many who survived, I often ask myself why I should have been spared when so many of my friends died. I think we may have squandered the opportunities given to us by the sacrifices of others.

One of the many ironies of war was the sad fate of John Schofield, who flew with me for so long as radio operator/air gunner. He stayed in the service a little longer than I, and was discharged just before Christmas 1945. On a visit to his parents-in-law, at Mannum on the Murray River, he dived into the water when his wife's cocker spaniel got into difficulties. The dog was saved but John was drowned, in a sad end to all those years of loyal and meritorious service.

My last active involvement with flying, except as an airline passenger,

75

was in 1946. A friend and I formed a partnership to buy five huge Short Sunderland flying-boats from disposals at virtually scrap metal prices of £1,000 each, plus twenty-two spare engines at £100 apiece. The aircraft formed the basis of Trans Oceanic Airways.

I was virtually a 'sleeping partner' and my friend, who prefers to remain nameless, formed the company and pioneered air services between Port Moresby, Hobart, Lord Howe Island, New Caledonia, the New Hebrides, the Solomon Islands, Grafton, and Port Macquarie.

The company was just struggling out of the red when the Federal Government of the day cancelled its licence. This put the company into liquidation, and Ansett Airways were able to take over all the routes and equipment for a paltry £20,000.

This was a hard enough blow for a man who had worked against all odds, on the proverbial shoestring, to build up a much-needed service. But worse was to come. Ansett put Catalinas on the service, and early one morning one of these blew up at its moorings in Rose Bay, Sydney.

My friend was accused of causing the explosion, presumably by way of revenge, and taken to court. He denied the charge and the jury found him not guilty, but the massive legal costs of defending his innocence stripped him of every penny.

Eventually he left Australia and continued his flying career in Europe and the West Indies. As a final irony, he found himself flying some of the same aircraft we had bought as war surplus, and which later were purchased by foreign operators.

10

Butterfat and Bulls

ON DISCHARGE from the R.A.A.F. I decided that I didn't want to return to a job in an Adelaide accountant's office. First, I applied for a job as announcer with the A.B.C. I still have an acetate recording of my test, in which I had correctly to pronounce such names as Kybybolite, Canna-wigara, Waukaringa, Ketchowla, Yudnapinna, Calpatanna, Koolywurtie, Algebuckina and Takamarinna. All are South Australian townships and the names could occur in news readings. When I hear that record today I can understand why I failed.

With this avenue closed, I decided to go on the land. I had a little experience, because Father owned a farm of several hundred acres at Mount Barker, about twenty-five miles from Adelaide. He was devoted to it although he had to leave it in the hands of managers. He had gone through a number down the years: some good, some not so good. One founded his fortune by regularly selling a quantity of Father's fat lambs, replacing them with vastly inferior animals, and pocketing the proceeds. In this way he set himself up in a different kind of business and never looked back!

After working an apprenticeship of six months under the current manager I started, early in 1946, to look for a place of my own. I found a property named St Magnus, of about 600 acres, near Mount Pleasant, thirty-five miles north-east of Adelaide. It had once been owned by the late Sir Walter Young and in its heyday had been a highly desirable property, but during the restrictions of the war years it had gone very much to seed.

I took over in March 1946, and rented a house from my neighbour, Robert Melrose of Rosebank, while the St Magnus homestead received a badly-needed facelift. The family which sold the property to me put all their furniture and implements into a clearing sale, which in those days was regarded as a social occasion.

A large crowd flocked to the sale from miles around, and the auctioneer proved to be quite a comedian. At one stage he held up a bundle of black roller window-blinds, and yelled 'Here we are, ladies—what am I offered for this lot? Don't forget—it's not the talk that makes the babies, it's the darkness of the night!'

He was addressing an audience which knew that sons are a farmer's finest asset—the more the better.

With unbounded enthusiasm I set about upgrading the entire property from homestead to pastures. Everything I needed was in short supply during that post-war year but I obtained an ancient Caterpillar tractor and kept this faithful workhorse toiling away for months, for fourteen and fifteen hours a day, re-seeding and fertilising areas that had been neglected for many years.

Always a good listener, I received invaluable advice from Ron Horwood, manager of Rosebank. Ron, a fine man who was a veteran of the first World War, kept this magnificent property in tip-top condition. I knew him and his family well. His son, also named Ron, went to school with me at St Peter's but died in 1943 as a P.O.W. in Siam. His sweet little daughter Marion, then only about ten, later married Alistair McGregor of the well-known South Australian wool-broking firm.

Ron was one of the old school in some ways and he tried to teach me the time-honoured method of castrating lambs by biting off their testicles and spitting them out. It is fast, effective, and somewhat nauseating, and I found it literally hard to swallow. I was relieved by the advent of the Elastrator: a tight rubber ring clipped round the testicle sac which causes it to atrophy.

Soon I was the proud winner of local contests for pasture improvement and general farm management. In my zeal I turned to the garden as well as the farm. John Ferguson, a skilled Scots gardener who worked at Rosebank, gave unstinting advice, and I employed Don Campbell from Mount Pleasant as my gardener. Don was a bachelor and a wonderful worker, and between us we soon restored the garden to superb condition. Before long, St Magnus became one of the showplaces of the district.

Don and I planted hundreds of trees around the garden and the paddocks, and flower bulbs by the sackful. I bought many of these new plantings from Stinsons, a well-known Victorian nursery near Geelong, and after dealing with them for about eighteen months I paid them a visit.

When I announced myself I sensed an aura of disbelief, and quite soon the staff dissolved in near-hysterical laughter. It seems that they had pictured me as a crotchety old gentleman in his eighties, but whether this was because of my near-illegible writing or my pedantic phrasing I do not know. However, they obviously got a kick out of meeting their 'best customer'.

I was able to find good help and advice for the outdoor work but Jean wasn't so lucky where our domestic economy was concerned. Household help was hard to find and we went through several rather unsatisfactory assistants. One woman always wanted Thursdays off, and we discovered that this was visiting day at Yatala Labour Prison. Her boyfriend had been 'public enemy number one' to the South Australian Police, and we learned that, until his luck ran out, she had assisted him by taking domestic work and spying out the job for him. When he had knocked off the contents of a house they would both disappear for a while.

Our best helper was a young Aboriginal girl, Rosie Brumby, but she left us after a year or so. Probably it was rather a lonely life for a young girl.

In 1947, when our second child Christopher was due, we were again without help. But while Jean was in hospital I heard of a recently-arrived young Englishwoman who sought employment, and I thought it would be a nice 'welcome home' present for Jean to find some assistance.

I engaged the young woman, who had a baby son of her own, but two days before Jean was due to return I walked into our newly-remodelled kitchen and was startled to find all the saucepans hanging on nails driven into the sides of the new fixtures. Strung across the kitchen, attached to yet more nails driven into the new woodwork, was a series of cords laden with her baby's nappies hung out to dry. On the electric stove reposed what Samuel Pepys called a 'shitten pot', in which her baby had performed. Alas, Jean never did get to see our 'new help'.

Beautiful Rosebank had magnificent gardens and a large animal reserve populated by deer, peacocks, rare white kangaroos, and other creatures. Many celebrities visited this renowned property and we had the pleasure of meeting some of them, including Sir Laurence Olivier and his then wife Vivien Leigh, who were playing a season in Adelaide's Theatre Royal.

Nearby Mount Pleasant, like most country towns, was a real 'Peyton Place' and one could write a novel about the goings-on (later including my own). There were plenty of local characters, including men like Ben Muster and Cyril Fullwood who sheared the St Magnus sheep, Harry Morgan the carrier, and Ken Hicks the butcher. 'Binks' Williams managed the local branch of Elder Smith & Co., the stock and station firm, and Ted Rodda managed the competition, Goldsbrough Mort & Co. The doctor was Lionel Cowling, and we had many a race if I happened to meet his Jaguar when I was driving my Bristol car or Vincent motor cycle.

In the nearby Mount Crawford district lived a remarkable elderly couple: Mr and Mrs Murray Dawson. They attended every clearing sale for miles around and bought up the most astounding collection of junk, including such things as great boxes of nuts, bolts, and sundry impedimenta. No one ever knew what use it could be to them.

They raised pigs on their land and the story goes that, one day, they couldn't find any trace of their swine. After a comprehensive search of the paddocks they tramped home again, to find most of them sleeping contentedly indoors.

They had a handsome home, at least from the outside. I was never invited inside. Today it has been renovated by its present owner, my cousin Sir Alexander Downer, former Australian High Commissioner in London, and I believe he has done a splendid job.

In those pre-myxomatosis days the district was infested with rabbits and rats. On cold nights the latter nested atop the cosily warm Jeep engine, and when I started up in the morning they went flying in all directions over my legs, shoulders, and face.

We had a stack of dogs on the farm: a couple of pet Irish setters named Mutt and Jeff; Spider the sheepdog; and Boris the Russian wolfhound for catching the vermin. They took some feeding, and on two nights a week I drove into the paddocks in my Jeep armed with spotlight and ·22 rifle. In about fifteen minutes I knocked off thirty or forty rabbits, skinned them quickly, and hung the carcasses in bundles inside hessian bags. Suspended from wire hooks on the boughs of silver poplars along the creek bed, where the kennels were located, these made a 'ready use' larder for the dogs.

Hec Bryant, who helped us at harvest time, earned his living as a rabbit catcher. One day he brought his sizeable catch of live rabbits onto our place, and our daughter Robyn watched him wring their necks prior to skinning them. After a while she asked 'Do they squeak because it tickles or because it hurts?'

Like most Australian farmers I suffered from lack of water. The Mount Pleasant area was notoriously dry, granite-based land, and the more I improved the farm the more water I needed. The only way to get it was by boring, which was a tedious and costly process in those days. The drill bit chunked monotonously up and down day after day, sometimes only drilling a few feet a day through the solid rock under the soil. Nowadays, such bores can be sunk in hours.

But at least we did strike water, very saline but good enough for watering plants. I wanted to surround the house with irrigated lucerne paddocks, both for feed and as a protection against bushfires which could not sweep through the green pasture plant. The paddocks were irrigated by fifteen-foot lengths of aluminium pipe coupled together in long lines with protruding individual sprinkler heads. Every few hours I had to turn on one section of the line and turn off another, always in that order in case water pressure split the pipes. During the summer I had to get up at least twice each night between midnight and dawn to adjust or move the pipelines.

My farm was basically sheep country and the rainfall declined markedly for each mile one travelled east from Mount Pleasant. It was ideal for woolgrowing but not so good for meat. However, with careful pasture management I ran crossbred ewes for fat lamb production plus a quantity of merino wethers. We produced some excellent wool as well as good quality lambs for export.

After a couple of years, through my friendship with Frank Macrow who ran a property named Stornaway on the Adelaide side of Mount Pleasant, I began to share his enthusiasm for Jersey cattle. I laid plans for the St Magnus Jersey Stud, and early in 1949 Frank and I went to the Royal Easter Show in Sydney to buy female foundation stock.

I was determined that the St Magnus Jersey Stud was going to be as modern and efficient as I could make it, and in this spirit I began by transporting the Jersey cows back to Adelaide by air.

This was practically unheard-of in those days, but my old friend Reg Rechner (who preserved me from the Surabaya suicide flight) was by that time Manager of Trans-Australia Airlines in South Australia. He arranged my charter of a T.A.A. DC3 freight aircraft, and I brought the cows back to Adelaide in the care of Ken Armstrong, who was a well-known stock agent and cattle judge. There was quite a crowd to welcome the novel cargo, including Father and Mother, reporters, and newsreel photographers.

Frank took my new herd onto Stornaway while we were preparing the dairy facilities at St Magnus, and while my new cows grazed the rich pastures I arranged to import my first sire, a two-year-old prizewinning bull of great breeding named Rochette's Rex. He came from Jersey in the Channel Islands, which is of course the home of the breed. When he arrived we were able to start production, but I had to milk my modest herd in an old timber dairy with a rough cobblestone floor, using a portable petrol-driven milking machine. In the meantime, one of the most modern and spectacular dairy buildings in Australia was under construction at St Magnus.

Frank and I, using ideas I picked up from dairy magazines and those we dreamed up ourselves, had designed a huge building with a saw-tooth roof. Everything in it was planned for convenience and efficiency.

At milking time the cows entered holding yards floored with non-slip concrete, kept clean by a constant film of running water. From the yards they moved into the milking area, which accommodated eight animals at a time. This area also was cleansed by water jets playing over the surface.

From the Alfa Laval Company of Denmark I imported a special milking machine that incorporated transparent glass cylinders, each hanging from a weighing scale. This automatically recorded the milk production of each cow, night and morning, throughout its lactation period. We had four such units, one to each pair of cows. As one cow was being milked, the animal on the other side of the unit was prepared by washing and sterilising so that the milking cups could be transferred without delay. While the cows were being milked, they munched contentedly at a concentrated meal containing linseed oil, which gave a rich lustre to their hides, and listened to recorded music which made life pleasanter for the staff and also, it was believed, increased milk production.

When each cow had given its milk it was moved forward into the middle bay of the dairy, where a special meal waited in each of sixteen stalls. This consisted of a chaff-like substance, produced from our own hay by a new machine called a Hammer Mill that I had seen in London, blended with grain put through the same machine, and enriched with mineral trace elements deficient in Mount Pleasant pastures.

The third bay contained store rooms, harness rooms, feed-crushing equipment, and stacks of tightly-compressed aromatic hay. Alongside the dairy building stood calf sheds, in which each calf had its own pen with a straw-covered cement floor, and the bull pen next to his exercise yard. Nearby stood a huge silo which we filled with ensilage (green fodder) harvested and chopped at the peak of its growth to be fed to the cows in summer.

From the main road, half-a-mile south, the whole complex was a sight to behold. Orderly buildings of white brick with red metal roofing were surrounded by the lush green of irrigated lucerne. Neat rows of trees and shrubs grew to maturity, and among them one could see the glossy, honey-coloured cattle around which the whole process revolved. I remember it all with pride, affection, and nostalgia.

As time went by, our success was proclaimed by an ever-growing canopy of red, white, and blue ribbons, won at various agricultural shows in South Australia and Victoria, which festooned the rafters of the milking area.

One of the most noted bulls I imported into Australia was Farineuse's Dreamer, affectionately known to his previous English owners as Jumbo. He was out of the beautiful dam Desdemona, who also was the mother of another of my imported cattle, Lactiflora 13th.

Jumbo, like all Jersey bulls, could be quite a handful. When he arrived by sea from England I accompanied his mobile pen as he was taken to the State Quarantine Station on Torrens Island, and I found the staff there to be somewhat apprehensive. They had had some unnerving experiences with my earlier imports, and Jumbo also gave them quite a time during his four weeks of incarceration. They were glad to see him go, and watched to see how I would handle him when I came to take him away.

But I knew something they did not—that Jumbo had a passion for Cadbury's Dairy Milk Chocolate. I took a half-pound block from my pocket, he devoured it appreciatively, and then followed me like the proverbial lamb as I led him up the ramp into Harry Morgan's truck. The quarantine staff watched in open-mouthed amazement until the truck disappeared down the road.

Jersey bulls have ferocious reputations but Jersey cows are among the most docile and beautiful of animals. Their placid temperaments and deer-like faces gave one the feeling of working among a herd of pets. I had tremendous pride in my Jerseys, so much so that, when Frank and I attended a farmers' meeting addressed by the Dutch geneticist Dr Haagedoorn, I spoke up in their defence.

Dr Haagedoorn preached the gospel of 'production at all costs', and at question time I asked why a farmer should endure working with crossbred, high-producing monsters when he could be the proud owner of beautiful Jerseys. Haagedoorn answered a trifle arrogantly 'Breed canaries for beauty —crossbreds for production!' But I am unconvinced. My milk production figures were among the highest in the State and I knew I was rearing beautiful creatures whose progeny would retain their inherent conformation.

I secured my first imported Jerseys on an overseas buying trip and holiday while the dairy was being built. Jean came with me, on our first trip together out of Australia, and I indulged my delight in speed by making the first of five visits to the famous Indianapolis 500 Motor Race. We stayed with Todd Dabney in Virginia and with the Eatons who then lived in Chicago.

From the U.S.A. we flew to London for a reunion with Tony Gadd of Nowra days, and after a few days he and his Australian wife joined Jean and me on a trip to the Bonython family area in Cornwall.

Cornwall is a beautiful county. Here we saw first the remnants of the Bonython mansion Carclew, burned down in 1934 just as Langdon Bonython was negotiating its purchase. The skeleton of the huge portico remained, but little else. As perhaps in the past, the former living area was inhabited by pigs! However, the glorious garden, with acres of massive rhododendrons and azaleas surrounding a great lily pond, spoke of the grandeur of the old days.

We drove on to Bonython Manor, near Helston. It seemed a pleasant though slightly forbidding house, but we were not to see the interior restorations I had heard about. Maybe the owners had had enough of Australian Bonythons turning up on their front door step, because they did not invite us in although we had a friendly talk.

Bonython Manor is said to have a ghost which appears only to Bonythons — or perhaps I should say is heard only by Bonythons. Father told me that he heard the non-existent horse and carriage crunching up the gravel drive one night, but it certainly did not manifest itself to me on that lovely sunny afternoon.

I planned our visit to Jersey to coincide with the annual Island Summer Show and we went there with Adrian Poole, a Jersey breeder from New South Wales. The wealth of beautiful cattle made my mouth water, and when I was taken to the breeding place of Rochette's Rex, the first bull I was to buy, his owners proudly displayed the calves that were his first progeny.

A trip to France and Switzerland gave me a breathing space in which to decide on my purchases. The Swiss mountain meadows, dotted with wildflowers, were breathtakingly beautiful. I was enthralled by the sound of cowbells drifting up from the valleys and bought a set, each bell having a different tone, to adorn my own cows at home.

On the return trip to Jersey I bought a number of superb cows. Surely the most beautiful ever to come to Australia was Haughty Belle of the Isle, who had been Reserve Champion of the Island. She became Champion of the Adelaide Royal Show in 1951 and one of her sons fetched a record price as a 1952 yearling. Haughty Belle was aptly named. She walked with a unique grace and poise and a quite majestic air, and she had a loose silky skin, a beautifully shaped head, and a superbly proportioned body. When she walked into the judging ring no other cow existed!

Later I bought Genuine Rochette 80th, Chez Nous Dreaming Beauty, and Lactiflora 13th from the stud which bred Rochette's Rex. Lactiflora 13th had the most perfect udder I've ever seen and she was a fine addition to the impressive herd I was establishing.

St Magnus was becoming a Mecca for the Australian dairy industry and it attracted many admiring stud cattle breeders who studied our equipment, methods, and results. I could be unashamedly proud of my efforts but they took some toll of my family life. I worked more than a sixteen-hour day, from four a.m. to after eight p.m., in order to take advantage of the ideal milking times of five a.m. and five p.m. with all the preparation and clearing-up that they involved.

There was much else to do on the farm and I became a real country boy. Trips to the city were rare, although I attended the weekly meetings of the Returned Servicemen's League, the Dairymen's Association, and the Australian Primary Producers' Union in Mount Pleasant. There was always so much to do on and around the farm that I did not like to leave it for holidays or during the bushfire season. No wonder that Jean became rather frustrated with this 'farmbound' existence.

But all this hard work did not distract me from my love affair with the internal combustion engine. In the late 1940s, when English production got into gear again, I bought a handsome four-door Triumph saloon with its distinctive knife-edged lines and also acquired one of the classic motor cycles of all time, the Vincent HRD Rapide.

I was so enthusiastic about the Triumph that the dealers soon sent one of their salesmen to Mount Pleasant in an attempt to sell me the new two-seater sports version. They thought it would be ideal for Jean. I tended to agree, and we went for a test-drive. The smart little car was an open two-seater with a dicky seat at the rear, but unlike the pre-war models the dicky 'lid' opened forwards instead of backwards. When it was open there was a clear space between the back of the front seat and the rear passenger's legs.

We set off with the salesman and me in the front seats and Jean in the dicky, but the rough country road made the car bounce a bit and this dislodged the catch of the dicky lid. It fell back, hit Jean a hefty blow on the forehead, and almost knocked her out. The poor salesman quickly reached back through the space between the seats in an effort to push the lid off Jean's head, but he was so flustered that his groping hand slid under her skirt and up into her crotch. How not to sell a car in three easy lessons!

I put my Vincent motor cycle to work in a way probably undreamed of by its makers. One of the tasks of a conscientious sheep farmer in wintertime is a daily ride round the flock, spotting ewes whose fleeces become so heavy with rain that if they rolled on their backs in the night they could not get up again. If you missed the daily ride you might lose valuable stock.

In my early days I made my rounds on horseback, but as life grew busier I used the Vincent to ride over the steep rocky pastures. Maybe I'm not unique in putting lovingly-made machinery to such use. One of my cousins, also a farmer, owned that most beautiful of motor cars, the Mercedes 300SL, whose two doors opened upwards like the wings of a bird. A vintage 300SL would command an enormous price today, but my cousin used to stow bales of hay and, I'm told, even a sheep into this masterpiece of automotive art.

Another proud Vincent owner was Ronald Angas, of the renowned pastoral family who lived at Angaston, about twenty-five miles to the north of Mount Pleasant. Obviously a lover of exotic machinery, he drove a Porsche in his late eighties, but in 1950 he seemed far too old for motorcycling. I thought 'Silly old bastard—fancy riding a motor bike at *his* age!' which must have been about the same age I am now . . . and I still ride my MV Agusta with gusto!

A by-product of the dairy herd was a lavish supply of natural fertiliser, some of which I used when I began to specialise in dahlia growing. I obtained tubers from leading Australian growers but none gave better results than those from Harry Brand, a dahlia grower with an international reputation. His tubers and my fertiliser, plus careful dis-budding, produced truly enormous blooms. I have photographs of my son Christopher standing in front of some which were twice as big as his head.

Thus, as well as a cattle exhibitor, I became a keen dahlia exhibitor and took many prizes at country shows. I didn't venture into the Royal Show dahlia contests, partly because they coincided with my cattle entries. When I tell people nowadays that I was once a successful flower exhibitor they think I'm joking!

11

Another Aerial Encounter

LIKE ALL farm kids my children loved to ride on the tractor, and like many doting fathers I allowed them to do so, although this practice has been the cause of many fatal accidents.

Christopher was about five when I took delivery of a new tractor. I attached a set of double disc harrows to the tow-bar and he hopped up onto the back step as I started off to harrow one of the paddocks.

The clutch was new and tight and as I raised my foot the tractor lurched forward. Christopher lost his balance and fell into the path of the oncoming discs. Instinctively my foot went down onto what I thought was the clutch pedal, but clutch and brake pedals were in reverse position to those I was used to on the old tractor. I was pressing the brakes, but the engine was still in gear and the tractor churned onwards.

By the time I realised my mistake the first set of discs had passed right over his body. The whole outfit shuddered to a stop with one disc of the second set just missing the top of his head, and another resting slightly below his neckline. By incredible good fortune the ground was rather soft and the discs somewhat blunt.

I eased the terrified boy out of the trap and rushed him to the local hospital, perhaps more frightened than he was by the thought of his possible injuries. Astoundingly, he escaped with only a broken collarbone.

For a long time after that he kept a wary eye on me when I was harrowing. He watched from the edge of the paddock, and as I came closer he hid behind the nearest tree. When I turned, his head peeped out, followed by his whole body as I went further and further away.

This near-tragedy was followed by a real one. We had acquired a marvellously industrious and cheerful German woman, Kitty Betlewski, to help in the house. She was one of the great flow of migrants then entering Australia on condition that the males worked two years on government projects. Her husband was working on the railway several hundred miles from Adelaide and they saw each other only for a few days every couple of months, but they accepted this good-humouredly as part of their investment in the future. He was considerably older than she was, and they had come to Australia because of the opportunity it offered to their only child, Ron.

Ron was a little red-head about the same age as Christopher, and they became great friends. One winter's night I was working in the dairy when a young farmhand who worked for me said rather casually 'I think you'd better go down to the house. There must be something up. Kitty's putting on a real turn!'

I hurried to the house and soon heard Kitty's anguished wails. They were so terrible that I began to run as fast as I could, and found her by the winter-swollen creek. 'My Ron! My Ron!' she sobbed, and I saw him floating face-down in the water. Still in the rubber knee-boots and overalls I used for milking I plunged into the water and in a few strokes retrieved the poor lad and carried him to the bank. Apparently he and Christopher had been playing by the creek and Ron had fallen in.

His face was blue and he showed no sign of life, but I yelled for my head farmhand, Laurie Dick, and we raced off to Mount Pleasant Hospital in the Bristol with Laurie attempting resuscitation on the back seat. We were too late. All the Betlewskis' dreams of a new life for their son had been shattered.

But farm life had to continue. The cows could not wait, whether it was for milking or mating. To succeed in the stud breeding business one had to watch conformation of body as carefully as the production figures. In those days the emphasis was on the total poundage of butterfat over a 305-day production period. Jerseys were supreme in this field because, being smaller than most dairy breeds, they did not eat as much. Their percentage of butterfat yield was infinitely superior although their gallonage was slightly less.

In addition to keeping faithful records of the milk production of each cow we also recorded their breeding habits, in order to anticipate when a cow would be ready for the bull.

The ideal was for most of the herd to be in maximum production during the lush months of late winter and spring, and dried off for their next calves at a time when feed was scarce. For a cattle exhibitor the best time to mate his star cows is nine months prior to the Royal Show, which in Adelaide takes place early in September. This ensures that the best-looking cows are in full production at show time, so that the ripeness of calving makes them look even better.

One night, after one of our rare visits to the city, I came home at two a.m. from the Lord Mayor's Ball in the Adelaide Town Hall to find that one of my best imported cows was *ready*! This must have been one of the few times in history when a cow was taken to a bull by an owner in full evening dress. It was well worthwhile, because Genuine Rochette 89th calved at just the right moment and was Grand Champion at the next Royal Show.

Preparation of show cattle was a long, painstaking affair. About six weeks before the event, we trimmed all the entrants' coats all over with electric clippers, and from then on they wore thick wool-lined canvas rugs to encourage an oily gloss on the coats. We fed them extra rations of linseed meal for the same purpose. A week before judging day we sandpapered and buffed their horns and polished them with Goddard's Plate Polish, treated their hooves with black shoe polish, and washed, combed, and plaited their tails. They were not combed again until just before entering the judging ring.

One year I had the seemingly bright idea of protecting the beautifully-prepared tails from the animals' own droppings by encasing the plaited locks in nylon stockings, fastened to the tails by lengths of darning wool. But heavy rain fell as we took the cows down from the Adelaide Hills, and this shrunk the darning-wool lashings which stayed on for a full twenty-four hours longer. I did not anticipate the harm this might do until two weeks later, when three tail tufts dropped off their owners and ruled them out from further competition in the show ring.

Sometimes we took our entrants down to the show grounds four or five days before the event, to give them plenty of time to settle down and gain peak condition for the great moment. On the night before judging I always stayed awake to make sure that none of them lay down in her own manure — rather like a keeper walking behind his elephants with a bucket!

Just before they entered the ring I added the final touch by fitting them with specially-made red patent leather halters with leads of pure white rope. Then I hung lengths of polished gold chain around the horns. Joined by small brass padlocks, they hung like glittering necklaces on the cows' foreheads.

One year I entered my maximum of nineteen cows and looked after them all by myself. They certainly kept me busy, and the exercising alone seemed a never-ending job. Milking them under the somewhat crude conditions also was a tedious task, especially for an amateur like me. It took me considerably longer than some of the old hands but at least my family and friends were supplied with large quantities of fresh milk during show time.

One day, when I was tugging away at a favourite cow, a little girl watched for a while and then asked her father 'That's a cow, isn't it, daddy? It's got more *things* underneath than a bull!'

At show time I could always count on the help of Alton Parks, a colourful old character who lived and dreamed Jerseys. A retired baker, he was a familiar sight wherever Jerseys gathered. With a 'Farmer Giles' brown hat and a rose in his lapel he was invariably on hand from the first day my beautiful cattle appeared in the Adelaide judging ring. He had a couple of fine old breeding cows 'farmed out' in the Adelaide Hills, and I allowed him to mate these with my imported bulls. He and Frank Macrow were two of

TOP: Milking time at Mount Pleasant. BOTTOM: The villain of the piece. The imported Jersey bull Rochette's Rex, which later gored Kym Bonython, at St Magnus Stud 1952

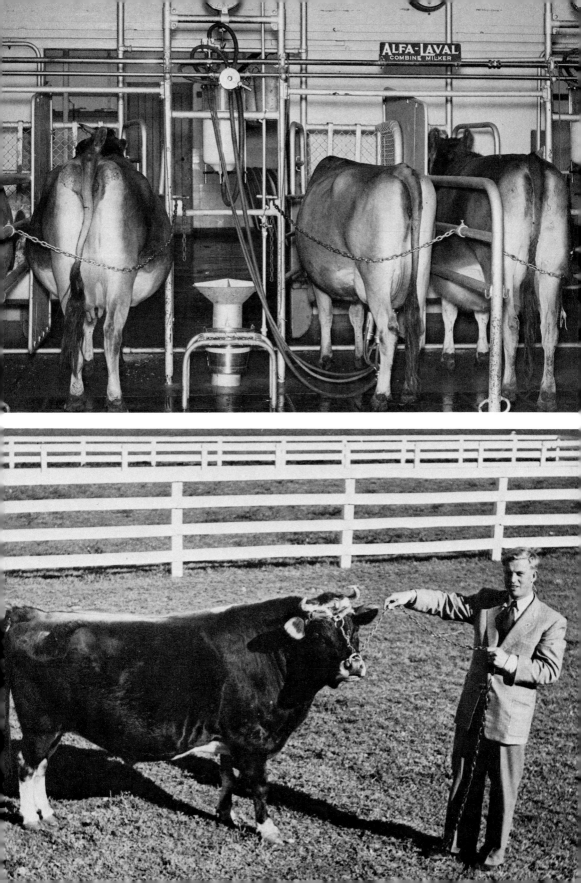

the most dedicated cattle men and most genuine friends I have had the good fortune to meet.

During my years as a stud breeder I made a number of unusual deals, but none so strange as that with a breeder who was equally involved with racehorses. For the sake of his reputation I'll call him 'Crippen'.

As time went by he became more interested in horses than in cows, but nevertheless he wanted to up-grade his dairy herd and asked me to sell him a very well-bred young bull from one of my imported cows. I asked 750 guineas for the animal, but with all his renowned persuasion he got me to give him the bull in exchange for a half-interest in a racehorse. He was preparing it for the coming season and swore it had great chances.

I was going through a brief phase of interest in horse-racing and I fell for the deal, but the horse had a bewilderingly checkered career. Its form was erratic, and although it won quite a number of races it seemed always to lose when Crippen had told me to back it to win. Whenever he advised me not to lay a bet, the confounded horse would win.

The creature was so unpredictable that Crippen and I, as the owners, were twice called before the stewards to explain why it lost when it should at least have had a place. I hardly knew one end of a horse from another and certainly couldn't justify its performance, but Crippen talked us out of it.

The horse actually got a start in the Melbourne Cup, and although it finished nearly last the acceptance showed it had some potential. By the time I wound up my interest in this equine extravaganza it must have cost me five times as much as the 750 guineas I should have pocketed for the bull, and I wonder sometimes whether I wasn't being used as the 'fall guy' for some complex con trick.

One more experience with friend Crippen left me with a distinctly jaundiced view of the 'sport of kings'. He phoned me at my office and asked me to meet him at a country racetrack about fifty miles from Adelaide. He indicated that he had 'a good thing' and that it would be worth my while to be in it.

I drove to the track and found him waiting in the car park in his usual rather furtive style. He said he had driven one of the jockeys up from the city, and that the 'hoop' had given him a surefire tip on a horse he'd be riding. We were not to put our money on yet, but to wait until the jockey emerged from the dressing-room immediately before the race. If the jockey scratched his left ear with his whip, it was *on*!

To while away the time I wandered into the betting ring and noticed the horse was quoted at eighteen to one, but I stuck to the bargain and placed no bet. In due course the jockey appeared, scratching behind his ear as arranged. I rushed to the ring, and found the price had dropped to five to four on. Usually I'm not a betting man but I risked a hundred pounds, and the horse actually won by a short head. It was a heart-stopping experience for a very amateur gambler, but I might have felt better (and probably

TOP: Flying in Jersey cows from Sydney for Mount Pleasant. Parafield Aerodrome, Adelaide 1949.   BOTTOM: American speedway ace Bob Tattersall (*Author's photo*)

wouldn't have placed a bet) if I'd known the story which Crippen hinted to me afterwards.

The race the horse had won was for allegedly untried horses which had never raced before. But the winner had raced at several country meetings under different names, and the owners knew just how good it was.

After that I stuck to cows. I felt they were more predictable and considerably more honest.

Always an ardent experimenter with new techniques, I had not been in the stud breeding business for long before I decided to try artificial insemination, which was quite new in Australia at that time. On one of my trips to England I bought the equipment and I taught myself by trial and error.

The advantage of artificial insemination is that the semen of first-class bulls can be used to impregnate cows any distance away, without all the trouble and expense of bringing the cow to the bull or vice versa. In fact I did not want 'outside' cows to be brought onto my property in case they carried some disease, and I preferred the convenience of the artificial technique.

Once learned and practised the method was straightforward. A cow 'on heat' was led into the bull yard, and as the bull mounted her I frustrated the mating by slipping a long rubber cylinder over the bull's penis. This cylinder contained a large prophylactic balloon with a small glass test tube on its inner end. The inside of the prophylactic was lubricated with a special oil so that the bull slid into it very easily and, in truth, did not know whether he was up Arthur or Martha—not that any of my stock were so unimaginatively named.

When the bull ejaculated, his sperm was collected in the test tube. Apparently he was satisfied and he was led away none the wiser, while the doubtless bewildered and frustrated cow was taken back to the paddock.

At various times our refrigerator was heavily stocked with assorted bottles of bull sperm, which tended to be confused with Jean's ingredients for homemade icecream. For a fee, I would go to often quite distant properties to insert the sperm into cows. This was done by using a long stainless-steel speculum to insert a plastic tube deep inside the cervix, and then using a hypodermic syringe to send the sperm into the womb.

I believe that the first pure-bred Jersey calf produced by artificial insemination, and recorded on the stud books of the South Australian Jersey Herd Society, was conceived with myself as go-between. Eventually a large artificial insemination centre in New South Wales bought Rochette's Rex and he begat many hundreds of calves in this manner.

Unfortunately my obsession with creating a perfect farm, stud, and dairy played havoc with domestic happiness, and there is no doubt that I put farm affairs well ahead of our private life. In 1952 I pushed our marriage even further downhill by making an overseas trip very much against Jean's wishes. I thought I could see an undesirable breeding characteristic developing in some of the latest calves, and decided to make a quick visit to Jersey to secure new and hopefully corrective bloodlines.

The home atmosphere was distinctly chilly when I departed: almost as bleak as the weather conditions my United Airlines flight encountered between Chicago and New York one dark February night. The eastern U.S.A. was blanketed with heavy cloud, snowstorms, and almost nil visibility. New York's La Guardia Airport was closed and the flight was diverted to Philadelphia.

We were one of many diversions and the airport lounge was jammed with frustrated passengers trying to reach New York. Eventually I was given a seat on an aircraft bound for that city, and as luck would have it I was placed next to Leona Jones. A vivacious, red-headed United Airlines hostess from Gadsden, Alabama, she had a ton of personality and a marvellous sense of humour, not to mention that appealing Southern accent. We got on like the proverbial house on fire during the short flight, and as I had a night to kill before flying on to London I asked her to do the rounds of the New York jazz spots with me.

The excitement of the music and her effervescent company blended into a dangerous brew. I surrendered, perhaps, all too readily, but before I left her that night I told her I was married. She was understandably upset, because the possibility had not occurred to her, and we decided the embryo affair must come to an end. Famous last words!

On my visit to Jersey I could not get her out of my mind, and five days later I cabled her to ask for another meeting on my way back to Australia. She agreed, and we met, and after two more days in New York a situation had developed that was hard to contain.

On the last night we went to the Coney Island Amusement Park, and found that one of the stalls had a miniature Chinese pagoda populated by a couple of dozen birds who would take a proffered dime from your fingers, fly it back to the pagoda, drop the coin, and return with a written 'fortune' wrapped round a matchstick, which it picked from a great heap.

Mine read 'You are going a long way—but you will return!' I did—only two weeks later! ·

The truth is seldom kind, and it would have been kinder of me not to have told Jean about Leona. It was an unenviable stituation for her, and difficult for both of us. I flew back to New York, but I had decided that I could not and should not leave my children, and once more Leona and I said good-bye.

Returning to Mount Pleasant, I tried to close my mind to everything but preparing the cattle for the autumn show season. I worked with fanatical determination, and on the day of the Mount Pleasant Annual Show I began to load the entrants into our cattle truck. First aboard was to be Rochette's Rex, whom I had been clipping, polishing, and generally aggravating for the past week. Undoubtedly his dangerous temperament was even edgier than usual as I grabbed the chain that led from around his horns, through his nose ring, and dangled loose to the ground. I took up the slack of the chain with a jerk and walked backwards out of the bull paddock, leading him to the truck. I had done it countless times.

The next thing I knew I was flying through the air with Rex's horn ripping into my left thigh. As I hit the ground he gouged me again, this time in the right thigh. It all happened in a flash, but I imagine I let out a yell that made my dairy hand, Ern Lambert, dash out of the shed to see what was happening.

He saw Rex about to gouge me again, and with admirable presence of mind snatched up a bull staff leaning against the fence and clouted Rex heavily across the rump. The startled bull jerked round to see what had hit him and this gave me just time to roll away under the post-and-rail fence of the yard.

I was smothered with dirt, my overalls were ripped open, and blood was flowing freely, but we did not realise the extent of the injuries until Jean had cut open my overall trousers and revealed them. The 'cornadas', as they are called in bull-fighting, consisted of two deep and jagged wounds. Jean hurried me to Mount Pleasant Hospital, where Dr Joy Seager was ready to give me a general anaesthetic and sew up the wounds with more than fifty sutures. My interest in the opposite sex had come within two inches of being terminated.

I had to stay in Mount Pleasant Hospital for nearly a week, and this was followed by a long period in an Adelaide hospital when the wounds became seriously infected. In my distracted state of heart and mind this period of enforced idleness was the worst possible thing for me and I asked poor Jean to stay away from me. She took the children to a seaside resort south of Adelaide.

Several weeks after the attack, when my wounds finally had closed, I returned to New York. I was torn in two directions but Jean executed the necessary surgery. From a drugstore pay telephone I put through a call to Australia to my friend Charlie Brewer, who told me 'The bird has flown.' She had taken the children to Melbourne, where our mutual friend Pat Forster took her under her wing and helped her through the first traumatic period of separation before we were divorced. Jean remarried later.

I returned to Australia with nothing settled so far as Leona was concerned. Naturally I had to finance Jean and the children and this meant drastic retrenchments on the farm. Five of us had done the work in the past but I cut down to Ern Lambert and myself. We managed, but it was very difficult on Ern's days off. In those days I had to keep on the run from four a.m. to nine p.m., and I remember a day when things became so hectic that I even had to empty my bladder on the move!

I had renewed my interest in speedway racing, of which I'll have more to say in the next chapter, and somehow managed to fit in a trip to Melbourne at least twice a month to race at the Maribyrnong Speedway.

Generally I seized the opportunity to see Robyn and Christopher, and I would take them to Pellegrini's restaurant at the top of Bourke Street and then to a children's movie matinée before I handed them back to Jean and went on to the speedway. On one trip we went to a suburban movie house where I set through no less than twenty-one Tom and Jerry cartoons, one after another. Greater love hath no man!

After a year of this kind of life Leona flew to Australia for a two weeks' holiday. She stayed with my old friend Neville Hemsworth and his wife at their farm near Camden, New South Wales, and then drove across country with me to Adelaide. After she had stayed a few days at St Magnus and with the Brewers at Birdwood I drove her back to Sydney to catch a Strato-Cruiser back to America.

The visit only served to convince us that it would not work out. Too much water had flowed under the bridge, and too many bridges had been burned. Deliberately she broke all contact and I have not heard from her again, although her sister once came to Australia and visited my Sydney gallery at a time when I was in Adelaide.

Undoubtedly this was the most heartbreaking affair of my life for everyone concerned, with all its moments of elation and misery intensified by the fact that it was never consummated.

By way of reaction I made up for lost time with a vengeance. A procession of ladies passed through my life, and one of the most hilarious periods was spent with a trio of acquaintances from Melbourne. Two were stockbrokers and the third was an ingenious villain with a nervous tic in one eye. They brought their own girlfriends and I had mine: a girl who ran a hairdressing salon in a Melbourne suburb. It was an Easter weekend, featuring the South Australian Speedboat titles. We enjoyed racing during the day and fun and games at night.

Ernie Lambert had taken another job by that time and I had engaged a recently-arrived family of Danes, the Pedersens. The father and his two sons worked industriously on the farm and in the dairy and the mother looked after the house, while I devoted more and more of my time to the speedway.

I felt it was time to go. I don't believe that any farm can succeed, especially such a specialised operation as St Magnus, unless 'the boss' is living and working there. It had all been a great and successful experience but my ambitions were moving elsewhere. My best friends, the Macrows and the Brewers, had left the district. My new speedway schemes were booming. I was tired of the lonely life on the farm.

I put the farm up for sale and among the prospective buyers (who did not buy St Magnus) were Mr and Mrs James McClure from Wilcannia in New South Wales. Two years later they were to become my parents-in-law when I married again.

On 19 September 1955 the St Magnus Jersey Stud was dispersed and the farm was sold. Occasionally I drive past the old place and feel like a character in one of those wartime movies where the pilots return to a former air force base only to find echoing hangars, disintegrating runways, and long-forgotten slogans on the walls. The purchasers put share farmers on the property and it lost the fine polish I had put onto it. Stock have eaten the lower branches of the trees I planted, the irrigated pastures have gone, and crossbreds roam in place of my glorious Jerseys. I do not write in criticism of the new owners because the management of the place is their business, but the heyday of St Magnus is only a memory.

Occasionally I wake up in the early hours of an inky black morning, hear the rain pelting down and the wind whistling, and thank my lucky stars that I no longer have to go out and bring in the cows for milking. I roll over and go back to sleep.

12

More Circuits and Bumps

SPEED WAS the god of most of my generation and it fascinated me from early childhood. Major (later Sir Henry) Seagrave was one of my earliest heroes, and a model of the Golden Arrow, the car in which he broke the land speed record in 1927, was among my prized possessions.

Dirt track speedway racing, the epitome of speed in all its spectacular excitement, began in Australia when I was very young. An Australian, Johnnie Hoskins, who in 1978 was still active in speedway in England, is generally credited with having promoted the world's first dirt track meeting.

Adelaide's meetings began in 1926, and a year or so later I persuaded my somewhat reluctant mother to take me along to what was known as the Speedway Royale at Wayville Showgrounds. One evening of that tumultuous excitement was enough to hook me for life.

Later I made friends with the Litchfield family, through Miss Lila Litchfield who was Father's secretary on the *Advertiser*. Her brother, Keith, was one of the better speedway riders of the day. He rode an AJS with considerable success, though he had a horrifying accident when he fell to the track and was run over by a competitor. The drive chain on the bike that ran over him almost cut his helmet in halves.

Keith was unconscious for some days but he recovered and was as good as ever. In 1929 I gave him a new helmet to wear when he went to England to race in the Australian team. He was a struggling mechanic in those days, with a little workshop in a shabby lane off Kensington Road, but his Litchfield Engineering Company is now one of the largest of its kind in Australia.

By the late 1920s I was a regular patron of the Saturday night meetings at the Speedway Royale, together with numerous other kids of my district. On Sunday mornings, inflamed by the action we'd watched the night before, we rode our pushbikes to a racing track we'd laid out under the gum trees around the western side of Victoria Park Racecourse. It was just across from the East Terrace house of my Uncle Peter and Aunt Elsie.

95

Our races were cut-throat and exciting, with feet trailing in the dirt in the true speedway style of the day and the roar of engines bellowing from our throats. Win or lose, I had a lot of fun plus a few skinned knees and elbows.

In those days, and until quite recently, Australian dirt track ovals were a quarter to a third of a mile in circumference and forty to fifty feet wide. The principle of the sport is that the power of the engine, whether in a two-wheel or four-wheel vehicle, tends to make the rear end swing wide. The rider or driver then directs the vehicle by increasing or decreasing power, although the front wheel is turning at an angle to the direction of travel.

This leads to some spectacular skids, and if the power suddenly cuts out the car or bike continues violently in the direction pointed by the front wheel. If the rider happens to be near the fence this can be very awkward.

There were no brakes on the bikes and no gears on either bikes or cars. The high compression of the racing engine was the only brake, acting as soon as the power was cut. The vehicles were either in gear or out of gear and the cars had hand brakes to lock the rear wheels in order to get the engine started before take off. In more recent years, however, speed cars and particularly super modified cars have been fitted with powerful braking systems.

The distance between competitors is minimal, with as many as twenty-five competing within touching distance of each other.

The professional stars of the day at Wayville were people like Jack Chapman, Paddy Dean, Alby Taylor, Frank Duckett, Vic Huxley, and Sprouts Elder. Many favoured the AJS while others rode the Harley-Davidson, the Indian, Douglas, or Matchless, until the all-conquering Rudge became the most popular. Their races attracted huge crowds, comparable with the terrific attendances we drew in the 1950s when the crash-and-bash stock car action was introduced onto Australian speedways. The air was thick with dust and heavy with the intoxicating smells of Castrol 'R' oil and 'Dope' fuel used by the riders.

To add spice to the programme, the promoters sometimes used 'Spot' Simmons, then known as 'Cyclone', who rode his motor cycle down a narrow runway from the top of the grandstand to the arena. Sometimes, with all lights doused, his clothes were set alight as he aimed his roaring machine down the inches-wide runway to the track. I was to become friendly with 'Spot' during my farming days, when he was the local electrician at Mount Pleasant.

Another attraction was a precarious array of ladders raised about 120 feet and swaying in the breeze. An intrepid character climbed to the top and dived into a little tank of water at the bottom of the ladders. The suspense of this attraction was prolonged for several weeks, with the promoters claiming that the wind would endanger the stuntman's life if he should attempt the leap.

In those days I met a number of men who were later to work with my speedway organisation. They included Wal J. Murphy, who for many years was the head of the motorcycling fraternity in South Australia, and Dick and Jack Wise who were notable riders. Dick later became my race manager at Rowley Park.

Race meetings also were held on the huge one-mile tracks at Gawler and Smithfield, north of Adelaide. When the speedway was moved from Wayville to Camden on the Anzac Highway, nearly down to the beach suburb of Glenelg, it was promoted by my acquaintances Gronwy Morris, a lawyer who was Secretary of the Sporting Car Club of South Australia; Kevin Lumbers; and Des Dwyer who later became an executive of the Royal Automobile Association.

When they had big crowds packing the Camden grandstands the promoters would retire to a spot behind the pits, sip nervously at their drinks, and offer up silent prayers as the fans leapt to their feet and roared their excitement at some incident on the track. The whole grandstand actually swayed a few inches from side to side. Years later, I was to know how Gronwy and his partners felt, when huge crowds rolled up to my Rowley Park Speedway.

Action at Camden was terrific. The stars of the day were the brothers Jack and Cordy Milne, and Putt Mossman, who were Americans; Morian Hansen the Danish rider; and local men like Laurie Packer, Les Fredericks, and Bill Maddern. Extra thrills were provided by the developing sport of side-car races, headed by Art Hubbard, Spence Miller, and Harry Butler. The most notable racing car drivers were Aub Ramsay, Alec Rowe, and the Englishman Bill Reynolds, who later sold me my most successful race car.

On most Saturday nights I rode my motor cycle down from Mount Lofty to Camden, and made an after-meeting ritual of stopping at Gibbs' Pie Shop on Anzac Highway. One night I lost a ten shilling note (a dollar now) and the significance of that sum of money in those days is shown by the fact that I took the trouble to retrace my tracks next morning until I found it.

Anzac Highway then was an ill-lit narrow road, probably the most dangerous in Adelaide, especially after rain. The road surface was treacherously greasy, as I discovered one night when my motor cycle slipped from under me and I slid fifty yards on my backside with the bike following in close formation, like some slow motion scene from a ballet.

After the war the action shifted to Kilburn Speedway, which opened in 1949. Youthful Jack Brabham, then National Speed Car Champion, clashed there with our local champion Harley Hammond. Jack, of course, went on to road racing and won three world championships and a knighthood.

Young Harry Neale also was making his presence felt, while George Robertson and Art Hubbard were the top side-car riders. Jack Young, the only South Australian to win a world speedway championship, was the back marker. His clashes with Bob Leverenz, the Jamieson Brothers, and Aub

Lawson were highlights of Kilburn programmes.

When my first marriage broke up and I could see the writing on the wall for St Magnus I decided to go seriously into the speedway business. A suitable speedway area was then already being used: ten acres in the heart of an old industrial suburb called Bowden, about two-and-a-half miles from the city. The area belonged to the South Australian Soccer Association and was known as Rowley Park because a supporter named Rowley bought it for £150 and gave it to them.

Originally the plan was to use Rowley Park for soccer in the winter and speedway racing in the summer, but the 'park' was mainly an old pug hole from which brickmakers had dug clay in Adelaide's early days. A slight fall of rain turned it into a quagmire and the earth was so saline that grass would not grow in the centre of the area. The Soccer Association decided it was better to use the rental money from the speedway to hire more suitable grounds.

Rowley Park had a rather rectangular layout in those days and interstate competitors gave it the derisive name of 'the butter box'. Few of them mastered the track until we changed its shape to the more conventional oval, and champions of the Sydney and Melbourne tracks rarely succeeded at Rowley Park. Andy McGavin, Australian Speed Car Champion, was one of the exceptions.

In daytime, Rowley Park looked like hell. No one could pretend that Bowden, with its narrow nineteenth-century streets of cottages dominated by the gasworks and gasometer, ranks among Adelaide's more attractive suburbs, and the speedway clearly showed its ancestry as a parched, dug-out pug hole. But at night it assumed an entirely different character. The blazing concentration of spotlights, the faint haze of dust thrown up by the racers, and the electric anticipation and excitement on both sides of the safety fence all blended into a hypnotic atmosphere.

Towards the end of my ownership I combined my loves for speed and art by commissioning the Adelaide painter Jacqueline Hick to paint a typical Rowley Park scene. The painting took her a long time. Whenever she went to the track to make preliminary sketches there would be a serious accident or even a fatality, and it would be a year or so before she tried again. But at last she finished the work and called it 'The Arena'. She saw the speedway as a kind of twentieth-century Colosseum, with gladiators in red uniforms and chrome-plated chariots around the perimeter.

Her painting undoubtedly glamorised the place, but perhaps she had captured the spirit of speedway. For the competitors it can be as frenzied as any chariot race performed to entertain the Caesars, and maybe the spectators haven't changed very much since gladiatorial days. They went there to be thrilled by the spectacle of men, and sometimes women, staking their lives on their luck and skill . . . and occasionally losing.

In 1978 I was amused to read, in the regular *Advertiser* feature captioned '25 Years Ago', that a quarter-century earlier I had won the heat and final of the Speed Car Handicap and revealed 'great promise as a future speedway star'.

That was in 1953, when I bought Dave Cooper's Ford A powered speed car and launched into speedway racing. A year later I tendered successfully for the Rowley Park lease and took the track over from Alf Shields, the promoter and an occasional contestant. A new occupation lay ahead of me, and for the next twenty years I was the promoter of Rowley Park and an active participant in speedway racing.

Encouraged by a few wins during that first season I commissioned Jack Brabham to design and build a twin-cylindered race car. It was revolutionary for its time but had the disadvantage of being almost impossible to maintain — especially for a non-mechanic like me. There was no way to obtain spare parts for its custom-made engine at short notice, because they had to be machined and assembled by hand.

But I raced the car, with its painted-on slogan of 'For Whom the Bulls Toil' (since I was still in my farming days), in many parts of Australia. I used the same slogan on its successors, although I changed 'Toil' to 'Toiled'. To emphasise the image I mounted a bovine skull on the bonnet of my various Bristol road cars and it became something of a trademark, to say nothing of the eleven assorted horns, bells, and whistles concealed under the bonnet.

One of them was a cattle caller, which I called a 'moo horn'. I discovered it during a visit to Texas, and have transferred it to every car I've owned, including my present vehicle. It has a remarkable effect on cows. Skilfully used, it will moo in a most seductive manner and cause cows to come galloping towards it from far and near, and rub their bodies lustfully along the fence separating them from the car. When I drive off they canter alongside the road, keeping pace with the car as far as the fences allow.

Another of my repertoire was an air whistle that sounded like an express train. Once, driving from Adelaide to Sydney, I sounded it as I was barrelling down the road alongside the railway. A group of workmen repairing the line leapt for their lives, picks and shovels flying in all directions as they evaded the imaginary express train bearing down on them.

My beloved Bristols always caused quite a stir in the 1950s. The most beautiful car I ever owned was a two-seater Bristol 404, and I still regret that I did not keep it. Twenty years later, it would be worth far more than I paid. It is literally true that 'they just don't make 'em like that any more'. I took over my beautiful car, canary-yellow in colour, from the Bristol factory in England, and Jack Brabham, who had recently started his English racing career at the wheel of a Bristol race car, went with me to pick it up. He watched the loving skill devoted to every detail of Bristols by craftsmen trained in traditional style, and exclaimed 'No wonder these cars are so bloody expensive! Talk about the horse and buggy days!'

I took the Bristol to Paris, where it created a minor sensation. For some reason most European cars were finished in very drab colours in those days and the Bristol 404 stood out like a peacock among barnyard fowls. Maybe it attracted a little too much notice. One day I was driving it in London from Piccadilly to Kensington and, as was my wont in those days, I weaved in and out of the heavy traffic until it banked up and stopped me. A big 30/98 Vauxhall had been among the following traffic and when I stopped this stopped too, and a tweedy gentleman stepped out and strode purposefully to the Bristol. In Colonel Blimp accents he reprimanded me 'I don't know where you come from, young fellah, but we don't drive like that over here!'

When I returned to Australia I drove the Bristol to the Sydney car showrooms of Bill Reynolds, an English speed car racing friend. A dapper little man, with well-tended moustache and goatee, he walked entranced around the Bristol and said 'What a beautiful car!'

I told him 'No good for screwing in, though.'

'No—but I bet it's bloody terrific for promoting them!'

Naturally I didn't risk any of my Bristols on the speedway, although I used them to tow my race cars, mounted on a trailer, from Adelaide to various tracks around the country. In those early years I racked up many thousands of miles of cross-country driving. Apart from the races, these trips usually were rich in incident of one kind or another. Jack Brabham came with me on one trip from Sydney to Brisbane, and on the return we kept passing and re-passing a large Ford sedan driven by a striking platinum blonde. We struck up acquaintance with her at our first fuelling stop, and when we stopped again I persuaded Jack to drive the Bristol while I accompanied the blonde. After an hour or so the euphoria of the previous night's racing had worn off and we decided to stop for a sleep. We found a quiet spot for a nap, but it could hardly be called restful.

I drove the girl to a hotel in Sydney, and she warned me against trying to see her again. She hinted at a connection with a well-known figure in the Sydney underworld, but this did not prevent a later meeting in different circumstances.

Some time later I was making another trip, from Adelaide to north Queensland, and I began to doubt whether I'd make it. I'd been involved in a speedboat accident shortly before leaving Adelaide, and had suffered concussion followed by persistent headaches. One of these had me in its grip and by the time I reached Brisbane I was in agony. The platinum blonde had given me her address in Brisbane, and with a feeling of 'Nothing venture, nothing gain', I called at her apartment. She put me to bed and looked after me until I was well enough to continue north with the rest of the team.

Rowley Park meetings were held on Friday nights, and as the crowds drifted away my mechanic Mac Diamond and I packed up our gear and headed east for the Saturday meetings in Melbourne or Sydney. If a Brisbane meeting was scheduled, we raced in Sydney and drove on to Brisbane for the following Saturday. I was 'into speed' in a big way. If

100

speedboat races were programmed for a Sunday afternoon in Adelaide I would race at Rowley Park on Friday night, drive to Melbourne for the Saturday meeting, and return home in time to compete on the Port River on Sunday.

The interstate roads were still mighty rough in those days and driving could be an endurance test. Early one Sunday morning, while Mac and I were speeding from Melbourne back to Adelaide, I suddenly saw a single wheel rocket past our car in the same direction. It was one of the trailer wheels. The axle had sheared, and as the wheel bounded like a kangaroo into the bush the trailer sagged sideways and dug in the remnants of the axle with a horrifying screech and shower of sparks.

We found the wheel when the sun came up but the trailer was unserviceable. Luckily a motor truck came rolling along with room for the trailer on its tray top. We loaded it on, I drove the race car fifteen miles to the nearest township while Mac followed in my car, and we left the race car there until we could pick it up with another trailer.

Accommodation always was a problem in our itinerant lives. I arrived in Sydney very early one morning and, realising there was no hope of getting into a hotel at that time, I knocked up a race track acquaintance named Bob Playfair. Bob, who lived in a little weatherboard cottage at Mascot, was something of a Don Juan. I found he had only one bed (a double one, naturally) but he told me I could hop in beside him. I enjoyed the rest, and later that day attended the opening of an exhibition of paintings by my friend Elaine Haxton. The newspapers covered the occasion, and my photograph, with Elaine, appeared on the social pages. Bob saw it and growled 'Cripes, if I'd known you was one o' them arty poofters I'd never have let you into me bloody double bed!'

There seemed very little time for sleep in those days. I was living a quadruple life, involved in speed cars, speedboats, music, and art. Sometimes they clashed, as when I shared a Parkside flat with a musician named Bon Maguire. He sang with Bruce Gray's Band, of which I was a member, but his other interests did not always coincide with mine. After one expedition out of Adelaide I drove 2,500 miles back from Cairns inside four days, despite primitive roads over much of the distance, and opened the front door thinking only of sleep. But the house was filled with cigarette smoke and wild wild women, and I practically had to fight my way through them to get to bed. After that I found solo accommodation.

The trip to northern Queensland was one I made in 1956, as part of a syndicate we called 'The Speedway Barn Stormers'. It was formed to take speedway for the first time to Rockhampton, Townsville, and Cairns. The other members were Frank Arthur, Managing Director of Empire Speedways, who promoted tracks in Sydney and Brisbane and was a former speedway champion; speed car drivers Frank 'Satan' Brewer and Andy McGavin; and motor bike riders Graham Warren and Lionel Levy.

101

Brewer, a New Zealander, had gained great success for his fearless driving on the California tracks. McGavin was known to his friends as 'Tripod' because of his remarkable physical equipment. Poor Lionel Levy later was killed on the Sydney Showgrounds track, trying to make a comeback. Unfortunately he was not unique in this. Motor bike racing is for those who are young and sharp, and I remember several other cases of men who died because they carried on too long. Harry Denton, the former side-car ace who was killed at Rowley Park whilst trying to make it as a solo rider when he was past his prime, was one of them. But who am I to criticise?

The Speedway Barn Stormers staged programmes on the showgrounds of the three Queensland coastal towns. It was a nerve-racking operation because the showgrounds were not fitted with proper safety fences, and only a flimsy barrier of wire netting fastened to wooden posts stood between the roaring cars and motor bikes and the crowd pressing close to watch them. The prospect of any of our vehicles going out of control and plunging into the crowd was a continual threat but fortunately it never happened.

To pad out the racing events, we recruited local lads for dirt track pushbike races, and put on spectacular fireworks displays that Frank Arthur set off with the help of local assistants.

Despite the fiercely rough roads, the constant travel, and the ever-present danger we had lots of fun. The two motor bike riders, Graham and Lionel, were a cheerful couple who took life easily despite their hazardous occupation and they loved to bait Frank Brewer's wife. Once we were having some delicious pawpaw for breakfast in Rockhampton when Lionel asked her 'Have you ever tried Worcestershire sauce on pawpaw?'

Mrs Brewer fell for it and tipped a quantity of the fiery sauce over her fruit. 'It *is* rather unusual, isn't it?' she asked as she gamely ate her way through the weird combination.

This period was marked by the best year I ever had in speed cars. In 1956 I disposed of the Brabham Twin and bought a Holden-powered car from Eddie Thomas, a Melbourne car builder and racing enthusiast. In this car I won the 1956 Australian Grand Prix, Australia's first fifty-lap speed car race. In the same year I won a title race at Toowoomba one night and an Australian championship in Brisbane on the following night. The car was not involved in any accidents during the entire season but I was not to maintain this trouble-free record.

I would not hazard a guess at how many accidents I was involved in during twenty-odd years as a competitor. As the speed and standards of racing increased the accident rate soared correspondingly. For about the first half of the time I promoted Rowley Park racing none of these accidents was fatal, but during the last ten years or so this unblemished record was broken and there were seven or eight fatalities.

Sometimes these deaths prompted people to make anonymous phone calls to me late at night. One such caller demanded to know how I could sleep at night 'With all the people you've killed?' But I could answer with a clear conscience. I said that I took exactly the same risks as the men who had died, and had done so for a number of years. Probably I had had more accidents than any of them, but luck had been on my side and in most cases I'd been able to walk away from the track. Nothing but chance had directed that I should live and they should die.

One of my most spectacular prangs was in the period when Walt Disney had popularised the American historical figure of Davy Crockett. All the kids were wearing Davy Crockett gear, and in tune with the rather flamboyant image that race car drivers projected of themselves I had a Davy Crockett hat, complete with 'possum tail', made for me out of rabbit skins. The first time I wore it I was charging down the main straight when I ran over the rear wheel of a competitor. My car did a series of flips that were captured on film by David Brock, our alert photographer.

One of his photographs, showing me upside-down with hands out-stretched as though to hold the car off the track and my head partly obscured by the furry tail of the hat, appeared in the *Illustrated London News* and numerous other publications throughout the world.

The accident cracked some vertebrae in my neck. Ever since then I have had limited movement of the neck and head, and I suffered severe pain in the neck and shoulder for a number of years. I had to wear a neck brace for some months after the accident and I was still obliged to wear it when I won my first Australian Hydroplane Championship, on Hume Weir in New South Wales.

The accident is only one of those in which I might have died. On another occasion I was planning a flight to Alice Springs and Ayers Rock with Sidney Nolan. On the night before our departure he came to watch me race, and saw my car leap off the track in another 'inversion'. Instead of going to Ayers Rock I went to St Andrew's Hospital with a badly dislocated shoulder. Sidney travelled by himself, and had the rather uncomfortable experience of flying in an aircraft which lost its way in fading light and only just reached Alice Springs before running out of fuel.

At a race on Fred Tracey's track in Melbourne my radiator hose burst and squirted boiling water over my legs. I crashed the car into the fence but suffered only minor bruising. Soon after that, on the same track, a competitor's car threw up a stone which penetrated my goggles and cut quite deeply into my eyebrow. Fragments of celluloid worked out of the lesion for two or three years.

I have had some other spectacular mishaps, but in my experience such accidents are less lethal than those which do not look nearly so dangerous. I have seen many apparently horrifying accidents but the worst injuries were inflicted in those which hardly appeared to be serious. Nowadays, speed cars are fitted with strong roll bars which carry their weight if they turn over, but drivers raced without them until the late 1960s and were liable to take the full impact on their heads. Slow rollovers, bearing fully down on the driver, seemed to inflict far worse injuries than fast flicks or somersaults.

Probably the Brisbane Showgrounds was my favourite track, and I felt the Sydney Showgrounds to be the most dangerous. It was comparatively big, but narrow, and I learnt to my sorrow that a driver only had to stray a little out of line to be in real trouble.

In one race I was 'crossed up' by another driver, and I crashed into the concrete wall near the gate into the pits. Petrol gushed everywhere but luckily did not explode. For years afterwards I was reminded of the impact whenever I saw the crack I had made in that massive wall.

Higher and stronger safety fences became essential with the advent of stock car and super modified racing, and we had a reinforced bank of earth between the main fence and the secondary fence that ran parallel to it. Cars screeching out of control could no longer crash through the fence—but occasionally a piece of them flew over the top. This happened during one stock car race at Rowley Park when two of the competitors collided. One car lost a wheel, which hit the north-east corner of the safety fence, bounced off, and rolled slowly across the centre from one corner to the other. It ran past the fire crew, who should have grabbed it, and when it hit the fence diagonally opposite it bounced off and rolled into the centre of the track. Another car ran over its edge and flicked it like a giant tiddlywink over the top of the rails.

The wheel flew into the grandstand and struck a woman nursing her child. Ironically, she was the wife of one of the fire crew, whose duty it was to stop such debris from becoming a danger, but she escaped with nothing worse than a bruise on the arm.

The Davy Crockett crash, Rowley Park 1954. Bill Wigzell in foreground, with Kym Bonython in the car rearing upright. (*David Brock photo*)

13

On a Broad Canvas

M AX HARRIS, the celebrated businessman—bookseller—poet—author—
journalist, whom I have known since schooldays, heard I was leaving
Mount Pleasant and looking for a house. He told me of one that had been built
by a designer named Gunter Niggeman. It was located on the edge of the
sandhills in what was then the new suburb of Tennyson, just north of Grange.
Niggeman was returning to Germany on the very day that Max told me about
the house, and Max sounded so enthusiastic that I inspected it immediately.
Its ultra-modern design, and the situation in what was then an almost
untouched area on the edge of the sea, appealed to me instantly.

I moved in without delay and hurried into my new activities, which
included a record bar in Adelaide. I felt I knew so much about records that I
could hardly fail, but it was not one of my happier ventures and I soon
discovered I was not cut out to be a storekeeper. However there are a few
pleasant memories. One is of a handsome young student from Sri Lanka
who was attending the University of Adelaide, but who seemed to spend
most of his spare time in my shop. Obviously his real love was music, and
soon I helped him to make ends meet by paying him a few paltry pieces of
silver to assist me on Saturday mornings. I daresay that, nearly a quarter-
century later, he looks back on this ill-paid activity with some amusement.
His name is Kamahl, and he is one of the most popular entertainers in
Australia who has appeared with equal success in Britain and America.

We received some strange requests, including one from a New Australian who asked for a recording of 'Spring Rissoles'. My two assistants and
I racked our brains until I made an inspired stab in the dark, and another
satisfied customer walked out—with a copy of *Rustle of Spring* under his
arm!

Soon after I moved to Tennyson, one of its greatest assets proved to be
the arrival of a marvellous couple named Ross and Ina Luck, who bought a
house directly facing mine. Ross was the Advertising Manager for David
Jones', the large Adelaide department store, and Ina was a fashion illustrator

TOP: 'Gelignite' Jack Murray, Bangkok 1956 (*Author's photo*). BOTTOM: 'The Bozz'
cops it again! Triumphant George Tatnell scores a direct hit on Kym Bonython while
Rowley Park Speedway manager Jack Self hides a smile

whose drawings were featured in a number of local and interstate journals.

One of our immediate points of contact was a mutual interest in art. Ross was a past president of the South Australian branch of the Contemporary Art Society of Australia, and I had been developing an interest in art, modern and otherwise, ever since I began to decorate the remodelled farmhouse at Mount Pleasant.

I imagine that this suddenly-awakened interest, like my love for music, was inherited from Mother. She was deeply interested in art, but I cannot say as much for the rest of my forebears. The walls of Carclew were hung with mediocre selections from the Victorian period, more notable for the massiveness of their gilt frames than for their subject-matter, but Mother accumulated a fairly steady flow of good paintings. Soon after Father's death in 1960 I visited her at Eurilla, where she had decided to live permanently, and she told me she had just finished hanging 120 paintings: souvenirs of 120 art shows which she had opened over the years.

They included three by Horace Trenerry, who lived first at Woodside in the Adelaide Hills and later in a supposedly haunted house, Wonnaminta, just down the road from Eurilla. The family knew him well and I met him occasionally in my youth. Poor old 'Tren' was the classic example of a painter unrecognised during his life but achieving fame after death. He lived a truly Bohemian life, existing on the proverbial smell of an oily rag, and if his works sold at all they went for ludicrously low prices. He died in 1958 of Huntington's Chorea, and since then his paintings have risen in value until they now change hands at prices that would have kept him in luxury. His landscapes of the Aldinga region, south of Adelaide, rarely have been bettered in Australian art. Mother opened two or three of his exhibitions but they made little impact outside Adelaide.

When I began to collect paintings my taste was predictably conservative. My first acquisition was a painting by a South Australian, Wright Harrison, and soon I bought others by such good but conventional artists as Hans Heysen, George Whinnen, and Max Ragless.

Eventually, however, I felt a vague sense of dissatisfaction with these purchases. Possibly I had been 'brain-washed' by the paintings in Mother's collection, many of which were by artists who had abandoned the classical style to paint in ways regarded in the 1930s and 1940s as revolutionary, experimental, or positively weird, but in any case my taste began to turn in that direction. When I saw an oil by Roderick Shaw, entitled *Capricornia*, I knew that it represented my real liking and I bought it with little hesitation. Eventually I sold it to a Sydney friend, Keith Bruce, and he used it as the foundation of his excellent collection.

I began to dispose of my early purchases and gave one of my Heysens to the drummer Gene Krupa when he came to Australia in 1954. It came to a sad end when his New York house was burnt to the ground shortly before his death in 1973.

In the early 1950s it was not easy to indulge a taste for contemporary art if you lived in Adelaide. The Royal South Australian Society of Arts mounted the occasional exhibition that appealed to my changing tastes, but most of the artists who were beginning to interest me never exhibited in Adelaide. There was no one on the gallery scene willing to take a chance on their type of work.

However, I received valuable guidance from the David Jones Gallery in Sydney, where I bought my first Sidney Nolan painting; from Lucy Swanton and Treania Smith of the Macquarie Galleries in the same city; and from two New Australian art dealers, Morley and Torda, also of Sydney. Vi Johns, of John Martin's Gallery, guided me in Adelaide.

In those days one could buy Nolans and Boyds for £20 to £50, and Drysdales for not much more. I paid only £10 for an Arthur Boyd ceramic tile that fifteen years later would have been worth $2,500, had it not fallen off the wall and shattered into a hundred pieces. Of course my judgement was not unerring, but most of the artists who appealed to me were to make their names in contemporary art and only a few sank into obscurity.

I bought my first Nolan painting in 1950. It was of the main street of the Queensland town of Gympie, and soon after that I bought one of his central Australian landscapes. It was a kind of aerial view of the harsh red terrain. He left for London later that year, and in 1951 he held an exhibition at the Redfern Gallery in London. He was anxious to make an impact there, and he wrote to ask if he could borrow the landscape for the exhibition.

Naturally I agreed, but a few weeks later I was perturbed by an impassioned letter from Nolan. He said that he had been out of London during the last few days of the exhibition, and during that time the buyers for the Tate Gallery had chosen the landscape for their collection. Apparently it was the one which appealed to them most out of his exhibition.

He begged me to relinquish the painting so that he might be represented in the permanent collection of this renowned London gallery. By way of compensation he said that I might choose any painting of his at any time in the future.

Rather reluctantly I let the landscape go to the Tate, and some time later I took up his offer of a replacement. I chose *Burke and Wills Leaving Melbourne*, which was to become one of Nolan's most famous works and was infinitely better than the one it replaced.

The Redfern Gallery exhibition gave Nolan a toehold in the international market but it took him some years to become self-sufficient financially. In 1954 he was anxious to drive to the Mediterranean and work in Greece and Italy, and he struck a bargain with me. I had a strong faith in his future and I advanced him £500, which in those days would buy a campervan for him to drive and live in. In return, he gave me the privilege of selecting any five of his paintings at a nominal value of £100 apiece.

This proved the best investment I ever made. I chose four of his second series of Ned Kelly paintings, and a large Italian landscape. When at last I had to part with them I sold each painting at between 1,000 and 2,000 per cent profit.

In those days I restricted myself with the narrow-minded intention to collect only Australian art, but eventually I learnt better. One of my rare exceptions in the 1950s was a Mathieu Mategot tapestry I bought in Paris in 1955. I bought it at a gallery named La Demure, and it appealed to me mainly because my love for cattle persisted in the form of collecting representations of bulls. From this gallery I had bought two statuettes of bulls, one in metal and the other in ceramic, and my imagination was captured by the large semi-abstract tapestry entitled *Linares*. It had been inspired by the death of the Spanish matador Manolete, who died from a cornada while fighting in the bull-ring at Linares.

The price was in the region of £2,000 sterling, and eventually I faced the problem of bringing it back to Australia. In those days Australia retained an iniquitous duty and sales tax on works of art, which more progressive countries such as the U.S.A. had abandoned fifty years earlier.

I thought about this long and hard, and finally folded the tapestry like a blanket and stowed it in the bottom of a suitcase. In Sydney, a gauche Customs inspector looked at it cynically. 'What's this thing here?'

'Oh—just a bit of rug I picked up while I was away.'

'Gawd—some people'll buy anything!'

He scrawled his chalked hieroglyph on the suitcase and I was home free!

Anyone who set out to purchase Australian art in those days was like a prospector mining a rich reef, although of course one had to have a lot of faith in the future. I bought a number of Arthur Boyd's *Wimmera* series for £20 to £50 apiece, and some magnificent Drysdales of West Wyalong and Sofala, together with some of his paintings of Aboriginal stockmen, on similarly advantageous terms.

My enthusiasm for contemporary Australian art developed into close friendships with many of the painters whose work I admired. One of these was 'Tass' Drysdale, and a chance visit to his house overlooking Sydney Harbour proved most providential. He had just undertaken extensive home renovations and was in need of a little ready money. Quite unexpectedly I was able to buy his most famous painting, *The Drover's Wife*, plus his superb portrait of Margaret Olley, and a typical Drysdale landscape of eroded soil with gaunt tree stumps, for £200 apiece.

Drysdale's wife Bonnie was an unforgettable person and I cherish many memories of her. One of my favourite 'Bonnie' stories concerns the 1954 Royal Visit. The Commonwealth Government wanted to give a Drysdale to Queen Elizabeth II, and persuaded 'Tass' to release a painting which was nominally in Bonnie's collection. On the night before the royal yacht was to leave Sydney a special function was held aboard and the Drysdales were among the guests. Bonnie, still smarting from the loss, cornered Prince Philip and told him 'If you find you don't like that painting when you get back to London, give it to Ma-in-law. *She* knows a good painting when she sees one!'

I gather that Prince Philip was not amused!

Clifton Pugh, who was almost unknown in those days, became another of my good friends during the mid-1950s. I bought one picture from him, now well-known, entitled *Collecting Dead Wool*. It depicted a farmer literally tearing wool from a rotting carcass, in that period when wool was fetching such high prices that even the odd tufts that clung to barbed-wire fences were worth salvaging. The greenish putrescence was most realistic, and Pugh told me that the picture was even more convincing when he first placed it on exhibition. He attached a piece of rotten meat to the back of the frame.

Years later I sold the painting to Mary Travers of the vocal group Peter, Paul, and Mary. She took it back to New York with her after a concert tour, but eventually tired of the painting and returned it to me in Adelaide. I was able to place it in one of the major Australian collections.

I was faced with a difficult decision about one of Pugh's paintings: *The World of Shane and Dailan*. I had bought it for £50, but before he handed it over to me he nominated it for entry in an art competition held in Adelaide. Apparently he did not realise that a condition of the competition ruled that the winning painting must be 'acquisitive', which means that the artist would receive the prize money but that the painting would become the property of the sponsor. The latter, by tradition, would present it to the State Gallery of South Australia.

While the judges were still deliberating, one of them confided to me that the result was in the balance between Pugh's painting and one by another well-known interstate artist. The prize money was considerable, and I felt I could not deprive him of the chance of winning it and of being represented in the State Gallery. And so, with reluctance, I did not insist that it should be withdrawn from the competition. The painting won the prize and I now have very mixed feelings whenever I see it on display in the State Gallery.

I presented a Clifton Pugh exhibition in Adelaide in 1964. One of the dominant paintings was called *The Rites of Spring*, portraying a rampant bull in company with a couple of very anticipatory cows. One of the great patrons of modern art in Adelaide, the elderly but enlightened Dr Mildred Mocatta, took an immediate fancy to the painting and was sorely tempted to add it to her collection, which had no parallel in Adelaide.

But she was in a dilemma, which she mentioned to Clifton Pugh. She told him 'I would dearly love to buy that painting, but I'm afraid it wouldn't go with my curtains.'

Pugh answered 'Well, change your curtains.'

109

'Yes, but even if I did, I don't think it would go with my furniture.'

'Well, change your furniture!'

Still uncertain, Dr Mocatta ruminated 'Yes, but what would my friends say?' and the exasperated artist replied 'Change your friends!'

However, she still did not buy the painting.

Another feature of the exhibition was the largest painting on display. Seven feet long by four-and-a-half deep, it was offered for the modest price of £225. A leading Adelaide insurance company was seeking a large painting for their new board room, and I tried to convince them that this one was exactly right. But they were not convinced and the painting went back to Pugh's studio when the exhibition closed.

Fifteen years later, the same company again asked me to recommend some work of art for their offices. With malicious satisfaction I was able to remind them of their previous rejection and tell them that the painting they could have had for £225 ($450) now would be worth at least $7,000.

But decisions always are difficult to obtain when boards or committees are concerned. Hal Missingham, the painter, photographer, and long-time Director of the Art Gallery of New South Wales, tells the story that when, as a new and rather nervous appointee, he attended his first meeting of that gallery's board, the aggregate age of the trustees was some 694 years.

The Chairman, aged ninety-three, on that day made the momentous announcement that he had decided to 'Step down for a younger man.' He then nominated another member whose age was eighty-nine.

The Board of the State Gallery of South Australia consisted of a similar collection of fuddy-duddies when I first became interested in art. The inevitable conservatism of advanced age was predominant and the representation of contemporary Australian artists was deplorable. This was brought into sharp focus during the 1954 Royal Visit, when our State Gallery was the only one scheduled to be visited by the Queen. The deficiencies of the gallery collection were so lamentable that they were rapidly made good by borrowings from art lovers. I lent nineteen modern paintings for this purpose, but when the *Advertiser* reported the borrowings my contribution was not mentioned. Perhaps the Board neglected to inform the newspaper that they had been obliged to include more contemporary art if they were not to be thought altogether behind the times.

The Chairman of the Board was the kindly Sir Edward Morgan, whose attitude to modern art matched that of his colleagues. Whenever I heard him opening an exhibition I was always rather heartened if he cited a particular painting or sculpture as being unworthy of serious consideration. Invariably he picked on a piece that was my particular favourite and I felt that, if he didn't like it, then it must be good!

Robert Campbell, himself a watercolourist of note, was then the recently-appointed Director of the State Gallery. He took a keen interest in South Australia's art world and made a point of viewing everything on the local scene, but I feel sure that his activities would have been constricted by the Board. His wife was Elizabeth Young, daughter of the founder of the Macquarie Galleries in Sydney, and she shared his interest in art. For a number of years she was art critic for the *Advertiser*, but although she was quite perceptive I am sure there are some comments she would like to forget. In 1961, for example, she wrote of Fred Williams' exhibition in my gallery 'One must believe that Williams has acquired some knowledge and understanding of his craft, in which case he must be singularly lacking in imagination and ideas.'

Fred Williams is now one of Australia's most widely acclaimed artists, both nationally and internationally.

In Robert Campbell's later years at the State Gallery, prior to his retirement and untimely death, his administrative effect on its collection seemed to diminish. Perhaps this was because of the pressures of his appointment, but Hal Missingham unkindly attributed it to 'knight starvation'. However much Campbell deserved a knighthood he did not receive one, although he was appointed O.B.E. and C.M.G. There is no doubt that the State Gallery took great steps forwards during his tenure as Director.

In the 1940s and 1950s one of the motivating forces in Australian contemporary art was John Reed, a wealthy collector who was, among other things, the original patron of Sidney Nolan. He founded the shortlived Museum of Modern Art of Australia, which despite his affluence always was run on a shoestring in somewhat nondescript conditions in Melbourne. However, the Museum set an enviable standard with the quality of its exhibitions and no doubt this was due to Reed's perceptiveness.

I was a Patron and Life Member of the Museum, but after one of the frequent changes of staff the secretary sent me a reminder notice that my annual subscription was overdue. I returned a reminder that I was a Life Member, and with good-humoured sarcasm enquired 'Just because the newspapers of Australia constantly refer to me as "the man with 99 lives" does this mean that I am expected to pay 99 life subscriptions?'

(Incidentally my speedway and speedboat activities so alarmed the insurance companies that my policies carried a clause exempting them from liability in the event of death by accident 'in any form of racing other than foot'.)

Reed encouraged members to donate works of art to the Museum, and I imagine I was only one of numerous collectors who obliged with major gifts. Now the Museum has closed I am sure I'm not alone in wondering what happened to all those donations. They were not offered back to the donors when the Museum was wound up and I am not aware that they've found their way into any of the major public gallery collections.

In a last effort to salvage the Museum, John Reed obtained space on the fourth floor of Ball & Welch, a Melbourne department store in Flinders Street. He asked me to provide an 'opening exhibition' in these new premises with a selection of paintings from my private collection—which I must immodestly admit was very impressive for that time.

I was glad to help and I put a lot of time into selecting and mounting the exhibition. Reed had invited Sir Rohan Delacombe, Governor of Victoria, to open the exhibition, and you may imagine my chagrin when His Excellency surveyed the exhibition with good-humoured contempt and remarked in his opening speech that 'As far as I'm concerned, the best thing to be seen here is the view out of the window across the Queen's Bridge over the Yarra!'

In the late 1940s art brought me into contact with Pam Cleland, a lawyer and excellent painter who was one of Adelaide's most interesting personalities.

She was a contemporary of Jeff Smart, and I first became aware of her ability as a painter when I attended an exhibition she presented in the loft of Mount Lofty House stables, just down the road from Eurilla. I bought a scene of Piccadilly Valley, which was actually overlooked by the loft of the stables.

At about that time she became a member of the conservative Adelaide legal firm of Genders, Wilson & Bray. The 'Wilson' was my brother-in-law Sir Keith Wilson, and the 'Bray' was my cousin-by-marriage John Bray, later to be Chief Justice of South Australia.

Pam had a great fund of legal anecdotes and she told me my favourite in this genre. The story goes that a man was charged with an indecent assault on a young girl, and when the case came to court he was defended by the noted Adelaide advocate Leo Travers. Apparently Travers presented a closely-reasoned defence for his client, including statements as to his ignorance of the opposite sex, but his opponent was a school contemporary of mine named Eb Scarfe. Eb was then the Police Prosecutor. He lived life pretty hard and was a tough adversary in court.

According to Pam's story, Eb said in his summing-up 'The defence claims that the accused is a person quite ignorant in sexual matters. In fact, if one is to believe the learned counsel, the defendant did not even know what a vagina was until he met Mr Travers.'

14

The Music Goes Round and Round

AFTER MY DIVORCE I lived the life of a bachelor gay for a while. There were plenty of opportunities for a good time in the speedway, art, and musical circles in which I moved. One of my more torrid affairs was with a leading Australian model. I was aware that she was leading me up the garden path to some degree, but perhaps it was a little further than I'd expected. On a number of occasions she would say that she had to have an early night because she was working the next day, and I dutifully returned her to her family home, but I learned that as soon as my car drove away it was replaced by that of a well-heeled bookmaker who also was escorting her.

Eventually she went to Paris to work for Givenchy. I was planning another trip overseas on various business matters and in my disillusionment I vowed that I would steer clear of her in Europe. But, quite by accident, I bumped into her when we were both strolling down the Champs-Elysées and for a couple of days it was all on again.

I was off on a tour of Scandinavia to talk to some speedway riders, and she promised to meet me in London a fortnight later. I duly arrived in the Big Smoke but she did not. Several days later she turned up with no apologies or explanations. I heard later that she had received an invitation to the Riviera to spend some time with the Aga Khan. Obviously an Australian speedway promoter was small fry by comparison!

With the feeling that two could play at that game I strung along with an Australian girl of my acquaintance, then living in London. When the model condescended to tap on the front door of my Brook Street apartment, the other young lady slipped out through the back. I have fond memories of the uses to which I put my Mathieu Mategot tapestry, which I was then using as a carpet in the apartment.

But these liaisons paled into insignificance when, for the second time, I met Julianne McClure. I met her first several years earlier, when we were introduced by Anne Kidman at a Spike Jones concert in Adelaide. We met again in 1956, when she was crowned Miss South Australia.

This title was a well-deserved tribute to her striking beauty and many achievements, but no such public recognition could ever hint at the special qualities that endeared her to me. Soon we were constant companions, and the time came when her family recognised that our marriage was inevitable. But there were two big problems. Julie and her family were devout Catholics, and I was a divorced person not of their faith.

Julie's parents asked me to discuss the matter with Dr Beovich, then Roman Catholic Archbishop of Adelaide, in case there was some way in which the marriage could be recognised by their Church. Of course there was not, but Dr Beovich and I spent a few pleasant minutes in his office comparing our injuries. He had broken his leg in a football accident many years earlier and I was in plaster from a speedboating mishap.

Despite this amicable meeting the Church still tried to influence Julie against our marriage. One evening she returned to her family home in St Georges, an Adelaide suburb, to find a young priest waiting for her. He had ridden over on his motor cycle.

First he tried reasonable arguments, and when these failed he made some veiled threats of 'eternal damnation' and quoted the case of another couple who had married against the wishes of the Church. He said that when the husband and his new bride drove off on their honeymoon they were involved in a car accident which killed one of them and crippled the other for life. The implication was that the Wrath of God had struck them down.

The Church was even more concerned about Julie marrying a non-Catholic divorcee because she was Miss South Australia, and they feared her action might set a poor example to other young Catholics. However, the young priest's arguments had no effect and he hopped on his motor bike and rode away. He had ridden only a couple of miles when he collided with a gum tree outside the Victoria Park Racecourse and broke an arm and a leg. Perhaps I will be excused a slight sense of satisfaction when I learned both of his arguments and of his accident. I felt a macabre pleasure whenever I passed that gum tree while en route to visit my family, who lived close by.

Julie and I had no doubt that we were right for each other and eventually our families agreed with us. In October 1957 we were married at the Adelaide Registry Office, with our friends Philip and June Jacobsen as witnesses. Mother had decorated the normally austere office with some of her distinctive flower arrangements.

This marked the beginning of many happy years. Julie's main sporting interest at that time was water-skiing, but I could not hope to emulate her in this skilled and graceful pastime. I tried to interest her in sports closer to my heart, and one night I took her and her father, who had been an amateur boxing champion in his youth, to the fights staged at the now-vanished Tivoli. The main bout was fought between the South Australian professional titleholder and an Englishman named Peter Read, programmed as 'former

R.A.F. champion'. Read took quite a pasting for several rounds, then suddenly unleashed a piledriver which flattened his opponent. In the few seconds of stunned silence before the audience realised what had happened Julie cried 'Oh, *good shot*, Peter!' This tennis phrase really broke up the boxing audience.

She joined me in watching my other love, cricket, but I think she enjoyed the barracking from the mounds rather than the subtler points of the game. The increasingly well-lubricated barrackers did not reserve their comments for the cricketers, and any sweet young thing who ventured within range usually passed on with a scarlet complexion. I heard one of the primest pieces of barracking at a match I watched with Julie. A vicious ball from a pace bowler rose sharply off the pitch and struck the batsman in the groin, and as he clutched himself in agony a stentorian voice bellowed 'Don't rub 'em, mate—count 'em!'

By the time of my second marriage I was deeply involved in the musical scene. I had loved music even before I could read. No doubt I inherited this from Mother, who was an ardent concert-goer and adored music until the end of her life, but I heard my first jazz records when my brother Jack began to collect them. I still get a kick out of such pieces as *Miss Hannah*, played by McKinney's Cottonpickers, which I first heard played on our spring-powered, wind-up gramophone.

I learnt to recognise some of the records in our family collection by the shape and colour of their labels. *Avalon*, for example, was easy to pick out because its label was a colourful reproduction of a sailing ship on a blue ocean. Others I knew by the length of the titles and the shape of the words.

On regular Sunday visits to Grandfather's house I entertained myself with his beautiful old music-box. In the gloom under the main staircase I extracted one or another of the dozens of spiky discs in its cabinet, locked it into position on the turntable, and listened to the tinkling tunes of the late nineteenth and early twentieth century.

Pianolas also were popular in those days. You fitted a drum of perforated paper into the mechanism, pumped steadily on the pedals, and as the drum revolved the piano keys moved up and down as though by unseen fingers while the notes of your selection sounded forth. In Grandfather's drawing-room I pumped out such tunes as *Paddlin' Madeline Home* while Father and aunts Edith and Ada drank tea, and at the home of my godfather, Alfred Corbin, I played *The Belle of New York*, *The Teddy Bears' Picnic*, or *The Doll Dance* while he stood behind me and whistled an accompaniment.

My musical tastes remained fairly conventional until I heard Ray Noble, who made a number of memorable records such as *Speedboat Bill*, *The Haunted House*, and the four-part *Turkish Delight*, featuring a number of jazz-influenced soloists. I added these to a collection of English recordings by such one-time greats as Carroll Gibbons, Lew Stone, Billy Cotton, and Bert Ambrose, but I was only dabbling in the waters of jazz until my friend

Dean Hay played me a number of newly-acquired Duke Ellington records.

They included *It Don't Mean a Thing if it Ain't Got That Swing*, and I could have taken that as a motto from then on. I became an instant addict. This record, together with the *The Dicty Glide*, *East Saint Louis Toodle-oo*, *Ring Dem Bells*, *Limehouse Blues*, and *Sophisticated Lady*, made me feel like an explorer looking upon new lands. I became an avid collector of every disc I could beg, borrow, or steal. Before long I was into Bix Beiderbecke, Frank Trumbauer, Henry 'Red' Allen, Louis Armstrong, and all the other practitioners of those seminal days of jazz. Rapidly I accumulated a weighty collection of the heavy 78s of that era although I'm ashamed to say that I treated them very carelessly. When I acquired my first car my faithful portable rode beside me on the sponge-rubber bench seat, with a selection of records including a couple of Count Basie discs that I swiped from sister Katherine when she brought them home from London. The bumps on the road and the gravitational stresses when cornering did nothing to improve the record sufaces but nevertheless my collection steadily increased in number. In 1973 I sold the bulk of this early collection to the National Library in Canberra, retaining only five for sentimental reasons. They included a Parlophone 78 of *Hot and Bothered* by the Harlem Footwarmers, a 1930s pseudonym for Duke Ellington. This was by far the loudest record I ever heard in my early teens and I used it as a handy way to cut short Katherine's telephone conversations. If I played it with my thickest steel needle and left the bedroom door open it was guaranteed to obliterate speech and hearing.

By the late 1930s the swing bands of Benny Goodman, Tommy and Jimmy Dorsey, Bob Crosby, Artie Shaw, Count Basie, Woody Herman and Chick Webb were spreading their influence far outside the U.S.A., to the delight of youngsters and the horror of their elders. Such bands seemed to me to be sparked by such incredible drummers as Gene Krupa, Cliff Leeman, Buddy Rich, Ray McKinley, and other notables, and to me they became the super-heroes of their art. Inspired by their intoxicating sounds I began to dabble in primitive rhythm, using a pair of tom-toms I had collected on a family cruise to Papua New Guinea in 1933.

Whenever a band performed at any of the dances or parties in East Terrace I inflicted myself upon the luckless musicians, sometimes led by a banjo player named Tommy Dorling or the pianist Isobel MacGregor and her sax-playing husband Val Spence. But the tom-toms were a poor substitute for the drums used by my heroes, and I cured this deficiency one day when my parents were away from home. Gathering up all my clothes except those I was wearing I took them to Trims the secondhand clothing dealer and flogged off the lot for ten pounds. I had my eye on a used set of drums on display in Pirie Street, and within a matter of minutes I had exchanged the cash for this ill-assorted outfit. It comprised an odd-sized narrow bass drum, decorated with an atrocious oil painting of a sunset, set inside a crude wooden box to which were attached a pair of tinny cymbals, sundry cowbells, and a set of Chinese wood blocks in orange, black, and gold.

Any parents less loving than mine would no doubt have reversed the whole transaction, redeemed my clothing, and administered appropriate chastisement. But I got away with it and joined other jazz addicts to play at various dances and functions around Adelaide. When Bryan Monkton was on piano we called ourselves 'Monk's Apes'. When he left for a while the group became 'Bonython's Pythons'. Undoubtedy our performance was on a par with such titling.

By various manipulations I upgraded my drum kit until I owned new white pearl drums fashioned in imitation of those used by my idol Gene Krupa, even to having my initials painted inside a small shield in the exact position used by the 'maestro'. The kit included a matching pair of tom-toms which Mother bought from the drum shop of the English percussionist Joe Daniels in London.

One Sunday morning in 1936 our group went to the Hedley Smith studios on the corner of Wakefield Street and Gawler Place and cut a number of recordings. With Geoff Williams on trumpet, Hughie Leonard on trombone, Gus Mumme on saxophone and clarinet, Colin Hamilton on piano, and Dennis Hookham on guitar we felt highly professional as we played in front of the heavy old-fashioned microphones, but the results were slightly appalling.

However, overwhelming enthusiasm and a little talent will conquer all obstacles, and during the next three years I made further recordings: with pianist Jack Young who was an announcer on 5AD, and with the A.B.C. Dance Band led by Jim Davidson. I cut two sides with some members of Jim's band, inspired by Artie Shaw's *Blues A and B*. We called the first one *Under the Bed (Traditional)* and the other *We're Sorry Now* as a variant on *Who's Sorry Now?*

Plenty of jazz records were reaching Adelaide by that time, and each afternoon after school I haunted the Rundle Street music shops of Allan's, Eddy's, and The Gladiola. But even these were not enough to satisfy me and I used to place special orders with Maxy Perch, Chief Steward of the P. & O. liner *Mooltan*. We made friends with him on the cruise to Papua New Guinea and he picked up new releases for me long before they reached Adelaide through normal import channels. By the end of the 1930s I was importing records direct from that most famous of all jazz outlets: the Commodore Music Shop in New York.

The proprietor, Milt Gabler, was recording some of the best jazz of all time on the Commodore label, and his manager Jack Crystal provided me with all their latest releases. They included names to conjure with nowadays: Bobby Hackett, Pee Wee Russell, Jack Teagarden, Wild Bill Davison, Jess Stacy, Bud Freeman, and George Brunis. And it was on a Commodore label

117

that I first heard that most wonderful of all jazz singers, Billie Holliday. I never dreamed that, thirty years later, I would bring most of these famous musicians to Australia.

No thrill could compare with that of unpacking a new consignment of discs from Commodore, with anticipation heightened by the long wait after making a choice from reviews in the American magazines *Downbeat* and *Metronome*, sending off an order by surface mail, and waiting for the shipment to arrive aboard a liner from San Francisco to Sydney.

My bedroom was lined with autographed photographs of my drummer heroes. Zutty Singleton, the New Orleans percussionist, wrote on his action photo 'To a real pal—and a Swing Man!' Gene Krupa wrote 'Your letter was a sender. Keep swinging!' And Cliff Leeman 'To my greatest fan—from your Yankee buddy.'

On later travels to America I looked up Zutty and his wife Marge, and they always seemed pleased when I arrived unexpectedly at their apartment in the Alvin Hotel, New York. They had all my Christmas cards from years back stuck to the wall of their living-room. Used by many musicians, the Alvin was a depressing hostelry but convenient to the New York jazz clubs.

My fan mail with jazz musicians soon developed into a two-way correspondence, especially with two of the 'orchestra wives': Ely, the wife of Jimmy Dorsey's drummer Ray McKinley; and Nita, the vocalist wife of Artie Shaw's drummer Cliff Leeman.

Ely is credited as co-composer of *Beat Me Daddy, Eight to the Bar*, which she told me was inspired by the writings of de Sade! Her letters always were amusing and full of low-downs on some of the great jazz names of the period. An extremely striking girl, she occasionally sent me photographs of herself wearing swimsuits far more daring than those seen in conservative Australia.

We lost touch during the war, but after a gap of fourteen years I visited America in 1954. I was staying at a hotel in San Francisco when my room telephone rang one night and a female voice enquired 'Is that Mr Bonney-thon? Mr Kym Bonney-thon?'

'Yes?'

'Well, you probably won't remember me, but I used to be Ely McKinley!'

'Of *course* I remember you—where are you?'

'I'm working on the switchboard downstairs.'

I arranged to meet her and take her out for a late supper when her shift ended at one a.m. We met in the foyer but I looked in vain for the svelte bathing-beauty. Instead I saw a rather blowsy redhead whose face looked as though she had seen everything. But the old spark was still there and we had a great time rehashing the past. She told me that she and Ray had divorced and that she was living with a taxi-driver, and I sensed many problems she did not mention.

We never met again, but there is a sequel. My brother Jack married a

New Zealand girl, Hope Rutherford, whose sister Airini married an Adelaide man. Airini had a son, Jim, but her husband was killed in the war. She was re-married, to an American serviceman, and went with him to live in California in Ely's old hometown. Young Jim eventually returned to settle in Adelaide, and in 1956 his stepfather sent him a newspaper cutting to pass on to me.

I read in it that Ely McKinley, the girl who during her final year at college was voted 'Most Likely to Succeed' and of whom it was thought that she might end up as a film star or a millionaire's wife, had been found battered to death in a San Francisco alley.

I never met Ray McKinley, who took over the Glenn Miller Army Band after the death of its leader and led it on world tours after the war, but I wrote to him in 1977. In reply, he told me that he learned about Ely's death in a way rather similar to mine. He and Ely once used the same dentist in New York, a man named Julius Reiser. When Ely moved to the West Coast her dentist there recognised Reiser's work on her teeth, and when Ely died he sent the newspaper cutting to Reiser. Reiser passed it on to Ray . . . surely one of the most macabre possible ways to learn of the death of an ex-wife.

In 1937, while I was still at St Peter's College, I began my long association with the A.B.C. as a jazz disc jockey. It was to last, except for the war years, until 1975. The first appointment was a big step for a seventeen-year-old, but at that time my enthusiasm for the subject had carried me into the innermost circles in Australia. Through constant reading on the subject, my almost daily correspondence with American jazz figures, and my ever-growing collection of records I suppose I may have known as much about jazz as anyone in Australia.

Those early broadcasts were a strange experience. The A.B.C. imitated the B.B.C., then under the influence of the super-conservative 'wowser' Sir John Reith, and announcers had to wear dinner jackets merely to present a programme! This, of course, was long before TV.

For a while I did a similar programme on an Adelaide commercial station, 5KA, but this soon faded out. Commercial radio stations always have been uninterested in jazz, with the exception of 5AD which for many years gave the great Adelaide jazz authority, William V. Holyoak, a regular spot.

When I was training with the R.A.A.F. in 1940 I went often to the A.B.C. studios in Sydney to watch their Dance Band, under Jim Davidson, broadcast their weekly programmes. Most broadcasting was 'live' in those days and it was good to see a band in action once again. I had known a good many of its musicians and singers for some years: people like clarinettist Keith Atkinson, trumpeters Norm Litt and Jim Gussey, drummer Tom Stevenson, and vocalists Dick Cranbourne and the Lester Sisters.

During the war my gramophone and records travelled wherever I went, and by 1945 I carted around scores of the heavy old 78s in cases made from the plywood air tails of aerial torpedoes. The records were one of the few sources of relaxation during some of those wartime periods but were not as popular with my squadron mates as they were with me.

During my farming years I began to broadcast again, now on National relay and also on Radio Australia, and the programmes attracted letters from as far afield as merchant seamen off the coast of China. Also I became a member of the jazz group led by clarinettist Bruce Gray and including trumpeter Bill Munro, trombonist Derek Bentley, pianist Lew Fisher, Bob Wright on tuba, and John Malpas on banjo. We did a series of live broadcasts for the A.B.C. and made quite a number of records.

On 8 February 1949 I played a recording session with one of the finest bands in the country, the Southern Jazz Group led by Dave Dallwitz, for Bill Holyoak's Memphis label. We made two sides: *Sweet Georgia Brown* and *Original Stump Jump Blues (in Hay flat)* composed by 'Massie Harres'. These elaborate puns, of course, derived from my farming activities.

The record was rated No. 2 in the Australian jazz polls and 'top-rated Australian recording' in the American polls. I was still much influenced by the Cliff Leeman style of drumming and one reviewer wrote 'If Kym Bonython hits that confounded Chinese smash cymbal one more time I shall scream!'

In 1950 Jean and I made our first overseas trip to America and Europe and at last I was able to visit the 'land of jazz' and see some of my heroes in person. In Los Angeles I heard the Kid Ory Band and Ben Pollock and his Pick-A-Rib Boys (so called because Ben owned a Spareribs restaurant in Beverly Hills) and visited the renowned Jazzman Record Shop run by Neshui Ertegun, son of the Turkish Ambassador to the U.S.A. Buying any of the goodies on display presented a problem. At that time Australia was still labouring under post-war currency restrictions, especially where U.S. dollars were concerned, and Australians were forbidden to order such luxuries as jazz records from overseas.

But we enthusiasts usually got around this problem. One could often buy a few spare dollar bills from travellers returning from overseas, and mail these to jazz speciality shops who would then return the selected items marked as 'Unsolicited Gift'.

Unfortunately a few sharp operators in the States simply pocketed the money, knowing that the would-be purchaser could not take action against them without revealing an attempted illegal operation.

I negotiated a couple of successful shipments from Ertegun, and then gathered some more funds which I despatched to him with a list of records. This order did not arrive and I assumed that he was playing the same trick that other dealers had played on friends of mine. I complained along these lines and Ertegun's Turkish honour was gravely offended. He had not received the money and the order, and he wrote me an extremely bitter letter.

TOP: Bruce Kelley, Australian and South Australian Sidecar Champion, takes a tumble at Rowley Park in 1957, just missing the outfit ridden by Stan Dyson (*David Brock photo*). BOTTOM: The 'Wonder Car' (Number 76) in action at Rowley Park 1969

Twenty-five years later he became Vice-President of Atlantic, one of the world's largest record labels. George Wein, my New York representative, is a close friend of Ertegun's and he thought it was time to heal the breach between two people with such close interests. I agreed, and George tried to act as peacemaker, but apparently Ertegun is not the forgiving kind. He gave George a message to this effect.

My 1950 trip to America recharged me with enthusiasm for the jazz scene. I heard the Elliott Lawrence Orchestra in New York, and we visited many of the Dixieland jazz joints such as Jimmy Ryan's plus the more modern spots like Birdland, where Woody Herman and his band were playing. But the greatest thrill was a night in Eddie Condon's Club in Greenwich Village. In this temple of jazz I heard Bill Davison, Edmond Hall, Cutty Cutshall, Jack Lesberg, and Gene Schroeder, with Cliff Leeman on drums.

When we returned home I rejoined the Bruce Gray Band but I soon began to suffer from divided loyalties. Often I was playing when I should have been supervising the birth of a prize calf on the farm, or busy on the farm when the band had an engagement. Finally one of my best cows gave birth to a stillborn calf in the early hours of one morning, when I was away with the band. I felt that I might have prevented this mishap if I had been doing my job properly instead of jazzing around with the band, and reluctantly told Bruce that I would have to pull out. I played again with him later, after my first marriage broke up and when I was involved in speedway activities, but I sold my drum kit in 1957 when I was still on crutches after a speedboat accident and unable to get within striking distance of a drum.

In 1952, en route to Jersey to buy stud cattle, I had the supreme pleasure of meeting my boyhood idol Gene Krupa. He and his orchestra were performing on stage in New York's Paramount Theatre and I went backstage after the show to introduce myself. I hardly expected him to remember me but he treated me like a long-lost friend and could not have been more charming. Only two years later he came to Australia for Aztec Services, for the first post-war tour by American jazz musicians. He brought with him the multi-instrumentalist Eddie Shu on reeds and Teddy Napoleon on piano, and Kenn Brodziak, the managing director of Aztec, engaged the Sydney drummer Keith Bruce as Gene's personal assistant for the tour. I met Keith when Gene came to Adelaide and he was to become one of my closest friends.

In the same year the clown prince of music, Spike Jones and his City Slickers, came to Australia for Lee Gordon who had started his meteoric career as a concert promoter for Australia and New Zealand. Spike was a great musician and I couldn't miss the opportunity to hear the man who'd turned *Chloe* into something that its composer never dreamed of, and so I went to his Adelaide concert. There, of course, I met Julie McClure.

I was to see a lot of Spike and his manager Ralph Wonders, with Ralph's

TOP: With Bill Wigzell (*left*) and the original *Bullo Bee* in 1954. BOTTOM: In the *Bullo-Bee-Low* with Mac Lawrie, Adelaide 1960, preparing for an underwater trip

wife Katherine, in the years ahead, and it transpired that I flew to America in the aircraft in which they were returning home in 1954. High above the Pacific, Ralph griped 'I love Australia! I love that scenery! I love those people! But where oh where do you get that goddam awful ass paper?'

Unfortunately Ralph's beloved Australia was still suffering from post-war shortages, and he had sore recollections of close encounters with the abrasive local product.

15

Over (and Under) the Waves

M Y LUST for speed extended to the water as well as the land, and while I was establishing myself at Rowley Park I had my first ride in a speedboat. It was a Holden-engined craft owned by Arnie Sunstrom, one of the Rowley Park drivers, and I enjoyed it so much that I said firmly 'That's for me!'

I'm surprised I hadn't thought of it earlier. In 1933 I had been an excited spectator at a celebrated powerboat contest on Adelaide's Outer Harbor. The Rymill brothers, in their speedboat *Tortoise*, pitted themselves against a New South Wales challenger named Harry McEvoy at the wheel of *Cettien*. McEvoy won the race.

Soon after my ride with Arnie I bought a potent piece of machinery from owner-driver Ward Bryce, who ran a drycleaning business in North Adelaide. It was a racing skiff powered by an eight-cyclinder Ford Mercury engine, and was among the fastest boats in the State.

In a skiff, the engine is fitted amidships and the driver and mechanic sit side by side in the stern. At low speeds the flimsy boat assumes a most awkward attitude, with the nose sticking high in the air, cutting out forward vision. As the craft gains speed the nose drops down and by the time it is skipping along in a series of leaps and bounds at 50, 60, and 70 m.p.h., only the last few inches of the hull are in the water. In boating circles this is known as 'prop riding'.

The skiff was the first of my *Bullo-Bees*. The name was inspired by my stud breeding activities, the first letter of my surname, and the appellation bestowed on me by a speedway character who for some unknown reason seemed to think there was a certain amount of flamboyance in my character.

I joined the Adelaide Speedboat Club and, helped no doubt by my speedway experience, I soon found myself as back marker in the programmes of handicap events held each Sunday at Snowdens Beach on the Port River. The club members included Roy Marten, an ex-R.A.A.F. type who was club secretary. Later to be Mayor of Port Adelaide, he became a staunch friend and is godfather to Timothy, son of my second marriage.

Before long, *Bullo-Bee I* gave me the closest shave of my life, whether on land or water. With Bill Wigzell as my mechanic and passenger, I was racing on a showery, overcast day. The final event was being run and the fast back markers were catching up with the slower contestants. As we came out of the final corner, heading for the checkered flag and with throttle flat to the floor, I saw that another boat had stalled directly in our path.

Instinctively I lifted my foot from the throttle, to cut power and avoid a collision. But the other back marker, chasing me down the course, could not see what was happening through the dense clouds of spray. In blissful ignorance he charged on at full speed, glimpsing my boat only an instant before he struck me side-on. His boat actually leapt over the top of mine. The whizzing blades of his propeller mangled my steering wheel, which I was still holding, and the side of his boat hit me in the face.

Dazed but still conscious I was able to work the throttle while Bill steered the boat. We made for the shore, where an ambulance took me to hospital. Luckily the damage was only two lovely black eyes, plus the persistent headaches of which I've written earlier.

Soon I was seeking even greater speed on the water. I disposed of the skiff and bought my first hydroplane from another enthusiast named Jack Odgers. *Bullo-Bee II* also was powered by a Ford Mercury engine, to which I fitted the newly-developed fuel injection system. This combination enabled me to establish a new State water speed record of 85 m.p.h. averaged over the two-way one mile course.

I also won my first national hydroplane title on Hume Weir in *Bullo-Bee II*, but I did not find her altogether satisfactory. She was a big boat, not especially manoeuvrable, and the hull had taken quite a beating over the years. I decided to look for an American hull on my next visit to the U.S.A., and Bryan Monkton gave me a letter of introduction to Stan Dollar.

Stan, President of the well-known Dollar Shipping Line, was a former Gold Cup speedboat racer. In boating circles the Gold Cup is the equivalent of the Melbourne Cup, and the waterborne thoroughbreds are powered by Rolls Royce or Allison aircraft engines. They push the boats along at speeds above 200 m.p.h., with an engine note that is pure magic to any speedboat enthusiast.

Stan introduced me to Morlan Visel, a former speedway racer of some repute. He ran a boating business on the shores of Lake Tahoe, a holiday and gambling resort near Reno. Among the craft at his marina I found a potent hydroplane named *Little Joe*, in which Morlan had set a class world speed record of 104 m.p.h. on the Salton Sea.

Little Joe had a very light plywood hull, powered by a souped-up Ford V8/60 engine. I tried her out on the icy unfathomable waters of Lake Tahoe and was sold immediately. As *Bullo-Bee III*, she was to win me my last Australian championship at Chicken Bay, Sydney, in 1956.

My Lake Tahoe visit coincided with some annual Gold Cup events, and these gave me a glimpse into another world. One of the residences of Henry Kaiser, the steel magnate, stood on the edge of the lake surrounded by acres of manicured lawns. His shocking pink *Hawaiian Kai* was driven into a special marina after each Gold Cup heat and raised out of the water by a submerged lifting device, so that mechanics could work on her and empty two 44-gallon drums of petrol into her massive tanks in readiness for the next event. Those engines devoured fuel.

While the boat was being serviced, white-clad chefs and waiters attended to the guests whom Henry Kaiser had invited to watch the day's racing. A scene from 'La Dolce Vita'!

My most vivid memory of that memorable day is not the full-throated roar of the huge engines, and the towering rooster tails of water thrown up by the competing craft, but the breathtaking *swish* as the spray fell back onto the placid surface of the lake many seconds after the engine noise had faded. Speedboat racing never seemed quite the same after that day on Lake Tahoe! Compared with my American counterparts I had to settle for 'beer tastes'.

Conditions for hydroplane racing were far from ideal in Australia, especially in South Australia. Hydroplanes have very light hulls and should be used on almost glassy surfaces for best results. When travelling at speed, the hulls make even less contact than those of skiffs. They are almost flying, with only the last inch or so of the sponson (float) and the bottom half of the propeller actually in the water. Racing such boats on Australian harbours or rivers has many dangers. Waters around the racing areas were not barred to pleasure boats, cargo ships, tugs, and other craft, and these threw up wakes which felt like a brick wall when a hydroplane leapt over them at 90 or 100 m.p.h. And, of course, the water could be choppy from sea breezes.

Repairs to the hydroplane hulls were inevitable after each meeting, not only because of the above hazards but also because of drifting debris such as bottles and pieces of timber. Lost propellers, costing up to $200 a time, were frequent casualties of such high-speed hits.

Just after Christmas 1956, these adverse conditions brought the career of *Bullo-Bee III* to a dramatic end.

On the Port River, Adelaide, I was defending my Australian title against some of the best drivers in the country. They included the outstanding woman competitor, Grace Walker, and one of Australia's most renowned racers, Ernie Nunn. Both hailed from Sydney.

My children Robyn and Christopher, over from Melbourne for the holidays, were among the crowds watching the races. It was easy for them to keep an eye on me because I was one of the first speedboat racers to wear a jet-type crash helmet, and I had painted it a psychedelic orange.

The usual uncontrolled mob of pleasure boats was floating around, and while I was travelling at maximum speed I hit the wash of a boat that had just passed over the course. *Bullo-Bee III* literally took off. She soared high in the air at close to 100 m.p.h. — so high that instead of smacking down flat on the water she nosedived. When the nose hit the water the whole boat simply disintegrated. One second she was there — the next she was gone.

I still don't know exactly what happened to me. I vividly remember the water changing colour from a dirty green to an ever-darkening brown as I went down and down to the bottom of the channel. I presume I was trapped in the wreckage, and there was nothing I could do until the buoyancy of my lifejacket suddenly pulled me free and I shot up to the surface — with a badly smashed leg that apparently had been doubled back under the dashboard. I was fully conscious, and my orange helmet helped rescuers to find me quickly in the choppy water.

Robyn and Christopher watched anxiously as I was transferred from the crash boat to a stretcher and then taken to hospital, but I was able to reassure them that I was not badly injured. After a few days in hospital I was discharged with my leg in plaster from toes to groin, but there was no way that my beautiful *Bullo-Bee III* could be patched up again. Mac Lawrie had salvaged the pitiful remains but the wreck was beyond repair.

My leg seemed reluctant to mend, perhaps because I gave it little opportunity to do so. I had more interesting things to do. I crutched around my usual beat at the double and had a series of levers fitted to my Bristol so that I could operate the clutch manually, but when I drove along the bumpy Grange Road en route from my house at Tennyson to the city, passengers were disconcerted to hear my leg-bones grating within the cast.

Six months after the accident I had to have a bone graft, involving ten screws within the leg. They are still there today. Altogether I was fourteen months in plaster, which was somewhat inhibiting especially when the dry skin itched maddeningly inside the cast. Sometimes I would pull up at a service station and use its compressed air hose to blow great showers of dried flakes of skin out of the plaster, but this gave only temporary relief.

In another attempt to alleviate the intense irritation I slid a Chinese backscratcher down inside the plaster. This was fine until the wooden rod snapped and left the little claw inside the cast, so that a window had to be cut in the plaster to remove this new irritation. The impossibility of scratching myself probably emphasised my contention that the greatest pleasures in life comprise the 'Three S's'. No prizes are offered for guessing what they are.

I worked up quite a speed on my crutches but I came close to disaster on a visit to the Sydney Showgrounds speedway. Jack Murray and I were standing in the centre of the arena during the running of a side-car feature race when one of the riders lost control. His bike came flying off the track directly towards Jack and me. I travelled backwards at slightly under a gallop, holding out one crutch in an attempt to ward off the charging machinery, but luckily it missed both of us. The principal damage was to my cast. When I had time to inspect it I discovered that my violent evasive tactics had fractured it all round and I had to go to hospital for a new one to be constructed.

Older and wiser friends frequently told me that I would live to regret all my racing indiscretions. I had cracked several vertebrae, damaged a shoulder, broken a leg, and suffered numerous thumps on the head, although none of them ever knocked me out. With the carelessness of youth I laughed perhaps a trifle scornfully at such warnings, but the years have proved them right. In 1975 we moved from one apartment to another at my Sydney gallery and I undertook to move such weighty items as my collection of long-playing records and art books. I had to carry loads of them downstairs, across a courtyard, and up another flight of stairs to our new apartment. After some days of this toil I thought I would crack up. My leg became very painful and for weeks after that I had to sleep with pillows at my feet to keep the weight of blankets off my toes. My Sydney doctor advised X-ray examination and this showed calcification of the bones, arthritis in the joints, and a thickening of the arteries.

But all that seemed impossible in the 1950s. Apart from speed track and speedboat racing I also had become involved in scuba diving. This came about through my friendship with Mac Lawrie, South Australia's leading marine salvage expert and an experienced scuba and 'hard hat' diver. Late one winter afternoon Mac took me out in one of his workboats and taught me the rudiments of underwater diving. I followed up this new experience by a visit to the Adelaide Skin Diving Centre, owned by the one-legged diver Dave Burchell. His exploits included locating and exploring the deeply submerged wreck of H.M.A.S. *Perth* in Sunda Strait, for which he was created O.B.E. I bought the necessary gear from him, but had to rely on other scuba enthusiasts for water transport because all my *Bullo-Bees* were far too small for bulky air bottles, flippers, underwater cameras, and other gear.

I dabbled in diving whenever I could spare the time from other activities, and this led the way to a new experience. In 1958 I resurrected *Bullo-Bee II*, had her completely rebuilt, and entered the Snowdens Beach races once again. She did not have the success of her sisters, but I managed to add a few miles per hour to the State water record. The final straw came when the Taxation Department refused to allow the deduction I was claiming towards the heavy maintenance of the craft. I claimed that my speedboat racing was part of my publicity for Rowley Park Speedway, but for some reason or other they refused to believe me. So I was ready to be tempted by a new toy when it was dangled before my eyes.

On a U.S.A. trip connected with speedway promotions I had planned a visit to the Virgin Islands, and had actually made a booking at a hotel run especially for underwater enthusiasts. It was owned by the parents of Leslie Caron, the French film star. But a Melbourne scuba distributor had given me an introduction to Gustav Dalla Valle, an Italian who rated only slightly

127

below Hans Haas and Jacques Cousteau as an underwater expert.

Gustav had a business which manufactured and distributed underwater gear, with branches throughout America. He also handled Italian two-man midget submarines, based on the wartime craft used so successfully against the British in the Mediterranean.

I stopped off in Los Angeles to stay a few days with Gustav, and the moment he showed me one of the submarines I knew I had to have one. I had to choose between it and the Virgin Islands and the latter lost. I placed the order and Gustav arranged for a submarine to be despatched direct from the Italian factory in Livorno to Adelaide.

The sub arrived several months after my return home, and as soon as it was released by Customs I had the speedway signwriter paint a name and design on the yellow fibreglass nose. Predictably, I named her *Bullo-Bee-Low*, and the design around the name depicted a rather dreamy-looking bull garlanded with flowers and afloat in a sea of bubbles.

Of course I had never ridden in an underwater vehicle and so it was a matter of reading the instruction sheets before descending into the depths —and hoping for the best! I felt some trepidation when I read 'Do not exceed a depth of 100 feet as, beyond this point, circumstances might arise which could cause the abandonment of the craft.'

The fifteen-foot fibreglass hull of *Bullo-Bee-Low* was powered by three 12-volt car batteries, which operated an electric motor capable of propelling her at five knots. Batteries and motor were contained in a watertight cylinder, beneath a compressed air cylinder with a nozzle leading to a plastic buoyancy chamber. When the submarine was fully assembled and floating, I followed the instructions and loaded her with the special lead ballast weights until she began slowly to sink. Then I released compressed air into the buoyancy chamber until she had a slight buoyancy characteristic.

After that, she operated on the principle of every submarine. To take her down, I let compressed air out of the buoyancy chamber so that it filled with water. This added sufficient weight to sink her. To ascend, I 'blew tanks' with the compressed air, thus expelling the water and replacing it with air.

Experimenting with these operations helped me to work out the meaning of the warning not to descend below 100 feet. Presumably the water pressure would be more than the buoyancy chamber could deal with, and she would continue to descend instead of rising.

Mac Lawrie agreed to join me in my first trip, and we launched the sub from the boat ramp at Outer Harbor. We settled into the seats and I released air from the chamber. Slowly we sank into the murky water and I turned on the motor, but for the moment I had my mind on other things than the directional compass and quite soon we saw timber pylons looming through the gloom. We had gone off course and headed underneath the wharf, and after a little backing and filling I brought her to the surface again. A group

128

of incredulous wharfies was peering down at us, and next day's *Advertiser* published a cartoon by Pat Oliphant showing the submarine enmeshed in fishing nets with one burly fisherman telling his mate 'Throw it back, Ernie! Nobody would ever believe you!'

Soon after this the Melbourne *Sun* featured a cartoon depicting two curvaceous mermaids talking to each other as *Bullo-Bee-Low* cruised past. One was saying 'I told Mr Bonython I wasn't 18 yet, so he threw me back!'

Bullo-Bee-Low was a lot of fun but she was cumbersome to launch and land, especially in some shallow Adelaide waters which are still only knee-deep several hundred yards from the shore. Two people could carry the hull but by the time it had been loaded and fitted with all its gear one felt more like going home for a rest than delving into the depths. This problem inspired us to design and build an amphibious trailer. It enabled us to tow the fully-equipped submarine behind a car on the road and down to the water's edge, and then tow sub and trailer behind a boat until we reached the chosen diving place. An added advantage was that the 150-minutes battery charge life could be used entirely underwater, instead of in motoring perhaps several miles out to sea.

A problem however was that a choppy sea made it very hard to re-load the sub onto the floating trailer. The fibreglass hull often suffered one or two holes in the process. Another hazard of the craft was that of the battery compartment. To avoid any possibility of seawater reaching the batteries the compartment had to be sealed tight by tensioning twenty-four nuts and bolts. This was an additional chore on top of manipulating the heavy batteries, and it had the inherent danger of explosive battery gases building up inside the compartment. I found this out the hard way.

Several times we took the sub to the water only to find conditions unsuitable for launching, and after one of these occasions I took her home and did not open the battery compartment before returning to the sea a couple of days later. With all systems apparently go, I switched on the motor and there was a loud explosion within the compartment. I was straddling it at the time, and the blast was fierce enough to make it bulge threateningly between my legs. Had it fragmented the results could have been too horrible to contemplate. They might have finished what the bull only just failed to achieve!

The explosion was caused because gases from the battery acid had accumulated in the airtight compartment. When I switched on the motor, the tiny electric spark set them off. To prevent this happening again I welded a gas tap onto the compartment, and on the way to a launch I always called at a garage and used its compressed air hose to force air through the tap and flush out any gases.

Bullo-Bee-Low enabled me to cruise the undersea off the coastline near Adelaide, use my underwater camera to photograph marine life, and explore the various wrecks and reefs. I could park the submarine on the seabed and

129

swim away to photograph the target for the day. I'm rather proud of the fact that I have never used a spear gun.

After I'd owned the submarine for a while, Dave Burchell and I worked out a stunt to publicise his skin diving business. He was to make his very first parachute jump from a light aircraft, wearing his aqualung gear, and rendezvous with me on the ocean bed. He would join me in *Bullo-Bee-Low*, and then we would cruise along to land at a predetermined spot where the media waited for us. To mark my position underwater I released a small red-and-white buoy incorporating the 'diver's flag'.

Things did not go entirely according to plan but we did manage to rendezvous about forty feet below the surface — although this was more by good luck than good judgement.

My great ambition was to take *Bullo-Bee-Low* to explore the waters of the Barrier Reef, but she was too big to fit into the freighter aircraft of the day and it would have been a massive task to tow her all the way by road. Eventually I sold her to a TV company and I have seen her featured several times in such children's serials as *Skippy*. On one nostalgic occasion I suddenly found myself driving behind her down Oxford Street in Sydney, 1,000 miles from her former abode and about eight years after I sold her.

Although I couldn't take *Bullo-Bee-Low* to the Barrier Reef I have enjoyed many aqualung dives in that area. The most spectacular region I visited was off Heron Island, where I had one of my more memorable encounters with a shark. I was swimming around about fifty feet down when I entered a cave about the size of an average room. The shark already was in occupation and it's hard to know which of us received the bigger shock. It came at me like an express train but fortunately was intent only in getting out of the way. It passed so close that it knocked the underwater camera out of my hands.

On one visit to Heron Island I met the divers Ron and Valerie Taylor. Ron's firm opinion is that sea-snakes are far more dangerous than sharks, because they are more aggressive and have a venom for which there was no antidote. He said that if you met six sharks and one sea-snake you should forget the sharks and get out of the way of the snake.

I told the Taylors about the amazing 'sink holes' near Mount Gambier in south-east South Australia. There is a number of uncharted subterranean rivers in the porous limestone of that region, and they fill great caverns which explorers have to enter through mere fissures in the surface, rather like entering a bottle through the neck. I'm not adventurous enough to explore them very deeply. I don't like losing sight of the 'light at the top of the tunnel', and exploration of the lateral crevices, so dark that one must have guide ropes to find one's way back, has no appeal to me. Several hardy enthusiasts, including the Taylors, have dived deep into the sink holes — and one or two have lost their lives.

Nevertheless, with Dave Burchell and some of his friends, I spent a breathtaking hour exploring Ewans Pond. It is like a small lake, only about forty-five feet deep, and at its lowest point the icy water bubbles into it through a patch of pure white sand. The water, filtered through deep limestone, is close to freezing even in midsummer. Before our activities stirred up the sediment the water was so clear that one more distant movie sequence I photographed showed five divers apparently suspended in space.

My underwater companions included John Brook, who taught me a great deal about scuba diving, and Bob Stone. Bob was as enthusiastic about underwater photography as I was, but his most notable attribute was that he was one of the greatest 'earbashers' I've ever encountered. The bubbles flowing from his face mask while we were under water showed that he tried to continue talking even under those conditions.

One day we were a couple of miles out to sea and were about to drop into the water when we saw two sets of tell-tale fins encircling our craft. We decided there was safety in numbers and agreed to dive simultaneously on the count of three. John and I dropped over the side, but Bob changed his mind and remained seated on the thwarts. The sharks were frightened away, and needless to say we gave Bob a good roasting on our return.

On one occasion, even Dave Burchell admitted some apprehension. Six of us were exploring the wreck of the *John Robb*, about 120 feet down and some miles off the coast, but I was having trouble with a faulty face mask. It kept filling with water, and when at last I got rid of the blinding salt water I found I was alone. I decided to ascend, and the moment I broke surface I was plucked from the water by a couple of breathless companions. Apparently that most predatory of all sharks, a White Pointer, had swum past our group on the ocean floor and missed me only by about two feet. With my vision obscured I had been quite unconscious of the fact—but it did seem a pity to have missed the chance of photographing the eighteen-foot monster.

16

88 Jerningham Street

LIFE OFTEN jerks onwards through a series of lucky or unlucky chances, and it was certainly a lucky chance for me that Ross and Ina Luck chose to live at Tennyson and became my immediate neighbours. They were ideal companions during that period when my interest in modern Australian art was expanding steadily, and my renewed association with Max Harris was equally prolific with good talk and good ideas. Through these friends I became enthused with the idea of publishing a book on the subject. None had been produced in Australia for almost twenty years, since the death of publisher Sydney Ure Smith.

I enlisted the aid of my friend Laurie Thomas, a former Director of the art galleries of Western Australia and Queensland and now art critic for a number of eastern States newspapers and magazines. He and I decided what artists should be included, then selected their most representative paintings or other works of art, and I contacted the artists to obtain copyright clearance and arrange for the photography. The whole procedure took two years and Ross Luck was an invaluable consultant as well as designing the book.

Most artists responded very quickly to requests to include their work but a few did not answer or gave reasons why they did not want to be represented. The strangest of these reasons came from Godfrey Miller, a senior figure in Australian art. I wanted to include three of his paintings, but he replied in spidery handwriting: 'I have given your request much thought and have now *finally* decided that I wish to be left out of the book *entirely* as my protest against the New South Wales government's decision to take over the Paddington Boy Scout Hall!'

Following this remarkable piece of logic I was obliged to seek representation of his work by using paintings in the possession of two State galleries, who had bought the copyrights when they acquired the paintings.

Godfrey Miller was a true eccentric. He had family connections with a shipping company, but lived frugally, and after his death was found to be quite wealthy. He taught at East Sydney Technical College, and one of the stories about him relates that, during a life class, he was peering over a student's shoulder. In an attempt to demonstrate what he wanted the student to achieve he used his pencil to make a number of quick incisive strokes on the student's pad. He then stepped back, gazed silently at what he had drawn, murmured 'H'm . . . that's not bad!', tore the sheet off the pad, and stowed it in his pocket.

At last the book, entitled *Modern Australian Painting and Sculpture: A Survey of Australian Art 1950–60*, was ready for the press. I had 2,500 copies printed by the Griffin Press, a subsidiary of Advertiser Newspapers, and released the book to coincide with the first Adelaide Festival of Arts. The price was five guineas a copy, quite substantial in those days, but the edition sold out quickly. I could not go into a second edition because of a bad under-estimate of the production costs, and the book never was reprinted. Sixteen years later it had become a 'rare book' and a copy sold at auction for $198!

Since then I have compiled two companion volumes, *Modern Australian Painting 1960–70* and *1970–75*. These were published by Rigby Limited in larger editions and sold out completely. The third, to be published by the same firm, will be *Modern Australian Painting 1975–80*.

While I was compiling the first book my artist friends often asked me 'Why don't you open a gallery in Adelaide? We'll support you because there doesn't seem to be a gallery there which likes our work.'

By this time I had become rather fed up with the ties that were part of being a small shopkeeper, but my involvement with Rowley Park Speedway, and my jazz broadcasts for the A.B.C., were insufficient to consume my nervous energy. I decided that a new venture would be a good idea, disposed of the record shop, and bought an old cottage in Jerningham Street, North Adelaide.

I converted the cottage into a small gallery and opened it in March 1961 with an exhibition by Lawrence Daws. After that, I presented Adelaide with a veritable flood of fine painters and sculptors of whom the majority had never exhibited before. The prices were very modest in those days before the art boom of the late 1960s and early 1970s, and sales were usually good, although the artists whom I wanted most to succeed often met with little success in conservative Adelaide.

Many of the patrons of my North Adelaide gallery will remember June Jacobsen. She came to Adelaide in 1955 when her husband was transferred there, bearing an introduction from my good friend Rosa Nicholls. June could not bear inactivity, and after trying her hand at a little gift shop in North Adelaide she joined the gallery staff. She was a tremendous asset because she was one of the most universally loved people I've ever met. After a while she decided to give herself the rather grand title of 'Personal Assistant to Kym Bonython'.

June was a ton of laughs and she had an answer for everyone. One day she received an obscene telephone call which began 'Hello, is that Mrs Jacobsen? Prick speaking.'

'I beg your pardon?'

'Prick speaking. P-r-i-c-k.'

'I don't know you.'

'You would if you saw it!'

Thereupon June snapped 'Listen, sport—this call's costing you sixpence. Fuck off!' and hung up.

She and her husband Philip built a house near the gallery, with an oddly-shaped swimming pool built around the trunk of a large gum tree. When Ina Luck saw it she said 'June, everyone in Adelaide will be laughing at your funny little swimming pool!'

'*Everyone* will not be invited to swim in it,' June answered pointedly.

June was godmother to my son Tim, and one year her ingenious Christmas presents to my boys gave them more pleasure than anything else they received. She saved her one and two cent pieces during the year and at Christmas gave each of them a little bag containing six or seven dollars' worth of copper coins. For little boys this was as thrilling as any of the treasures of Midas.

But, since they were little boys, it prompted them to badger the indulgent Jacobsens for even more money. Once as we were on our way to visit them I threatened Tim 'If you ask Auntie June for any more money I swear I won't take you there again until next Christmas.' Five minutes later, almost as soon as we'd walked into their living-room, Tim with innocent face and upturned eyes began to sing a melodic ditty whose sole lyrics were the word 'money' repeated over and over again.

I could only remember similar tactics that I had used on my parents and think 'Like father, like son!'

June died under the anaesthetic during a fairly minor operation in 1971, and many of us lost a great and dear friend.

A regular visitor to the gallery from the time I opened it was Bernard Hesling, who is talented in many fields but especially as a raconteur. In his earlier years, when he was working in Paris, he hob-nobbed with the leaders of contemporary art and he had a thousand stories to tell about them—which he invariably did and at very great length. He wrote a number of books, and became quite well known for his South Australian radio broadcasts, but achieved his greatest fame for his whimsical vitreous enamel works done in vivid colours. Many visitors to Adelaide found them irresistible souvenirs.

Bernard's wife Flo died in 1970 and when Bernard next visited the gallery June asked solicitously 'How are you feeling, Bernard?'

He answered 'To tell you the truth, June, since Flo died I've been absolutely *miserable* . . . but come to think of it I was miserable when she was alive, too.'

134

John Brack was one of the artists whose work made little impression on Adelaide when I opened my first gallery there. He made the telling comment that 'The trouble with my customers is that they all like what I was doing *last year* best.' But many people must now be sorry that they failed to snap up his paintings at prices that were ludicrous by comparison with what they sell for nowadays.

Some of the notable exhibitions included Sidney Nolan's 'African' paintings, presented during the 1964 Adelaide Festival of Arts. The author George Farwell, then public relations man for the Festival, remarked that 'If a bomb had fallen on the Bonython Gallery during the Nolan opening, Australia would have lost most of its major painters, writers, composers and critics.'

At this time I had already launched into my entrepreneurial activities on the jazz scene and I had brought Eddie Condon and his All Stars from America on an Australian tour. We threw a memorable party at our Tennyson house, attended by most of the people who had been at the Nolan opening.

Other exhibitions during those early years included a large collection of paintings by Albert Tucker, produced while he was living in New York. He was a striking-looking man with a beautifully tended brown beard, which caused the painter Charles Bush to remark on the TV programme *My Fair Lady* that 'Tucker uses more dye in his beard than Perceval uses paint in his pictures.' (Perceval was noted for his thickly textured paintings.) Tucker was a favourite with the ladies, and some of the Adelaide girls whom he pursued so ardently named him 'Mr Tuck-'er-in'.

Lloyd Rees presented a fabulous exhibition of his Italian paintings in 1962, and Albert Tucker returned in 1966 with a series of bushland paintings. In succeeding festivals I was proud to exhibit some of Charles Blackman's *Cat in the Garden* series and the world's first exhibition of Arthur Boyd's *Nebuchadnezzar* series.

Arthur Boyd was the senior member of the immensely talented Boyd family which comprises painters, potters, writers, poets, and musicians. At that time he lived and worked in London, not far from Lawrie Daws. Lawrie saw the collection just before it was shipped to Australia and was vastly impressed by the exciting series, but was puzzled by some of the details. Boyd did employ a great deal of symbolism which made some of his work rather obscure. Lawrie said 'Arthur, these paintings are absolutely terrific, but why have you given Nebuchadnezzar red, yellow, and blue balls?'

In a typical Arthur Boyd response the artist replied 'Well, of course you know Nebuchadnezzar was mad!'

Boyd hated to fly and on one of his rare ventures into the air he flew from London to Paris with Sidney Nolan. It was a rough trip, and the story goes that Nolan asked Boyd whether he was feeling nervous. Boyd allegedly replied 'No. Everyone knows that God looks after Sidney Nolan.'

135

Louis James, who *could* have been one of my oldest friends, became a regular exhibitor in my galleries. I say 'could' because we were born only a week apart, we spent our boyhood within 200 yards of each other in Wakefield Street, we were members of the same pre-war Militia company, and we even shared the same tent at Woodside Army Camp immediately after the outbreak of war. But I volunteered for the R.A.A.F. and Louis stayed in the army, and after the war he and his wife Pat lived for seventeen years in London. We did not make real contact until after he returned to Australia in 1964, but we did not even recognise each other from our youthful days.

Mother demonstrated her artistic perception by purchasing the very first painting ever sold by Louis, from an exhibition in John Martin's Gallery. Today it is one of eight of his paintings I am proud to hang in my home.

For Christmas 1973 Louis painted a wonderful design on my motor cycle crash helmet, though he found great difficulties in adapting to a rounded rather than a flat surface. Wearing the helmet always gave me an added incentive to ride safely because I'm sure he would never have forgiven me if I'd damaged his creation—though I came close to it on one occasion. I was riding across the Sydney Harbour Bridge, and a driver became so intrigued by the helmet that he forgot about the other traffic.

Francis Roy Thompson was another Adelaide painter who added lustre to the local scene. Roy's philosophy was that 'The most important things in life are Art and Fun—and the greatest of these is Fun!' He was the life of every party, in which he was apt to throw off his clothing and perform a wild dance. He once did this at the house of fellow-painter Wladys Dutkiewicz, in the Adelaide suburb of Rose Park, and then collapsed exhausted on a sofa. Apparently he woke in the early hours and walked naked from Rose Park to his studio, about two miles away, went to sleep again, and when he awoke had to call plaintively from his window for someone to go and retrieve his clothes, as he had no others.

Roy was best at figurative paintings but towards the end of his life he ventured into a series of not entirely successful abstracts. One day one of his friends was driving a Land Rover through the Flinders Ranges, far from Adelaide, and remarked to his companion 'This is where Roy Thompson and I went through the fence last year, and rolled the car down into the gully.' He stopped to inspect the scene, and they saw a solitary figure seated at an easel in the dry creek bed. They walked down to talk to this lonely artist and discovered that it was Roy Thompson, busily painting an abstract in the very spot where he had crawled from under the vehicle twelve months earlier.

Among the artists I encouraged was Stanislaus Rapotec, a former Yugoslav resistance fighter. 'Rappy' lived for some years in a boarding house, with a rather formidable and outspoken dame as his landlady. Her house was near my gallery and my contacts with 'Rappy' inspired her to drop

The newspaper cartoons which appeared after Kym Bonython's first ventures in the *Bullo-Bee-Low (reproduced by permission of the Adelaide Advertiser and the Melbourne Sun)*

THE ONE THAT GOT AWAY

OLIPHANT
CARTOON

"Throw it back, Ernie! Nobody would ever believe you!"

"I TOLD MR BONYTHON I WASN'T 18 YET — SO HE THREW ME BACK!"

in from time to time. One day I was presenting what was, for Adelaide, a startling exhibition of abstracts, and I could hear her walking around with disgusted clicks of her tongue. Soon she cornered me in my office and commanded 'Mr Bonython, you must *not* show this work! You are driving people to Parkside!' (Adelaide's hospital for the mentally disturbed).

The comments of visitors to the gallery sometimes caused me to wonder. At one exhibition I showed a collection of original prints, simply mounted by having each corner pinned onto softwood boards. One buyer collected his purchase on the final day of the exhibition, leaving a blank board with a red 'Sold' sticker alongside the number. Two ladies stared at the blank board, and one asked the other 'I wonder what this means?' Obviously she thought it was the ultimate in modern art.

Two of Marc Chagall's stained-glass window prints, later to become world famous, were in the same exhibition. I heard one visitor ask another 'What do you think of this?'

'This modern art won't last,' was the reply.

In the early 1960s I became acquainted with Brett Whiteley, then a precocious young Sydney painter but now one of the major talents in Australian art. I believe his reputation will live alongside Tom Roberts and Frederick McCubbin. He was working in London when we first corresponded, and I bought several of his paintings by mail. Bryan Robertson was staging an exhibition of 'British Paintings of the Sixties' at his Whitechapel Gallery, and from this I bought one of Whiteley's major works, *Summer at Sigean*: a seven-and-a-half by fifteen foot masterpiece painted in the South of France. It became my favourite painting of all time and I even planned two houses around it, but eventually I was forced to sell it, for $30,000, to keep my Sydney gallery going. I had bought it for £400, quite a substantial outlay at that time.

Like many great artists and performers Whiteley was the supreme egotist. Mounting one of his exhibitions was a major operation. He would insist that the gallery be completely repainted, that windows should be covered, and even that a wall should be removed if it didn't suit his idea of how the whole exhibition should be displayed. Naturally these demands caused a good deal of argument before we reached a compromise, but the exhibitions invariably were superb and were highspots of my gallery career.

Awarded a Harkness Fellowship to visit America, Brett worked in New York and produced a ninety-foot monster that summed up his love-hate feelings about the United States. In those days he was much concerned with the political scene, although in his maturity he seems to have mellowed. The mighty work incorporated flashing lights and sirens, the seedier aspects of New York's night life, and a bit of pornography, and his strong protest against America's involvement in Vietnam.

It cost me $2,000 to bring the artwork from New York, but there were no bidders when it went on display. Eventually it went for exhibition in a

TOP: What goes down must come up! Kym Bonython being fished out of the Port River after his speedboat accident.   BOTTOM: Recovering the wreckage of the speedboat— alas, beyond repair. Snowdens Beach, 1956.

Perth gallery run by John Gild, who had no more success in selling it than I did. He presented it to the Western Australian Art Gallery as a gift from himself, and soon thereafter took his own life in despair at mounting debts.

When Brett heard that John Gild had given the painting away he was naturally rather upset, because so far he had not received a cent for the work. He felt, justifiably, that the Western Australian gallery should not have accepted a gift without ascertaining that it was the donor's property, but he was told that it would take an Act of Parliament to extract his work from the gallery's collection. He vowed he would never again exhibit in Perth and so far he has stuck to that resolution.

A story about Brett Whiteley concerns his period in New York. He ran short of money, and persuaded Qantas to commission him for a series of posters to publicise Australia's international airline. When he delivered the finished sketches he was somewhat put out by the negative attitude of the company officials, but this is not altogether surprising because each of his designs included an aircraft crashing in flames.

On his way home to Australia from his years overseas he decided to stop off in Fiji for a few months and paint in those tropical surroundings. He found himself a hut in the jungle, and one day he was busily working amid the lush greenery when a representative of his New York dealers, Marlborough Galleries, emerged through the undergrowth. Brett's opening remark was 'Jesus, another fucking dealer!'

Artists often regard art dealers as bloodsuckers interested in their work only for what they can get out of it, and it is said that when the famous but somewhat eccentric Australian artist Ian Fairweather heard that a Sydney dealer was about to visit his studio on Bribie Island he promptly leapt into his dinghy and rowed furiously out to sea. He remained there until the disillusioned visitor had departed.

Fairweather, of course, is the man who crossed the Timor Sea on a raft, and occasioned a full-scale search when he was thought to have been lost.

Sam Fullbrook, a much-respected Queensland painter, looks more like a shearer than an artist, and may often be seen wearing singlet and trousers and a brown felt hat, even on quite formal occasions. When I first met Sam he sold me a charming evening landscape painted in the Kimberleys, for which I paid about £10. Sam considered such paintings to be minor works and said 'I call these me little fucking Strauss waltzes.'

Sam, a true Australian, loved cricket and racing, and when I bumped into him I quite often found he was on his way back to Brisbane from a Test Match or race meeting. In 1978 he rejected my offer to present an exhibition of his works from 11 November onwards and said 'Anything after Melbourne Cup Day is rat shit! Gallery owners might as well have a holiday and start again in the autumn!' Se we settled for early in 1979.

In 1963 John Brack painted my portrait, but although we got on very well together he is one of those artists who does not like the subject to see how the work is progressing. When at last I saw the finished work I was a trifle disappointed, because I thought there was overmuch emphasis upon a rather ill-fitting sports coat and my gold wrist watch and identity bracelet.

However, I realised that Brack had sought to bring out the more extrovert side of my character, and so I wrote to him and asked whether he would be willing to add at least a portion of my celebrated checkered cap in what I unwisely referred to as 'that blank area in the top right-hand corner of the picture'.

Of course I could not have chosen a less tactful phrasing because an artist regards every part of a painting, including the 'blank spaces', as part of the composition. Brack replied '*There is no blank area in the top right-hand corner of the painting*! . . . But, just to show that I am not lazy, if you care to send over the object referred to I will paint a special small painting which you could then hang alongside your portrait.'

I sent him the cap, he painted it, and the large and small paintings now hang side by side.

Portrait-painting often can be a slightly tense activity, especially if the painter follows the more unconventional style of representation, and some empathy between painter and sitter is important. Sometimes this comes about in an unlikely manner as in the case of Noel Counihan and Colonel Aubrey Gibson.

Noel Counihan is an avowed Communist and a renowned social realist painter. Colonel Gibson was an equally avowed capitalist, besides being an astute collector of Australian and international art. He was for many years a Trustee of the Victorian State Gallery.

When he decided to commission a portrait of himself he asked Hal Missingham to recommend the best possible man for the job. Missingham asked 'How do you want to be seen in your portrait?' and he answered emphatically 'As a tycoon!'

Missingham recommended Counihan, who accepted the commission but felt it necessary to make his sympathies abundantly clear. He approached Gibson's desk, flung down his Party card, and said defiantly 'My card!'

Gibson rose, produced his Melbourne Club card, and threw it down beside Counihan's. 'And *my* card!' he replied.

Thus the ice was broken. They became good friends and a fine portrait resulted.

Sir William Dobell's first major self-portrait was commissioned by an American, Harold Mertz, for the then record price of £5,000. Mertz put a condition on this commission: that any preliminary sketches for the portrait should be offered to him before being sold elsewhere. Dobell agreed but perhaps absent-mindedly ignored the condition, because prior to his death at least two such sketches found their way into private collections without being offered to Mertz. However Mertz was not a man to drive a hard bargain and he overlooked this outcome.

I first met Harold Mertz, who was to do a great deal for Australian art, in 1964. I was setting up a sculpture exhibition, which involved the movement of great concrete blocks from the back yard into the gallery, when a jaunty Chaplin-like figure approached me. He wore a red check sports coat and a green porkpie hat set on a mass of curly white hair, and carried a walking stick. 'Where's the boss?' he enquired.

'That's me!'

His expression seemed to show some disbelief but he introduced himself as Harold Mertz of Port Washington, Long Island, New York State. He and his wife LuEsther were on holiday in Australia and he had decided to buy four or five Australian paintings for his office. My friend Laurie Thomas had kindly recommended him to me.

Mertz had become a wealthy man from a business connected with magazine distribution. But I was a little wary of wealthy Americans at that time because I had had an unnerving experience with Raymond Burr, alias 'Ironside' of the TV series. Burr had an art gallery in Los Angeles and he had approached me to assemble a comprehensive display of Australian art, which appealed to me as a rare opportunity to 'invade' the United States with Australian talent. For this reason I agreed to assemble the collection for a nominal two-and-a-half per cent commission on sales plus the costs of freight, insurance, and so on.

Expense seemed no object to 'Ironside'. He phoned me almost daily and sent me a cablegram of over 500 words relating to the exhibition. In high excitement at this possible breakthrough into the American market I persuaded most of Australia's leading modern painters to provide works for the exhibition.

But sales were negligible and I found it very difficult even to recoup what little money was due to me and the artists. In the end I had to go to Burr's Beverly Hills premises and wring the money out of his manager. Far from helping Australian artists, I alienated many of them. Artists who had loaned their paintings became increasingly impatient when, after six months, their work was still 'somewhere in America'.

One well-known artist, who was very irate, took me to task. As usual, he thought that the 'dealer' had profited while the artists lost. In an effort to explain the situation I wrote to him, concluding 'All I got out of the exercise was 2½%—not even enough to cover the phone calls and postage.' When I came to sign the letter I added a postscript: 'No! That's not all I got out of the exercise! I also got *the shits*!'

So, after this experience, I was a little wary of American deals. But Harold Mertz soon changed these feelings. During his few weeks in Australia he became more and more enthusiastic about Australian modern art, and the 'four or five paintings for his office' grew into 183. He was determined that fellow-Americans should share his enthusiasm, and he was perhaps the greatest thing that ever happened to Australian art.

140

Over a two-year period I assembled a formidable collection for him. It included many works now acknowledged to be the best ever produced by some of the artists. One of them was a beautiful Wimmera landscape by Arthur Boyd. When my son Timothy was very young he had decided to improve it by touching it up with Julie's nail polish, and the painting later was reproduced by a well-known Australian publisher and sold in large quantities throughout the country. Whenever I see these reproductions I can't help smiling at the sight of the bright cerise 'additions' perpetrated by our incorrigible child . . . and perhaps now accepted as the artist's concept.

Mertz proved rather naive about having the collection exhibited in America. He believed the New York Museum of Modern Art, or the Guggenheim Museum, would leap at the chance, and I was in no position to disillusion him. But it proved a forlorn hope. Such galleries apparently like to make their own decisions rather than exhibit a ready-made collection in which they had not been involved—even if all expenses are paid.

The collection ultimately was launched at the celebrated Corcoran Gallery in Washington, D.C., in March 1967. Mertz insisted on bringing Julie and me, together with Ross and Ina Luck, to Washington for the opening. Ed Clark, former United States Ambassador to Australia, was highly enthusiastic about the exhibition—more so, I am ashamed to say, than our own Embassy staff in Washington.

Mr Clark brought Lady Bird Johnson, wife of Lyndon B. Johnson, along to the opening. He introduced us, and she promptly invited us to the White House for afternoon tea.

I believe that Harold Mertz was paying income tax in America's highest bracket, something like ninety-three cents in the dollar. The cost of buying and importing the paintings, plus the printing by the Griffin Press of an elaborate catalogue which reproduced every painting in the collection, must have amounted to around $500,000. Under American tax laws he was able to write this cost off against tax, and perhaps reduce his commitment to something like eighty-eight cents in the dollar, but there were strings attached. He had to give the entire collection away to some institution or he would lose the tax rebate. Eventually it came to rest in the University of Texas. This was a felicitous choice because it is the only American university to devote a part of its curriculum to Australian studies.

Mertz made several visits to Australia while I was assembling the collection. On one of these, Geoff and Dahl Collings produced for Qantas a thirty-minute film on the Mertz collection. Whenever he was interviewed by members of the Australian press, their eternal fascination with money made them ask him 'Mr Mertz—are you a millionaire?'

He answered 'Well, I'm *half* a millionaire.'

'Half a millionaire? What do you mean by that?'

'I've got twenty thousand dollars, and if you've got twenty thousand the rest is easy!'

141

He was a man of many surprises. When the exhibition was well and truly launched he sent me a brand-new Chevrolet Impala as an 'unsolicited gift', and insisted on paying the accompanying freight, sales tax, and duty, as well as the cost of steering conversion for Australia. He considered that if it cost me even one cent it would not be a gift—but the Australian Tax Department had other ideas. They made me pay provisional tax on the value of the car in anticipation that I would receive a similar gift in the next financial year.

When the exhibition was over, and the collection safely housed in the University of Texas, Harold Mertz seemed to lose interest in Australian art. He moved on to other things: buying antique furniture in France, icons from Russia, and vast quantities of Scotch whisky as an investment.

Very different from the Washington exhibition was one which I presented in Broken Hill at the request of the Shell Oil Company—but it led to an unexpected result. Shell was opening a super-duper new service station in that city and its public relations people came up with the idea of an art exhibition in the lubritorium. I took about fifty works to the Silver City and with the help of Mae Harding, an art teacher at the Broken Hill Technical College, I mounted this show in what must have been one of the most unusual art venues of all time.

While in Broken Hill I noticed a number of humorous and unusual paintings displayed in various hotels and cafés. Each was signed by someone named 'Pro Hart'. They sparked my interest and I tracked him down.

He proved to be an extremely likeable and unassuming person who then worked as a driver down in the mines. He had been a compulsive sketcher since childhood and he painted in his spare time. His nickname 'Pro', short for 'Professor', was bestowed on him by his workmates because of his constant experimentation and invention, and because they thought him 'a bloody know-all'. He designed and built a machine-gun in which he attempted to interest the Australian Army, and he showed me an amazing telescope. When he focused it on a church crucifix about a mile away I could even see the weld marks in the metal. After I had returned to Adelaide he sent me a newspaper cutting showing a photograph of him with the telescope, with a caption stating that 'with his homemade telescope he intends to study the planet Mars'. Pro had written in the margin 'Also the nurses' quarters across the road.'

Through this first contact I took a collection of his paintings to Adelaide and presented his first exhibition, 'Down South'. Prices ranged from £5 to £60, but nowadays I wouldn't be surprised to learn that he makes more money than any other Australian artist. Nevertheless his personality has not changed and he still remains the same simple and likeable personality. In 1977, when I was guest of honour on the TV programme *This Is Your Life*, he was good enough to remark 'If it wasn't for Kym Bonython I'd still be picking rocks down the mines.'

142

One of my earlier Adelaide exhibitors was a young artist and sometime art critic named Robert Hughes, now an internationally known figure and art critic for *Time* magazine. One of his earliest patrons was Major Harold de Vahl Rubin, whom Hughes in his usual colourful way describes as having 'ridden through Australian art like a combination of Louis XIV and the Phantom of the Opera'.

Rubin was an amazing man, with a great eye for paintings. In a 1964 issue of *Nation* magazine Hughes wrote a piece entitled 'The Birdman of Toorak House', in which he described the Major's 'acquisition' of an entire exhibition of Hughes' paintings that had been displayed in a Sydney gallery. Apparently the only way that Hughes could secure payment for the paintings was for him and his current girlfriend to accept an invitation to Rubin's mansion Toorak House, 650 miles to the north in Brisbane.

On arrival, Hughes found that Rubin had gone away for the weekend. He left instructions for Hughes to look after the house while he was away.

A huge aviary, full of hundreds of screeching birds, adjoined Toorak House, and when Hughes made a tour of inspection he found one of the birds dead on the floor of the aviary. He buried it in a corner of the rose garden, and when Rubin returned he naturally told him what he had done.

Rubin immediately demanded that he should produce the corpse. Feeling rather foolish, Hughes dug it up. By that time, ants were crawling in and out of its eyes, but Rubin took it and proceeded to carry out an autopsy with a knitting needle. This seemed to satisfy him as to its cause of death and he attacked Hughes with 'You accept my hospitality and repay it by killing my birds! You bird murderer! I know—you strangled it in a fit of drunken frenzy! It was a very valuable bird. It cost five guineas—and now you've killed it!'

Hughes' girlfriend had had enough by that time. She remonstrated with Rubin until he signed a cheque for the paintings he had bought, and they took their leave. Rubin later bought another entire exhibition of Hughes' paintings, but he continued to refer to him as 'a killer of birds' right until his death in 1964.

By that time, I could call my gallery venture a success. Harold Mertz had continually urged me to become 'Number One in the Australian art world', but I realised that if I was to make further headway I would have to move out of Adelaide. Many of the painters whom I had encouraged in their early years had now been taken up by dealers in the eastern States, and if I was to contract new artists and obtain works by those already well-known I would have to work on their own ground. So I was very open to persuasion when Betty O'Neill, a sister of the Australian Olympic swimmer Frank O'Neill, came to Adelaide in 1965 to sell me on the idea of taking over her Hungry Horse Gallery in Paddington, Sydney.

Modern Australian art had come to stay and I felt that I had played a useful part in breaking down some prejudice against it . . . although a certain amount remained. When our youngest son Michael was about eight years old a friend of his called for him, but when Julie told him to go up to Michael's room he refused to come in the front door. 'My mother says I'm not allowed to play in Michael's house,' he said. 'It's full of bums, titties, and dicks.'

This was a formidable description of my art collection, but I must admit that ever since then I have tended to evaluate any possible purchases against this rather dubious assessment.

17

Champs and Chumps

MAX HARRIS once wrote of me as 'the Cecil B. de Mille of Bowden'. Maybe it was intended sarcastically but I've no reason to be other than proud of the appellation. Showmanship is the name of the game in speedway as it is in every other aspect of entertaining the public from ballet to bull-fighting, and the public always responds to glamour, drama, excitement, and above all, the spectacle of men literally taking their lives in their hands as they thunder round the track in a speedcar or on a motor cycle. If, by showmanship, I could attract audiences to Rowley Park, then I was doing my job properly and ensuring a living for a number of people including myself.

The riders and drivers understood the value of showmanship and to a large degree they were all showmen themselves, who thoroughly enjoyed displaying their skills and daring to a roaring crowd.

A prime example was Jack Murray, commonly known as 'Gelignite Jack'. He rose to fame (or notoriety) because of his exploits during the 1954 Redex Round-Australia Trial, which he won in the Ford he called *Grey Ghost*. Among the many rough stretches the drivers had to cover was the road across the Nullarbor from Kalgoorlie to Ceduna, which in those days was unsealed. The bull-dust was so thick that the speeding cars threw it up in great red plumes that hung in the air and completely obscured forward vision. If a driver became stuck behind another vehicle he dared not pass him for fear of a head-on collision with another car approaching through the blinding dust.

Jack soon solved this problem. He carried a few sticks of gelignite, and when he could not pass he lit the fuse on one of them and tossed it out of the car. The explosion would make the leading driver think that he had a blowout and pull over to the shoulder, thus leaving Jack room to sweep past him.

Jack came to Rowley Park to race in one of our first stock car feature nights. Inevitably his entry onto the track was presaged by a stick of gelignite

145

tossed over the fence, a stunt which greatly appealed to me. We soon became firm friends, and our relationship was strengthened by the fact that he also was a teetotaller who believed in the best of food and confectionery wherever and however it might be obtained. His flamboyantly outrageous behaviour struck a responsive chord in me and I enjoyed every moment of his company—even though I was often the fall guy for his pranks. Once when we were together I felt an urgent call of nature and disappeared into the bush to relieve it, followed about thirty seconds later by a stick of gelignite which, to say the least, upset my bodily functions considerably.

He and his brothers operated a Bondi garage and owned a string of taxis. They took it in turns to get the cabs on the road each morning and then attended to their various hobbies, which seemed more important than dull business affairs. If a customer turned up at the petrol pumps while Jack was busy inside, and began impatiently honking for service, Jack was apt to say 'Let him go—he'll soon get sick of it and find somewhere else!'

Jack was the old-fashioned type of practical joker who planned his stunts far ahead. One night he was driving me and some other people along the Parramatta Road when a police car drew up alongside and waved us over. Apparently we were not only speeding but driving without a tail-light on the boat trailer. Jack drew up, the policeman alighted purposefully, drew out his notebook and leaned his elbow on Jack's door frame.

Jack looked him straight in the eye and commanded 'Take your dirty hands off my nice clean car!'

The argument continued for a couple of minutes, with both parties becoming more and more heated, while we in the back seat tried to shrivel into invisibility at the thought of a night in the cells. But suddenly both Jack and the cop burst out laughing. They were old friends, and this was a well-rehearsed act that they put on to the consternation of innocent bystanders.

Jack's garage was lined with true and fictitious souvenirs of his exploits, including newspaper headlines and photographs of incredible wrecks by land, sea, and air in which he allegedly had been involved. The garage served as a club for his mates from all over Australia, who sat around yarning in deckchairs. Woe betide anyone who tried to work on a vehicle. Strings of crackers and similar missiles were tossed into the pit to drive them out again. In mid-morning another of his friends, who was a pastrycook, would turn up with a great array of cream cakes, buns, meat pies, and pastries, to be set upon by the gathering.

Jack was one of the pioneers of water-skiing in Australia and on his free days he revelled in this sport up on the Hawkesbury River beyond Windsor. There was always a band of beautiful girls in attendance, together with assorted eccentrics. Everyone had a nickname, such as 'Narra' for his narrow-gutted brother and 'The Ox' for one of the taxi-drivers who was a physical giant. The Ox was once water-skiing on a very long line when he spotted a draught horse wallowing quite deep in the water. Positioning

146

himself skilfully he sped closer and closer until he could cast off the line, make a mighty leap, and land squarely on the horse's back.

Unusual characters abound on the speedway circuit. The vast majority are male, at least in Australia, although I remember three very distinctive females. One was Fay Taylour, an Irishwoman who earned an enviable reputation as a solo motorcyclist on the English tracks in the 1930s. When she came to Australia, just before I took over Rowley Park, her best days were behind her but she was making a gallant attempt at a comeback. She had taken to speed car racing and various Australian promoters had arranged to provide her with cars in which to race on their tracks. I don't know how she was treated elsewhere but there was little gallantry displayed when she appeared in Adelaide, where the male competitors, mostly in much superior cars, set about her mercilessly.

Her presence in the Sydney pit area posed some problems, but the promoter, Frank Arthur, followed the harem principle and appointed a eunuch as her guardian. He was a well-known Sydney character and stock car driver known as 'Nutless' because, in a prank involving a door-jam, he was robbed of his masculine attributes. 'Nutless' stood custodian at Fay's dressing-room door, but this may not really have been necesssary. 'Fay' means 'fairy' but there was nothing very fairylike about Fay Taylour. Already in her fifties, she was a solid and muscular woman, probably well able to take care of herself.

Some years later, Australian promoters brought out a diminutive Japanese girl named Nanae Okamoto. She rode an inferior machine of smaller engine capacity than her rivals but nevertheless put up a most creditable performance, particularly in handicap races where she was given a start by the second level of competitors in the Adelaide bike ranks. She later abandoned racing after running over and killing a male competitor in Japan.

For one season I brought out a fast-talking, voluptuous Italian girl, Bobby Borghese, who was one of the stars of Duke Donaldson's Freeport Track on Long Island. Powder Puff Derbies were a regular feature on the American scene and she was a big favourite with Italian-Americans, but she was a novelty in Australia. She drove one of our company cars and had a number of great victories during her stay in South Australia.

Attracting such visitors was an important part of my job as the promoter of Rowley Park and a vital component of my identity as 'the Cecil B. de Mille of Bowden'. To keep the customers happy one had to provide a constant flow of new attractions. These were hard to find in Australia and so I made a number of scouting trips overseas, looking for new talent just as I used to seek new candidates for my stud. I went several times to Sweden and Denmark as well as to Britain and the U.S.A.

In Sweden I stayed with Ove Fundin, who had been five times World Solo Champion, or with Ulf Ericson, an extremely handsome young man who looked rather like a youthful Omar Sharif. I brought Ove and Ulf to

Australia several times.

On my first visit to Sweden I could not find any accommodation in Stockholm and Ulf kindly lent me his family's country cottage which he said was 'only seven miles from town'. Little did I know that one Swedish mile equals three English miles. I thought my taxi would never get there.

One night at Rowley Park I saw Ulf completely demoralised immediately before the start of an important Sweden v. Australia 'Test Match'. Just as he was getting ready for the start, one of the other Swedish riders gave him the news that Ulf's girlfriend, back home in Sweden, was pregnant. He exclaimed 'This shouldn't happen to a good clean-living boy like me!' and he wasn't worth a damn for the rest of the evening. Some years later I heard that he was killed while working as a crop-dusting pilot in the U.S.A.

Among my Swedish acquaintances was Lasse Akeby, a well-known speedway writer and editor of the magazine *Fart*. Believe it or not, that's Swedish for 'speed'. Lasse certainly believed in speed and he was undoubtedy the most hair-raising driver it has ever been my misfortune to accompany. In the 1950s Sweden had just changed from left-hand to right-hand driving, but most cars still had their steering on the right of the car. This was strange enough to me, but it was far worse when Lasse was driving at just under 100 m.p.h. on unmarked greasy dirt roads and constantly turning to talk to me instead of watching where he was going.

Lasse had been a milliner, in those days when girls still wore hats. I stayed a few nights in an apartment where I suspect he entertained his many friends, and one room was filled with boxes of hats. Apparently he broke off each *affaire* with a parting gift of a hat and several times I was able to pick out his past lovers by their headgear.

In 1957 I brought Roger Forsberg, Arne Carlsson, and Gote Nordin out from Sweden to ride at Rowley Park and when they arrived I staged a special practice race so they could display their talents to the local press. It was a disastrous move. On the very first lap of the demonstration Carlsson clipped Forsberg's rear wheel and crashed onto the track. He fractured his skull and that put an end to his appearances in Australia—and possibly to his speedway career. Until the accident he was freely tipped as a potential World Champion, but after that he never achieved the same degree of success.

On visits to England I examined the local speedway scene and I was staggered by the vast difference in costs. At that time, each Rowley Park meeting set us back about £2,000, which was quite a lot of money in the 1950s, whereas the English promoters would not pay more than about £400. However they did not present a mixed programme, with several sections on the same bill, in the spectacular style to which Australian audiences were accustomed.

My trips overseas enabled me to present a number of attractions for the first time in Australia. There was always a big financial risk involved but it paid off when, for example, I presented Australia's first Demolition Derby. Gate figures soared, from the average 10,000 spectators we could expect during the summer season, to over 20,000, and we gave them all value for money. We could have admitted even more people but the police ordered the gates to be closed and when I saw the gigantic crowd I was glad that no more could enter. Like the promoters of the old Camden track, I was in fear and trembling lest the terraced mounds of the viewing area should collapse under their weight.

As the name implies, a Demolition Derby is an event in which the last car still mobile is the winner. It's a 'no holds barred' contest that may be run anywhere within the safety fences with the object of putting all other contestants out of action. In the States, such events were contested by old bombs that could be bought for as little as five dollars. From the public's point of view the fun lay in seeing the cars crash into one another, and there was no point in writing-off good cars. Usually when one car crashed into another a door would fly open and the next car would promptly tear it off. All good harmless fun which gave the spectators the basic human pleasure of seeing things smashed up . . . and maybe gave them the emotional release which prevented them beating up their wives.

But the Racing Drivers Association, the body which controls speedway in South Australia, was so fanatically concerned with safety that they made incredible demands for the modification of the cars. All doors had to be welded shut, all seats removed except for a driver's bucket seat, and safety harnesses fitted. By the time these modifications were made each driver had about £100 tied up in his vehicle and he was rather wary about having it written off. Naturally this made his driving a bit more cautious than the slam-bang American style.

Nevertheless, the Demolition Derbies still provided a great spectacle. About seventy cars entered for the first event and they took off with a mighty roar of engines. One after another fell victim as they battered their way around the track, and the crowd shrieked its delight at the rending of metal, spurts of steam from burst radiators, clouds of smoke and dust, blow-outs, and spectacular crashes in which one car seemed to leap upon another as though to devour it. Doubtless many of those who watched would have liked to do the same kind of thing on the open road.

At last only one car was left to crawl wheezing around the track, battle-scarred but victorious.

Another great attraction was Figure Eight Stock Car Racing. I saw it first at Indianapolis, run on a track called the Speedrome. This was operated by Leroy Warriner, a driver I imported for a couple of seasons in Australia.

Figure Eight racing used only the corners of the main circuit. The track then took a cut into the centre in the form of a figure eight. Cars roaring around this configuration could meet at the intersection, all going in different directions.

149

The American drivers charged across this intersection with throttle feet flat to the boards, presumably on the principle that the faster they roared across, the less chance there was of collision. But there were plenty of crashes and I saw cars rolling over and over until they were brought up by the perimeter fence. Warriner had added spectator interest by ploughing a furrow right through the centre, so that the speeding cars would bounce high in the air as they approached the lethal intersection.

But Figure Eight never really caught on in Australia. The competitors tended to slow down as they reached the intersection, thus robbing the event of much of its spectacle, and I'm sure this was because of the amount of money they had to invest in their cars.

The Customs Department also created problems for Australian speedway promoters by insisting on a huge bond covering the sales tax and duty that could be payable on any vehicles imported, just in case the drivers sold them in Australia. Added to the freight charges this caused a prohibitive barrier and so I usually brought the drivers into Australia and had them compete in my own race car. One who drove it was Jim Maguire, who had built up a great reputation on American tracks. He had lost an arm in a racing accident but he drove with a special attachment fixed to the steering wheel and grasped by a hook fixed to the stump of his arm.

Another of the American drivers I imported was Jimmy Kirk, who had great success driving modified stock cars and 'midget cars', which is the American name for speed cars, in Pennsylvania. He drove twice for me, and while he was in Adelaide he stayed at a motel owned by Roy Sands, another Rowley Park driver who was also an airline pilot. Like me, he was taught to fly by Alan Clancy. Roy had two race cars, one of which he drove himself while the other was jockeyed by a driver who took a percentage of any prize money.

Rightly or wrongly, Roy had a reputation for frugality although he had a good income as an airline pilot and owned the motel which I used to accommodate 'imported' drivers. He was having some trouble with his Offenhauser race car and Jimmy Kirk, who was a capable mechanic, volunteered to see what he could do. For two days he slaved free of charge on the Offenhauser until he felt it was running properly, and when at last he straightened up he wiped his greasy hands and fished out a cigarette. 'Got a match, Roy?' he asked, and Roy went to the counter of the motel for a box. Handing it to Jimmy he said 'That'll be two cents, please.'

Another 'Jimmy' whom I brought out from America was a former American National Champion: Jimmy Davies. He was a sensational driver and during his career he had run third in the Indianapolis 500 as well as being twice National Midget Champion, the equivalent of a world championship because this type of racing is run only in Australia, New Zealand, and the U.S.A. He lived up to his reputation on his Australian visits in 1963 and 1964 because he won fifty-three out of fifty-four starts at Rowley Park.

150

But no one could call him popular. He was arrogantly outspoken and he riled his opponents by calling them 'squirrelly' drivers and telling them, before a race, exactly how he was going to wipe them all off the map. To begin with they tended to dismiss this as 'Yankee bull' but he would promptly go out on the track and leave them for dead.

The *Advertiser* motoring writer who covered our meetings described Davies' first Adelaide success in distinctly ungraphic terms, saying that he 'Slowly passed the opposition on the outside'. This hardly conjures up the image of a daredevil driver in full flight, especially since Jim's technique was to hold back until he saw an opening, dart around outside his opponents, and pick them off one by one until he hit the lead.

My first drive in an Offenhauser was in Jim Davies' car and it was a revelation to one accustomed to the more cumbersome and less responsive Holden-powered cars. The Offenhauser was a particularly light and man-oeuvrable vehicle with one of the most potent engines used in speedway racing. In June 1966, Davies died in the car he allowed me to sample. During an American race he crashed headlong into a concrete wall at something over 100 m.p.h. No one could understand why the accident happened and it was first thought that he must have been overcome by carbon monoxide fumes, but the man who bought the wrecked car for reconditioning discovered that the butterfly of the carburettor was stuck wide open. Davies would no doubt have taken his foot off the throttle to negotiate a corner, but the engine would have kept going at full power and crashed the car into the fence. Thus ended the career of one of the most accomplished race drivers ever to appear on Australian speedways.

Good as Jim was he met his match in the incomparable Bob Tattersall, who was without doubt the best driver I imported. He was recommended to me by Joe Barzda, a former sprint car and championship driver who owned a speed shop organisation in New Jersey. Joe provided parts for my cars and from time to time gave me the names of drivers worthy of a trip to Australia.

When I first met Bob, in 1958, he used to wear colourful cowboy clothes and in the spirit of showmanship I introduced him to Australia as 'Two Gun Bob Tattersall'. The name stuck to him during the first few years of the fourteen that he visited Australia.

On his 1958–59 visit he appeared only at Rowley Park but in some subsequent years he appeared also for other promoters. On that first appearance I put him into a V8/60 Ford-powered speed car brought to Australia by the New Zealand champion Ross Goonan in 1957. On Bob's very first race in this car the steering locked and he crashed into the safety fence, and spent his first racing night in Adelaide in the Royal Adelaide Hospital.

In 1960 he returned to Australia with his wife Delores and his own Offenhauser. I had brought out Peter Craven, the magnificent young English solo rider, with his wife Brenda and their young son. The Tattersalls and the Cravens shared a seafront cottage at Grange, quite near my own house at Tennyson, and the two speedway stars were strangely contrasting characters. Bob seemed larger than life with a rough and aggressive personality, while Craven was rather shy and retiring. Nevertheless they were both superb exponents of their own styles of speedway and I believe they were two of the three greatest whom I ever brought to Adelaide.

Craven was a truly phenomenal motorcyclist. Small and agile, he threw his weight around in the saddle in a way rarely seen in Adelaide and he was probably the most spectacular rider ever to compete at Rowley Park. During his whole career he had never fallen off a bike or had any kind of accident, but two years later he had a fairly minor mishap which resulted in his death.

Speedway fans always will remember an incident during Bob Tattersall's visit in 1962. Speed cars are designed so that the bulk of the vehicle's weight bears upon the back wheels and the outside front wheel, with only negligible weight on the inside front wheel. When a well-balanced car is at power this wheel hardly touches the track and often rides several inches above it. The purpose of this seemingly strange adjustment is to place the maximum car weight on the driving wheels.

Bob collided with another car during a championship event at Rowley Park and broke his front axle. The inside front wheel flew off the car and for a lesser driver that would have been the end of the event. But, by skilful manipulation of the throttle, Bob completed the remaining twenty-one laps on three wheels by maintaining power and keeping the axle stub up off the track. He was negotiating other speed cars, who certainly did not give him any special consideration because of the accident, and his completion of the course must surely have been one of the most amazing driving exhibitions ever seen.

On one of Bob's subsequent visits he had to enter an Adelaide hospital where tests confirmed that he had been afflicted by cancer. He returned home and died some months later in his home town of Streator, Illinois, which proclaimed a Bob Tattersall Day shortly before his death. He was their most famous son.

Third in my trio of great American drivers was Marshall Sargent, a stock car driver from San Jose, California, whom I introduced to Australian speedway for his first full season. He gained a number of exceptional racing victories and became a certain drawcard, with the crowds about equally divided for and against him. This is the ideal recipe for an attraction in such a controversial sport as speedway, because the ones who don't cheer a contestant will derive just as much enjoyment from barracking against him. But when Marshall returned to the States after one of his subsequent visits he was involved in a racing accident causing head injuries from which he never fully recovered. He gave the game away and when I last heard of him he was operating a bar in his hometown.

With Julie on the Eurilla verandah, overlooking Piccadilly Valley from Mount Lofty 1978. (*Milton Wordley photo*)

I was hardly surprised to learn that he'd been in an accident. During my visits to America I'd been appalled by the casual safety precautions compared with the far more stringent procedures in Australia. Once I went to a sprint car meeting at a place called New Bremen and noticed there was only one warning light in the middle of the main straightway. The fire engine and ambulances were parked at one end of the ground, and when an accident occurred at the other end there was no way of warning the contestants that there was an obstruction on the track. A few flag-waving officials tried to warn them off but by the time everyone realised what was happening there'd have been a multiple pile-up, with one driver dead and another seriously injured.

TOP LEFT: Kym Bonython with Lionel Hampton in a Los Angeles recording studio 1955. TOP RIGHT: With Dave Brubeck 1960. BOTTOM LEFT: With Gene Krupa in Sydney 1954. BOTTOM RIGHT: Clarinettist Pee Wee Russell with one of his 'hand-made' paintings

18

'Hello Central. Give Me Dr Jazz'

M Y ART and speedway involvements were of course accompanied by my lifelong affair with my earliest mistress: music, and particularly jazz. Before long this was to extend into other fields of entertainment but for a while my main preoccupation was to be the A.B.C. jazz programme, *Tempo of the Times*. After a war-long gap it had once again become an established weekly programme, and a fairly good flow of correspondence (not all of it complimentary) assured me that it had a wide audience.

One listener wrote to suggest that I should be 'banished to the middle of the Nullarbor Plain, with instructions to support myself from the sale of alto-saxophones to the Aborigines'. Another letter came from 'Moppy' McCubbin, brother of our family friend Louis McCubbin, former Director of the State Gallery of South Australia. 'Moppy' remarked that my use of the word 'listenable' in one of my programmes was 'assassinable'.

Once the tape-recorder became established my life was made a good deal easier, because I could tape my broadcasts at almost any time. At first, however, the A.B.C. was fanatically law-abiding about putting recordings on tape. They feared the possible transgression of copyright and indulged in some incredible examples of bureaucratic idiocy. On one occasion I had to be out of Adelaide on a date when my programme was scheduled, but instead of pursuing the logical course of taping my entire programme they insisted only on recording my spoken comments. In between these were gaps of the appropriate length for each jazz record to be played.

I had some apprehensions about this method, and they were fully justified. I listened to the programme from Brisbane and as soon as I heard the voice of the announcer on duty I predicted chaos. It was the full moon period of the month: a time when his behaviour was notoriously unpredictable.

Things went well for the first ten minutes, until he forgot to switch the turntable speed from 45 r.p.m. to 33 r.p.m. for a new record. After that everything went wrong. There would be long periods with no sound,

154

followed by a mixture of voice and music. From 1,600 miles away I listened in anguished horror.

My jazz contacts, and my personal friendship with Frank and Rosa Nicholls of Melbourne, resulted in an invitation to become a member of Aztec Services, a company that specialised in importing overseas musical and theatrical talent to Australia. Frank and Rosa were two of the twelve shareholders of the company, and I became their Adelaide representative. My responsibility was to make all the necessary local arrangements for the entertainers, from booking the theatre to checking them into hotels.

One of the many people whom Aztec brought to Australia over the years to come was the West Indian pianist Winifred Atwell, who eventually settled here permanently. She was not a jazz pianist but still a very versatile and talented musician. We became firm friends, and one day she and her rather massive Jewish husband Lou Levisohn came to our beach house for lunch. Lou asked me to name my favourite pianist, and I thought the best way to answer was by playing some of my record collection. After hearing four of them he remarked 'You don't like pianists. You like drummers!'

My frequent trips to America to scout for speedway talent soon had a double purpose. I used them to check out possible entrants for the Aztec circuit also. One of these was a variety show, Sam Snider's Water Follies, which I ran to earth in Albany, New York State. The show consisted of a number of 'water acts' involving precision swimming, high diving, and comedy turns, mingled with singers and other performers who worked on a stage alongside the two portable pools. Wily Sam Snider assigned one of his girls to look after me and I soon found that we had a lot of things in common, not least of these being that her father was a speedway driver. However, I could never have claimed to match her in agility, because she was the show's contortionist.

We brought the Follies twice to Australia and they were a huge success. My favourite among the cast was the rotund comedian Eddie Rose, an expert diver whose 'belly flops' from the tower into the pool were a highlight of the show.

His wife, Mary Dwight, a former champion swimmer in her home state of Florida, led the water ballet. They stayed in my house during their Adelaide season and I treasure a tape recording made by Eddie in which he sang along to a recording of Erroll Garner playing *I Can't Give You Anything but Love, Baby*. Eddie sang his own lyrics, entitled *I Can't Give You Anything but Babies, Love*, with words running something like:

> Gee, I hate to see you start to swell, baby
> Clothes that looked so well now look like hell
> Until that lucky day when you're unwell . . .

In 1954 I made my first individual venture as a theatrical entrepreneur.

155

The Sydney promoter Bill McColl offered me the services of the famed American vibraphone player Red Norvo, with the black singer Helen Humes. Red's trio included a promising young guitarist named Bill Dillard and the genial black musician Eugene Wright on bass. Bill died in a hotel fire a couple of years later, but I was able to bring Eugene several times to Australia as a member of the Dave Brubeck Quartet.

Financially the concert was a disaster in Adelaide, but it started me on a road which was to make and lose considerable sums of money for me in the future.

My trips to America, armed with my newfangled tape-recorder, enabled me to keep up with the jazz scene as well as scouting for drivers and entertainers. In 1956 Gene Krupa invited me to stay with him and his wife Ethel at Yonkers, a suburb of New York, in their handsome house with music piped into every room. All of it was Bach.

Gene was playing in New York and I used to end my working day with a couple of hours in his club, taking in his performance before we drove home at three or four in the morning. Two legendary jazz figures dropped by the club at that time and Gene introduced me to both of them. One was Miles Davis, then in my opinion at his peak as a trumpeter, who crept into Gene's dressing room like a black ghost. His quiet gravelly voice was unlike anything I'd ever heard before. While we were talking, in walked Ben Webster, the famed tenor-sax player. He told us that he'd just left the ex-heavyweight boxing champion Joe Louis, and recounted how the Champ had tapped him playfully in the kidneys. According to Ben, Joe's fist had travelled only two or three inches but he felt as though he'd been kicked by a mule!

I taped a number of interesting interviews with famous jazz musicians from San Francisco to New York and Chicago to New Orleans, and augmented them with interviews made in Europe. I was to bring several of these musicians to Australia.

Gene Krupa kindly lent me his Jaguar to drive south to Atlanta to stay with my wartime friend Fred Eaton, and Fred arranged for me to make a quick flight to New Orleans in the aircraft owned by his employers, the Sears Roebuck Company. It was an opportunity to see and hear some of the New Orleans bands such as Santo Pecora and the legendary Preservation Hall Band, which I later brought to Australia.

On the same trip I met Norman Granz of Los Angeles. He is the only man reputed to have made a million dollars out of jazz—but not by playing it! He organised and presented 'Jazz at the Philharmonic', which featured most of the big names of the day and drew huge crowds in numerous countries during the 1950s and 1960s.

I soon learnt the secret of Granz's success. He drove a ruthless bargain and expected a promoter to accept all his conditions even if it meant breaking the law. For example, he wouldn't allow his artists to sign a

156

contract unless the figure quoted was tax-free. I knew that the Reserve Bank of Australia, which had to approve all contracts with visiting performers, would never accept such a document and I told him so. Granz made it plain that if I couldn't accept his contract then I might as well forget the whole deal.

In 1960 I made my first really big plunge into presenting overseas jazz groups in Australia when I brought the Dave Brubeck Quartet from America. At that time I had no experience in organising a nationwide tour and so I turned the arrangements over to Aztec while retaining a majority financial interest.

1960 was the year of the first Adelaide Festival of Arts. I had accepted the responsibility of arranging its jazz performances, and so the Brubeck tour tied in very neatly with this. The whole venture was phenomenally successful and apart from the money it earned me I enjoyed close rapport with Brubeck and his boys, especially his distinctive saxophone player Paul Desmond. Eugene Wright, who had made a previous visit with Red Norvo, was on bass, and the drummer was Joe Morello.

Joe was a hell of a drummer—and a lot of laughs. He wore bifocal glasses as thick as the bottoms of beer bottles and the press never knew whether to take him seriously when he said his hobbies were pistol-shooting and home movie-making. In fact he was very good at both of these.

I brought the Quartet out again in 1962 for an equally successful tour, but when the next Festival came around in 1964 I thought it was time for a change. I contacted the bass player Jack Lesberg, whom I had met in both America and Australia, when he came out with Louis Armstrong for Lee Gordon. Between us we set up a band of some of the greatest names in jazz.

Eddie Condon, the guitarist and raconteur, was the nominal leader and the master of ceremonies. Three members of the original Count Basie Band, trumpeter Buck Clayton, trombonist Vic Dickenson, and the famous blues singer Jimmy Rushing, known as 'Mr Five-by-Five' because of his proportions, seemed surefire attractions. Another was Pee Wee Russell, the greatest clarinettist of them all and my favourite jazz musician. Bud Freeman played tenor saxophone.

The piano chair was hard to fill but we finally settled on the multi-instrumentalist Dick Cary who not only plays the 88 but also some very exciting alto or 'peck' horn. Lesberg, of course, was on bass, and I brought out my longtime favourite Cliff Leeman on drums.

As soon as the word went round that this great band was to tour Australia I was approached by the Sydney jazz pianist and journalist Dick Hughes, jun. He pleaded for some involvement in the tour and I arranged for his quartet to open the concerts in Sydney. I also used him as a kind of 'band boy' to help with the general arrangements and, I hoped, to send glowing reports to the Sydney press of the musical banquet coming their way.

The tour opened in the Regent Theatre, Adelaide, with concerts at eight p.m. and midnight. Despite the mediocre audience at this late show it featured some of the best music of the whole tour, with Dick Hughes making an unscheduled appearance when he wandered on stage clutching a whisky bottle and exited unsteadily on the other side. I still don't know whether the music excited him or whether he'd celebrated too vigorously during the early show.

The Sydney concerts were played in the old Sydney Stadium, a monstrous wood and galvanised-iron edifice built in 1907 for the heavyweight contest between Bill Lang and 'Boshter' Bill Squires. Dreary by day, this gigantic building exuded great atmosphere when it was filled with up to 12,000 people and the lights were low except for those illuminating the performers. The acoustics were surprisingly good unless it rained, when the loudest music would be drowned by the barrage on the iron roof.

The band performed on a revolving stage set within the perimeter of the boxing ring. It made about three-and-a-half turns in one direction, stopped, and then took off with a jerk in the opposite direction. I thought it seemed slightly rickety and my fears were realised during a Saturday afternoon performance. 'Mr Five-by-Five' was performing *When You're Smiling*, and to emphasise the last note he brought his considerable weight to bear in a resounding stamp of the foot.

The stage promptly collapsed. It was as though the spokes of a cycle wheel had let go at the hub. The whole centre stage dropped about six inches and the grand piano began to slide ponderously across the floor, with Pee Wee Russell hanging on apprehensively. 'You can't top that!' Eddie Condon quipped.

The tour was a great musical and emotional experience but a financial let-down. Among its most pleasant memories is that of Eddie Condon's vivacity and good humour. He was a publicist's dream, who always came up with the right comment at the right time.

Stories about Eddie are legion. When asked what he thought about electric guitars, he replied 'Very dangerous!'

His opinion of Ted Lewis, the so-called King of Corn, is quoted as 'Ted played very bad clarinet. He made the clarinet talk, and it usually said "Please put me back in my case!"'

The clarinettist Joe Marsala says that he once had a seven-piece group, including Eddie Condon, working at the Hickory House Club in New York. After a year's engagement the manager told him 'I just can't understand why people like your music so much. Why, there's one guy comes in here listening and drinking every night of the week.'

Joe replied 'Oh, that's Eddie Condon. You've been paying him to play the guitar for the last twelve months.'

When the tour ended I went with the group to Sydney Airport to see them off, and one by one they all said good-bye except for Pee Wee Russell.

He stood to one side, but at last he came sidling towards me in his characteristic way. Shyly he grasped my hand in both of his and said 'Kym . . . I want to tell you . . . I've come ten thousand miles to meet a gentleman!' With that he turned and shuffled off to the aircraft.

As the saying goes, that really broke me up, especially since it came from a man whom I so much admired.

I met Pee Wee once again, about nine months before his death. He had taken up painting and I tried very hard to arrange an exhibition of his work, but he didn't like to let his beloved paintings out of his hands for the length of time required. However, I determined to acquire a painting by this man whom I consider to be one of the greatest improvisers in the history of jazz, and I went to his apartment with cheque book at the ready. He let me look at all the paintings stacked around his living-room and I decided on the one I liked best: a canvas about four feet by three. I asked 'How much would you want for a painting like this, Pee Wee?'

He looked at me with his rather hesitant expression. 'Oh . . . about twenty-five hundred dollars?'

Somewhat taken aback I said 'That's a little more than I really meant to spend, Pee Wee.'

Instantly he asked 'How about four hundred?'

So I acquired *Paradise Found*, undoubtedly the only genuine Pee Wee Russell canvas in the southern hemisphere. And this story reminds me of the time when another acquaintance asked him 'How come your paintings are so expensive, Pee Wee?'

'Well . . . you know . . . they're all *handmade*.'

I understand that his entire collection of paintings eventually went to Rutgers University, New Jersey, of which he was a faculty member until shortly before his death.

I got a lot of fun out of the Condon tour but lost a lot of money. Exactly the reverse applied when I brought out the big Ray Charles Orchestra for a three-State tour later that year.

The blind singer-pianist was then at the zenith of his fame. His country-style music topped the charts everywhere. He was the Number One jazz singer, a talented instrumentalist, and he led a magnificent band.

But I felt no empathy with Ray or any of his band. In fact it was difficult to do so. The twenty-plus people were ruled with a rod of iron by his manager Jeff Adams, a black man who was quite militantly hostile towards 'honkies' in the way that was then coming into fashion.

Trouble started immediately they arrived in Australia. They came by air from Europe, where they had been making a film, and at one a.m. on the day of their arrival I received a phone call from Jack Neary, a director of Aztec Services. Jack, a former policeman who had broken into show business as a member of a singing group called The Four Guardsmen, said 'You'd better get down to the airport in a hurry. Ray Charles was seen giving himself a shot in the men's room at Darwin Airport, and there's talk about putting him on the next plane out of Australia.'

My heart took a nosedive. I had staked my shirt on the tour and if Ray Charles couldn't perform there'd be no point in going on with it. I would lose more than $40,000 in advance payments and forward publicity.

But when I turned up at the airport Jack told me that he had dropped a few words in the right ears, and that so long as Ray could get himself off the aircraft and act fairly normally there'd be no hitches. Fortunately Ray had come down from his high and there were no more problems at that time . . . but another was yet to come.

The first Sydney concert went like a bomb, and I was euphoric as we travelled through Melbourne and Brisbane before returning to the old Sydney Stadium for the final performance of the tour. I wasn't even perturbed by the fact that I saw very little of Ray Charles. He spent the entire day in his hotel room and would not appear on stage until the band had played the first half of the concert. After the intermission the band would break into his theme, and the blind musician seemed to appear out of nowhere, on the arm of his valet. After the final encore he just as suddenly disappeared.

Ticket sales for the Sydney Stadium indicated another full house for the final concert and it seemed nothing could go wrong . . . until someone told me that two policemen had gone to Ray Charles' suite in the Chevron Hotel at about four p.m. that afternoon.

I really sweated out the next few hours. The crowds poured into the weird old Stadium and the atmosphere of excitement and anticipation was almost tangible. It even increased during the first half, when the band played superbly. Then, after intermission, and about thirty seconds before he was due to go on, Ray Charles and his valet turned up as though nothing had happened. The audience went wild when he appeared on stage and the evening was a stunning success.

I never learned what happened in that hotel room and I'm not sure that I want to. The word was that the police had been paid off, and that may be so.

A couple of years later, Ray Charles was arrested in Canada for being in possession of a quantity of heroin. I was in New York at the time and I said to my agent, George Wein, 'I bet I know where he stashed the drugs. In his portable radio.'

'What makes you think that?'

'Because I noticed that whenever Ray left an aircraft he was worried about his radio. He always told his valet to make sure that he didn't leave it behind. I always wondered why he was so concerned about an ordinary little radio.'

Later I was told that my hunch was right!

The Ray Charles concert was a highspot in my promotional career. The old Sydney Stadium was torn down a few years later, though not before Ed

Sarkesian, the very sharp American manager of the folk-singing trio Peter, Paul, and Mary, discovered a lurk that probably had been perpetrated upon unwary promoters for many years. He checked out the rows of seats against the printed seat plan, and found two rows of ringside seats not shown on the plan.

This solved the mystery of why there were always so many 'scalpers' outside the Stadium, offering tickets to the queues shuffling towards the box offices. A 'scalper', of course, is a man who buys tickets for good seats well ahead of time, and sells them at grossly-inflated prices to people who have not booked or who fear they may not get a seat.

Apparently one of the staff had been operating a nice little sideline from this simple deception for some time, and it's a wonder the owners had not spotted it long before. I remembered bumping into the gentleman in question on one occasion when he was actually stuffing notes into his pockets, but despite his embarrassed expression when he saw me the penny still did not drop.

In the year after the Ray Charles concert I combined with my Sydney friend Brian Nebenzahl to bring out to Australia that enigma of jazz, the pianist Thelonious Monk. This tour might be described as a controlled disaster.

Even though I was a member of Aztec Services, all of us planned so badly that I brought Monk out during Dave Brubeck's third concert season under the Aztec banner. Monk's tour seemed slightly bizarre from the very start. Even as he and his wife Nellie stepped off the aircraft from Rome I was handed an account for excess baggage charges on twelve bottles of Coca Cola, an ironing board and an electric iron, and the fourteen suits and seventeen pairs of shoes in Monk's luggage. 'I don't want the Aussies to think I'm a bum,' he mumbled through clenched teeth in accents reminiscent of Marlon Brando.

As the promoter I was responsible for all such charges and there was nothing to do but pay up. We had booked our guests into the best hotel in Sydney, the Town House at Elizabeth Bay, and we drove them there and hurried off to make everything ready for the concert. We had not been able to book the Town Hall, at that time the normal venue for jazz concerts, and so we'd taken a chance on a well-known dance hall called the Trocadero. This had been the headquarters of the fine Australian trombone player Frank Coghlan and his band, but I think it had never before been used for a concert. We had to hire hundreds of wooden chairs (hundreds more than there were bottoms to place on them, as things turned out) and we spent the afternoon arranging them in neat rows facing the stage and chalking the row numbers on the floor. An hour or so before the concert began we realised that the seats were not numbered and frantically tore sheets of paper into little strips and wrote numbers on them. We placed these on the chair seats and at last all was ready. With fifteen minutes to go we opened the doors, and the blast of wind from George Street blew every number off the seats and onto the floor.

After Monk's first Sydney concert we prepared to move on to Melbourne. We went to pick him up at the hotel, he admitted us to his suite, and we stood gaping on the threshold. A mountain of garments was heaped in the middle of the floor, as though suitcases had simply been upended and emptied out. Crowning this tangled heap a contraceptive device reposed coyly.

There was no time for the Monks to pack their bags and so they simply had to pick out whatever they needed. We had to book the suite for another four days and leave it empty until their return.

We should have gone to Adelaide, where I had booked the Centennial Hall for a concert, but our bad planning meant that Aztec had nowhere to present Dave Brubeck in that city. Kenn Brodziak persuaded me to transfer the Centennial Hall booking to Aztec and to present Monk in Newcastle, which he assured me was 'a good jazz town!' Maybe it is, but we lured less than 200 to hear Thelonious Monk.

However, it was cheaper to go from Sydney to Newcastle than to Adelaide, and to trim costs a little further we decided to go by car. Publicist John Collins, who had done such a fabulous job on the Ray Charles tour, drove us the hundred miles north while the others, and the equipment, followed in a van. We were driving through the countryside between the two cities, with Monk as taciturn as ever in the back seat, when he boomed suddenly 'Where the hell's all the fucking kangaroos?'

The reason for this startling demand was that someone in New York had told him he should buy a kangaroo-skin coat in Australia, and he was becoming perturbed by the apparent dearth of marsupials. Later we took him to a Sydney dealer where he bought no less than three kangaroo-skin coats. Some time afterwards I told this story to my New York agent George Wein. He laughed and said 'I'll lay odds he never took the coats out of their boxes. Probably they're still in his apartment, stacked up with all the other souvenirs he's brought back from overseas trips and never uses.'

George Wein was the promoter of the famous Newport Jazz Festival and a man with deep knowledge of the American jazz scene, as well as being a fine pianist himself.

I stayed out of jazz promotion for a couple of years, because the Monk tour was another financial disaster and I had no better luck when I brought out the Modern Jazz Quartet for the 1966 Adelaide Festival. Then in 1969 George offered me the Duke Ellington Orchestra for an Australian tour.

I hesitated a bit, because my efforts to promote jazz in Australia had been full of worries and frustrations and I'd lost far more money than I'd made out of such ventures, but the magic name of the Duke was irresistible. He was seventy then, and his band was one of the best he had gathered together during the whole of his illustrious career.

With fingers tightly crossed I signed the contract. I need not have worried, because the tour was a roaring success. The band included the incomparable Johnny Hodges (who died only three months later), plus Russell Procope, Harry Carney, Cootie Williams, Cat Anderson, and the organist Wild Bill Davis.

They played to big houses in all capital cities, and it was a triumphal progress for one of the greatest musical figures of the twentieth century. Once more the highspot of the tour was a concert in the Sydney Stadium, played to a packed and wildly enthusiastic audience.

It was a typically hot and humid February night and the temperature under the floodlights must have been well over the century. All the musicians of the big group packed onto the revolving stage were streaming with perspiration, but the tremendous enthusiasm of the audience seemed to inspire them to even greater efforts. Harry Carney, the baritone saxophone player who had been with Duke Ellington for over forty years, obviously made a hit with a pretty young thing in the front row ringside. She offered him a cool drink as the revolving stage carried him slowly past her, and he drank it down and waved her a cheerful farewell. When the stage brought him back again two or three tunes later he began waving in happy anticipation and the whole procedure was repeated.

Harry Carney was one of the most pleasant and unassuming jazz players that it has been my good fortune to meet, and I've met a lot of them. He returned with Duke Ellington when I brought his band to Australia again in 1972, but this return visit did not repeat the success of the first. Obviously the packed audiences on the first tour had consisted largely of people who wanted to see this legendary figure, but once was enough. Audiences were barely half the size and I was made painfully aware that in our population of 13 million the number of true jazz fans is depressingly small.

Harry Carney died soon after that visit and Duke Ellington died in 1974. I consoled myself with the thought that at least I had brought them to Australia before it was too late. To my mind, visits by such incomparable artists more than compensated for all the problems involved.

In between the two Duke Ellington visits I brought in an equally famous orchestra, the Count Basie Band. George Wein made this visit possible too. The band was visiting Japan and he arranged for them to come on to Australia, and travelled along with them to make his first visit to this country.

The tour opened in Perth, with an open-air concert presented as part of the Festival of Perth. Immediately after the concert the group packed up and boarded the midnight flight which brought them to Adelaide at around six-thirty a.m., but when they reached the hotel they discovered that their visit happened to coincide with one of Australia's greatest sporting events: the England v. Australia Test Match, played once every four years in Adelaide.

163

Hotel accommodation was at a premium, and the receptionist told George that the musicians' rooms would not be available until ten a.m., the check-out time when other occupants would vacate their rooms.

George erupted into an incredible outburst, with expletives flying regardless of the crowded lobby and his voice just slightly below a shriek as he told the management exactly what he thought of them. I doubt whether placid Adelaide has heard such an outburst before or since. I suspect it would have been just as violent if the rooms had been reserved from the night before and George had been obliged to pay an extra day's accommodation for the entire band.

But George, as always, rapidly simmered down and before long was his normal cheerful self. The great success of the tour was a big consolation.

He had never been exposed to cricket before his visit to Australia. Every time he turned on the TV in his room it seemed that the screen was filled with the actual game or with commentators talking about it, and he could not understand how a game could last for three, four, or even five days.

About six months later, when we made one of our numerous telephone calls between New York and Adelaide, he opened the conversation with 'Has that goddam game finished yet?'

164

19

'Bonython's Fame or Folly?'

IN 1965 I made the big decision to extend my art galleries to Sydney. I took over the lease of the Hungry Horse Gallery, but I did not make the move without some misgivings. The location of the gallery, on the corner of Elizabeth and Windsor streets in what was becoming the fashionable suburb of Paddington, was fine. But the proportions of the gallery were not. It consisted of several rooms on the top floor of a picturesque old building, and included the use of two small rooms at street level and an office halfway up the stairs, but its proportions were frustrating. The rooms were quite unsuited to the display of large-scale paintings, and the division into the top-floor and ground-floor rooms meant that it was impossible to supervise the whole area.

Light-fingered visitors found it was very easy to steal pieces from the rooms at street level and slip out of the door. There was no storage space and the whole building suffered from a plague of cockroaches. When you entered the little kitchen at night, and turned on the light, the whole place seemed to start moving.

But the gallery gave me a toehold in the art world of the eastern States and I determined to make the best of it for the time being. The lease had only eighteen months to run, and I began to look for alternative premises while mounting some attractive small-scale exhibitions at the Hungry Horse.

Among the earliest was an exhibition of drawings by Robert Dickerson, known as 'Dicko', whom I first encountered during air force days at Darwin. Dicko was a tough nut. He had taken up painting after the war but before this he had been a boxer of some note. He carried this aggressiveness into his art. During the 1950s he produced some of the most powerful 'social comment' paintings ever seen in Australia.

In those days he did not suffer criticism gladly when he had a few grogs under his belt. On the opening night of his Sydney exhibition he heard some derogatory remarks about his work above the babble of the assembled multitude. He turned on what he thought to be the critic, grabbed him by the scruff of the neck, and threw him down the stairs. Unfortunately he had grabbed the wrong man. The one to whom he gave the bum's rush had just bought one of his drawings, whereas the real culprit was nervously looking on.

I found the site for my ideal gallery when a land agent led me through a 'right of way' piercing a row of Paddington terrace houses and showed me a vast open area surrounded by rows of terraces. The open space once had been the site of a sulphuric acid works, but when Paddington became more densely populated the residents lodged a petition for its closure because they feared it might blow up at any moment. When I first saw the area it had long been deserted and was occupied only by a few rusty petrol drums, some timbers rotted by acid fumes, a mountain of broken bottles, and an old rusted horseshoe which I took as a sign of good luck. It now adorns a cedar tree in the Eurilla garden.

From the streets running around the terraces one would not have dreamed that the area even existed, and the narrow entrance was a bit of a problem, but I saw the site as perfect for my 'dream gallery'. Betty O'Neill introduced me to Stan Langton, an Englishman who had been a builder and had turned to designing buildings, and he was just the right man to turn my ideas into reality. After closing the deal for the site I bought a twelve-foot-wide terrace house in Victoria Street. The rear of this terrace was opposite the right of way. We gutted the house to provide an entrance foyer to the gallery through the ground floor, and I converted the top storey into a flat for use during my visits from Adelaide.

In the incredibly short space of four months Stan directed the clearing of the area and the building of the gallery, which formed a hollow square around a great courtyard. Twenty feet wide, the gallery gave ample space for exhibiting the largest works and for presenting several exhibitions at once.

The speed of the work was all the more remarkable in that we encountered numerous obstructions. Some might have been extremely expensive to remove if the ways of the big city had not been very different from those prevailing in little old Adelaide. It was amazing how fast some of the bureaucratic regulations could be waived if one was prepared to grease a palm or two.

On 18 November 1967 we opened the new Bonython Gallery, Sydney. Five hundred guests paid ten dollars each to attend the opening and the resultant $5,000 went to the Art Gallery Society. As each group of people arrived in the gallery they encountered the charm of its complete surprise. They entered through the narrow foyer constructed through the terrace house, with the initial reaction of 'Well, what's so different about this?' and then descended four or five steps through the former back yard of the house. These led them past running water, miniature Japanese maples, and flowering fuschias into the courtyard, of which the *pièce de résistance* was a great willow tree about twenty feet high. We had imported it from suburban Ryde shortly before the opening, and the publicity we gained by blocking all traffic on the Ryde Bridge more than compensated for the cost of buying and transporting the willow.

Then, as the visitors gazed around them, they were faced with the stunning sight of the gallery built all round the courtyard, with great windows revealing the brilliantly-lit interiors and giving a first glimpse of the paintings, sculptures, ceramics, and tapestries on display.

Visitors remarked that the view was equally breathtaking from within the gallery, especially when the courtyard plantings and other works were fully established. Eventually two great willows rose from the floor of red ceramic tiles and there were waterfalls, hibiscus bushes, and ivy. The whole place was a haven of peace and beauty, and if it was not the largest commercial gallery in the world, as some admirers claimed, it was certainly one of the most beautiful.

The visitors to the opening exhibition drank champagne, ate exotic foods, listened to the jazz music of the Don Burrows Quintet, and feasted their eyes on one of the most splendid exhibitions of contemporary art ever seen in Australia until that time.

Earlier that year I had flown to London to select the exhibition from the vaults of the Marlborough Fine Art Gallery. The paintings included works by many world-famous names: Ben Nicholson, Victor Pasmore, John Piper, Ceri Richards, Graham Sutherland, Francis Bacon, and Oscar Kokoschka. Among the sculptors were Henry Moore, Barbara Hepworth, Kenneth Armitage, and Lynn Chadwick.

The upstairs gallery featured an exhibition of Japanese ceramics, selected by Betty O'Neill on a visit to the East. In another court of the gallery hung three magnificent tapestries, woven in Aubusson to designs which I had commissioned from John Coburn. These were the first tapestries ever woven in France to Australian designs.

Yet another display presented a mixed exhibition of works by Australian artists who had been associated with me in the past, and whose work I intended to feature in a series of one-man exhibitions in the new gallery.

It was a most spectacular launching although, like every launching, it caused a few waves. Victoria Street, like many Paddington streets in those days, was dirty as well as narrow, and its residents were not as sophisticated as they might be. They resented their street being crammed with Rolls Royces, Jaguars, and Bentleys, and the sudden influx of the 'upper crust' into their then humble suburb. Some of them discharged a barrage of raw eggs over adjoining roofs into the courtyard, and I had to settle a few claims for new shoes and dry-cleaning during the following days.

The crowd also contained a few knockers, including the architect Harry Seidler. He is renowned for the Australian buildings he has designed but not for his patronage of Australian art. First he complained about the acoustics of the gallery, which after all was not planned as a venue for jazz concerts, and then he rather contemptuously kicked one of the skirting boards. 'These skirting boards,' he commented. 'Are they new, or did you pick them up somewhere second-hand?'

Standing in the group listening to Seidler's comments was John Roche, Stan Langton's brother-in-law. Once Lord Mayor of Adelaide, he is a noted South Australian property developer. With a slightly sardonic smile he remarked 'Listen, old chap, if you'd like me to start on a list of *your* dissatisfied customers, I'll be only too happy to oblige!'

Later I was flattered by a remark from Sir Roy Grounds, who designed the huge National Gallery of Victoria. After congratulating me on the success of the project he said 'How wise you were not to have used an architect. Otherwise it would have cost you twice as much and would not have been half as good!'

I thought the compliment had added value in that it came from an architect.

It was a hectic night, and when the last visitors had departed I felt the unusual need for something stronger than a soft drink. I drank a full bottle of champagne all by myself and quickly fell into a deep sleep in my tiny apartment.

The success of the opening was proclaimed by headlines in the Sydney and interstate press during the next few days. One of them said 'Gallery in World Class'. Others said 'Breathtaking' and 'An Act of Faith in our Art'. while a more sombre observer queried 'Bonython's Fame or Folly?' One reviewer remarked that I had 'moved from a cultural dog box to an artistic Mecca'.

One of the less approving critics was Ross Lansell, then the art reviewer for the *Sunday Telegraph*, who disparaged my practice of playing modern music through the gallery speaker system. I felt that such music was quite appropriate for exhibitions of contemporary art. Also I believe that an art gallery should be a place of relaxation and enjoyment, not a kind of cathedral crypt demanding tiptoe progression and hushed voices.

After a few exhibitions Lansell mounted his hobby-horse again and wrote that he found it hard to review exhibitions against a background of 'Hollywood-style mood music'. I could not resist this challenge and wrote to his editor that 'Whilst many of us in Sydney harboured grave doubts about Mr Lansell's abilities as an art critic, one is left with no doubts whatsoever about his musical knowledge. What he chose to call "Hollywood-style mood music" was in fact Ravel's "Daphnis et Chloé".'

This letter happened to coincide with one from another Sydney gallery owner, complaining about Lansell's destructive criticisms of the work of a promising young artist. The editor published both letters but I never discovered whether they had anything to do with the fact that Lansell's art

TOP: Kym Bonython with jazz catalyst Eddie Condon (*left*) and trombonist Vic Dickenson. BOTTOM: With Duke Ellington and Sir James Harrison, Governor of South Australia, in Adelaide 1970

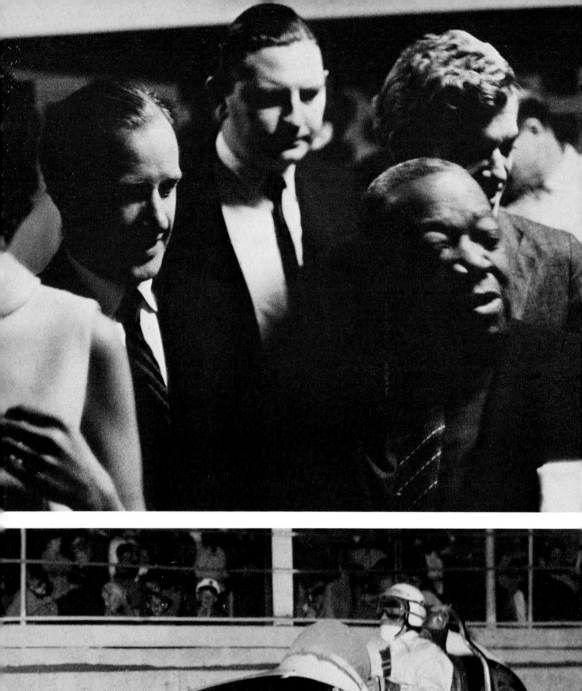

criticisms did not appear in the *Sunday Telegraph* thereafter.

Despite the acclaim given to the gallery's opening, public response to the magnificent Marlborough exhibition was lukewarm. However, that tended to be par for the course in Australia in those days when contemporary art appreciation was in its infancy. How wrong this attitude was! Few people praised the Francis Bacon painting, priced at $34,000 in that exhibition, but on the very morning it arrived back in London it sold for $75,000. Today it would be worth at least twice that sum, and in 1978 the Art Gallery of New South Wales paid $150,000 for a Bacon painting of similar size and quality.

Marlborough Galleries, with outlets in London, New York, Rome, and Tokyo, was then the largest gallery chain in the world. It was owned by Lloyd and Fischer, two Jews who had been booksellers. They were notoriously tough businessmen. One story about Lloyd says that when a new exhibition opened one of his brash young assistants asked enthusiastically 'Mr Lloyd, are you going to reserve one of these paintings for your own collection before we offer them to the public?'

Lloyd exploded 'How many times do I have to tell you? I collect *money*, not paintings!'

I never had the pleasure of meeting the two gentlemen, whom Brett Whiteley called 'the undertakers of art' because they dealt almost exclusively in works of art from deceased estates. I dealt through their modern art section manager, Tony Reichardt.

My own attitude is slightly different from Lloyd's. I believe it is bad for business to 'pick the eyes' out of an exhibition before it opens and I never buy anything for my own collection until it has closed. In fact I tend to collect paintings, not money!

However I think I have built up a fairly impressive collection from the 'leftovers' still unpurchased after exhibitions closed. I sold my Nolans, Drysdales, and Boyds to finance my Sydney ventures, but the empty spaces soon were filled by the works of younger and less established artists in whom I had faith. As usual, some reached the heights while others fell by the wayside . . . but one can rely only upon 'gut feeling' as to the likely future of any artist.

Naturally I made my share of mistakes, sometimes because I acted against my better judgement. On one of my visits to London I was bombarded with messages left at my hotel to 'Contact Laurie Hope', an Australian painter then living in England, but I had planned every moment of my time during a brief visit and did not manage to return his calls. On my last night in London I returned to the hotel at two a.m. to find Laurie waiting for me outside in a battered Volkswagen van. He invited me into the van and I found it was loaded with paintings. Rain dripped onto them through the roof and I had to inspect them by matchlight, but finally I made three purchases. As I suspected I might, I lived to regret them. I have not been able to sell any of the paintings, although Laurie has built up a modest reputation.

TOP: Jazz party at Tennyson 1964. *From left* Artist Sidney Nolan, jazz musician and journalist Dick Hughes, singer Jimmy Rushing, art critic Robert Hughes (*Robert McFarlane photo*). BOTTOM: The celebrated 3-wheel-drive by Bob Tattersall, Rowley Park 1962

The opening of my new gallery made life busier than ever. Despite the shortage of buyers for paintings from the Marlborough Galleries, art was becoming a big business in Australia and I needed eight to ten people to handle all the various aspects of the gallery operations. Every three weeks I had to organise and set up new exhibitions in Sydney and Adelaide, and in summertime I had to organise and attend a new 'spectacular' for each Friday night at Rowley Park. This involved a great deal of planning and administration, but I used my own race driving as one of my few relaxations. I had to plan and present my weekly jazz programme for the A.B.C., and I was running regular concert tours by overseas musicians. These involved frequent travel to all the capital cities.

It was difficult to find time to yarn with visitors to the galleries but still possible to extract some fun out of life. In 1968 I was brave enough to mount a 'retrospective exhibition' by Barry Humphries.

As an entrepreneur I had brought Barry to Adelaide for his first visit, and presented his now famous one-man show for several nights in the Adelaide Town Hall. Consequently I knew him quite well and was aware that he had started life as an art student. When his career as a satirical comedian began to flourish he abandoned painting and became a collector instead, concentrating on earlier Australian and European art.

The exhibition in my Sydney gallery comprised a selection of Barry's early drawings and paintings, executed from his student days onwards. These were not startlingly original, but by that time he had already achieved a certain reputation and this attracted a crowd to the gallery. Obviously they were more interested in what new ways he had discovered to shake up the bourgeoisie than they were in his early paintings, and he did not fail them.

In the Sydney exhibition he mounted three giant panels, each about eight feet high by eighteen inches wide, with a single letter on each panel. Collectively they spelt B-I-G. Alongside these were five tiny sections, also bearing a single letter apiece, spelling out S-M-A-L-L. Two other noteworthy paintings were 'Lambscape' and 'Beefscape', which were representations of butcher shop windows. The former contained woolly lambs gambolling in lush grass, with sprigs of wattle dotted around the perimeter, and the latter depicted fat Hereford calves.

His *objets d'art* included two leather boots joined together at the toe and entitled 'Siamese Boots'; and my favourite—a pair of brown trousers equipped with a fly extending from knee to ankle. This was called 'Nigger Brown Pants'.

The highlight of his exhibition was a canvas wading pool, eight feet in diameter, filled with 250 secondhand books which I bought for him from a junk shop. Onto this mountain of volumes he emptied forty-eight tins of Heinz Vegetable Mayonnaise, and captioned the result 'After reading these books I felt sick'.

On the opening night Barry stood by this masterpiece, and as the crowd gathered around him a waiter approached with a large tin of sweet corn on a silver salver. Accepting the open tin he announced 'It is not often that an artist such as myself is given the opportunity of completing his major *oeuvre* in the presence of such a large and distinguished gathering.'

With that he flung the contents of the can over the top of the repulsive mass in the wading pool, and observed triumphantly 'Yes, it needed that little touch of yellow!'

Yet another incident in which I participated was when I was guest of honour on the TV show *This Is Your Life*. Barry was one of the guests, and when he appeared he had a pair of large black leather boots brought on camera with the pretext that he was going to create a special work of art for me to mark the occasion. With that he produced a jug of yellow custard, poured it into the boots, and announced 'There you are! Pus in Boots!'

20

Art Mixed With Craft

IT SEEMS that whenever anyone thought about me they remembered the old slogan 'If you want anything done, ask a busy man.' I was invited to sit on a number of committees and found it hard to refuse because many of them coincided with my personal interests. By 1970 these commitments included the Council of the South Australian School of Art, the Encyclopaedia Britannica Awards Committee, and an appointment as Art Advisor to the Broken Hill Proprietary Company Limited, Australia's largest company. B.H.P. was constructing a massive skyscraper on the site of the old Menzies Hotel in Melbourne and they asked me to advise them on buying suitable paintings and other works of art for installation in the building.

The Encyclopaedia Britannica Awards Committee was chaired by the well-known academic Sir Leonard Huxley, and its function was to select outstanding achievements in the fields of art, science, and literature. The awards consisted of a gold medal and a cheque for $10,000 for each prizewinner.

Such substantial awards are rare in Australia and they were forerunners of the Australia Council subsidies, which often went to finance (perhaps over-generously in some instances) aspirants in various fields of the arts who had yet to prove themselves.

Perhaps because of the composition of the Awards Committee, its meetings were more serious than those of the Australia Council, but Sir Macfarlane Burnet once told us a story that enlivened our deliberations. It came from a young relative and concerned an Administrator of Papua New Guinea. According to the story the Administrator was entertaining an important visitor, but when tea was served the houseboy produced a most dilapidated teapot. The administrator demanded 'Where is Number One teapot?' and the houseboy replied 'Number One teapot bugger up finish. Him now piss like missus, not mister!'

During the 1970 Adelaide Festival of Arts I met Dr H. C. Coombs, former Governor of the Reserve Bank of Australia and then Chairman of the Australian Council for the Arts (now the Australia Council). He asked me if I would care to become a member, and assured me that it would involve only one day a month.

The Australia Council and its Boards comprise the main funding body for the arts in Australia. It subsidises the Australian Ballet, the Elizabethan Theatre Trust, the Australian Opera, the Aboriginal Arts Board, the Literature Board, and a number of similar organisations.

Quite soon I found that my responsibilities consumed considerably more than 'one day a month' because I was co-opted onto several sub-committees. To begin with, Dr Coombs had offered me a choice between Community Arts and the Experimental Film and Television Fund. As an inveterate movie-goer from an early age I naturally chose the latter, and found myself Chairman of this new committee which for the first time was empowered to give financial assistance to aspiring young film makers.

Membership of the Council provided a great intellectual stimulus. Dr Jean Battersby, the Chief Executive Officer, was an inspired worker and an indefatigable administrator. I have the greatest respect for her and for Dr Coombs, although both had plenty of knockers inside and outside the organisation. Other Council members included such outstanding members of the Australian creative community as the poet Judith Wright, playwright David Williamson, artist Clifton Pugh, jazz musician Don Burrows, writer and film producer Phillip Adams, Barry Jones the former quiz-whizz turned parliamentarian, and George Johnston the novelist.

From time to time the Experimental Film and Television Fund Committee included young men who were to become directors or producers of fine films, made during the great blossoming of the Australian film industry from the mid-1970s onwards. The Committee played a considerable part in fertilising that new growth, and some years later Peter Weir, who directed *Picnic at Hanging Rock*, kindly acknowledged that we assisted him to produce one of his earliest films.

Barry Jones and Phil Adams could be relied upon to prevent Committee meetings from becoming too tense, even when we were under siege from a vociferous minority who claimed they were not receiving their just dues.

Their applications for assistance were processed by the Council's professional staff, who made recommendations to be discussed during our monthly meetings. One assessor felt that the Committee should know more about the types of scripts being submitted, and he detailed one of these entitled *The Phallic Forest*.

One scene depicted a bored and frustrated housewife watering her back garden with a hose. You could see that she was missing something in her life. But suddenly a giant penis thrust through a knot-hole in the tall wooden fence surrounding the garden. This phenomenon was followed by a quick close-up of the wildly spurting garden hose—and her ecstatic smile.

Our brief was that we should be concerned only with the artistic merit of any submission and that we should never reject any worthwhile script because it was 'agin the Government' or 'critical of the capitalistic society which provides this financial aid'. But the assessor was worried about this scene in *The Phallic Forest*. He feared that the then Prime Minister, John Gorton, might object to it. 'Object?' remarked Barry. 'I thought we might even ask him to provide the props!'

At another meeting, Barry told us that on the previous evening he had attended a new production of the opera *The Rape of Lucrece*. He said 'The singing was adequate, but the acting left a lot to be desired. In fact the rape was more like coitus interruptus!'

Another member, the lawyer and parliamentarian Peter Coleman who in 1978 was to be leader of the New South Wales Opposition, asked Barry 'How is it that when the newspapers used to print your photograph they called you the "former quiz-whizz", but when they use it nowadays you're called a "parliamentary wit"?'

Barry replied expansively 'Well, you know, in the world of the bland even the one-barb man is king!'

During my Council activities I seemed to be appointed with remarkable frequency to various finance committees. I told the Finance Chairman, Dr Dick Downing, that my only qualifications for such appointments was that I had escaped bankruptcy by a hair's breadth for so many years.

In October 1971 I received a telegram from Prime Minister Billy McMahon inviting me to be Chairman of a Committee of Enquiry into Crafts. Later I learned that by one of the usual bureaucratic foul-ups an identical telegram had been sent to each of the five people who were to make up the committee. Eventually this situation was resolved, but we soon discovered that a far more important error had been made. The committee did not include a single craftsman or craftswoman. No such enquiry had ever been carried out anywhere in the world, there was a great deal to be learned, and it seemed totally inappropriate for us to commence our deliberations without at least one representative of the crafts joining the committee. We refused to begin work until this omission had been made good.

This stubbornness was not well received by the Government of the day and I was summoned to a confrontation with Peter Howson, Minister for the Environment, Aborigines and the Arts. (Barry Jones suggested that this department should use the acronym ABFARTS.)

My reception was chilly because of an article by Laurie Thomas which had appeared in that morning's *Australian*, concerning the Enquiry Committee and headed 'Government long on dithering, short on concern.'

Howson was backed up by two 'heavies': Neil Townsend from his own department and Sir Lenox Hewitt from the Prime Minister's staff. This trio laid it on me hot and strong, claiming that it would be improper for people who might benefit from our decisions to sit on the committee. I countered this by saying that the Commonwealth Arts Advisory Board included such practising artists as Fred Williams, Sir Russell Drysdale, and Sir William Dargie, and pointed out that well-established artists could be relied upon to set aside personal prejudice and act with honesty and impartiality.

I felt that I made little impression, but two days later the mighty had fallen. It was November 1972 and the Labor Party under Gough Whitlam swept into power. A few weeks later, our committee was bolstered by the potter Marea Gazzard, who was head of the Crafts Board; the jewellers Dick Richards of the Art Gallery of South Australia and Howard Tozer of the Royal Melbourne Institute of Technology; and Ian Templeman, the Director of the Fremantle Arts Centre.

For Executive Officer we secured the services of Felicity Abraham. I long admired her sterling work on the theatrical side of the Australia Council's activities and she proved equally enthusiastic and competent on the Crafts Enquiry Committee.

After all these birth-pangs the committee began work in earnest in August 1973. During the next two years we travelled to many parts of Australia, interviewed more than 400 men and women involved in all the crafts, and sent questionnaires to about 2,000 more. On top of this, we received and analysed 350 written submissions.

Felicity Abraham crammed all this work into just over eighteen months. That included the collation of our final report and recommendations, which was presented to Parliament in March 1975. But by that time the economy had started to slide, Whitlam was fighting for political survival, and most of our recommendations could not be implemented for lack of funds.

However, the Crafts Board of the Australia Council already had been acting upon many of the problems uncovered by our committee, and our two-volume report was received enthusiastically by several crafts organisations throughout the world.

My involvement with the Australia Council and its various committees and sub-committees added considerably to my work load, and I doubt whether many people in the country spent as much time in aeroplanes as I did in the early 1970s. Before I joined the Council I used to claim that I dealt with three of the most difficult sections of the community: artists, jazz musicians, and speedway riders. But now I was able to add yet another category: film makers. Some of them could be just as paranoid as people in any of the other three categories, but when one occupation became too hard to take I could absorb myself in the others.

I was a member of the Australia Council for four years. During this period, Whitlam increased the funds available from $5 million to $25 million per annum. The various activities, previously the responsibility of but one organisation, were split into seven different boards, each being responsible to the Australia Council. Membership of the Council was doubled, and the whole system seemed to become more impersonal.

I met Whitlam only once during my tour of duty. He attended one of the Council meetings, and when we were introduced he remarked 'I always imagined you to be a much more venerable gentleman!' That was my first and only conversation with a Prime Minister.

Constant travel around Australia with all its interruptions to my home and business life had become very tedious and I was relieved when I was allowed to stand down from the Australia Council, although I was co-opted for a further year to the Crafts Board pending the completion of the Enquiry Report. Also I had become very concerned about some aspects of my Sydney operations which were increasingly difficult to handle from my home base in Adelaide.

My main market was in Sydney and I decided the time had come to dispose of my Adelaide commitments and move permanently to the east. I sold my North Adelaide gallery to Richard Llewellyn, who was thus able to move from his small suburban premises to much more spacious and centrally-located quarters. Richard had excellent but very specialised tastes in art, and I wondered whether they would be palatable to conservative Adelaide. After about a year my fears were realised when he was obliged to sell the gallery to Andris Lidums. Lidums told the local press that he would 'give Adelaide what it wanted', and when I later visited the gallery and saw his display I remarked 'If this is what Adelaide wants then thank God I've moved to Sydney.'

The move was not without traumas. Adelaide real estate values in those days were still very low by comparison with Sydney, and by this time we had moved from Tennyson to establish a beautiful home in Leabrook. When we sold it, the proceeds would have been no more than enough to buy a dilapidated terrace house in Paddington with no front garden and precious little at the back.

For our last three months in Adelaide we lived at Eurilla, and this period in our family's former summer home, which had so many happy memories, was quite a sentimental experience. Just before we left for Sydney we held what we believed would be the last of our family Christmas dinners ever to be held in the old house. Mother, who in her advancing years lived in North Adelaide, bedridden and paralysed by a stroke, was brought up to join us at Eurilla for what proved to be her last visit there.

Two days after Christmas, with my brother Warren and sister Katherine, I began dividing up the contents of the house. The plan was for each of us to take a share of the contents and then for Eurilla to be auctioned, but I soon realised that I could not abandon this important part of my life so casually. The thought of Eurilla going to strangers, and being closed to me thereafter, was too much to accept. I decided to buy the house from the rest of the family, so that it would always be waiting for me if ever I returned to Adelaide.

We let Eurilla to friends and left the garden in the capable hands of Frank, a New Australian who worked on the railways during the week but took on gardening jobs in his spare time. He lived at Henley Beach, not far from our previous home at Tennyson, and when we moved to Leabrook he established a magnificent garden there.

Frank must be the hardest and most dedicated worker I have ever met. When we moved to Sydney he agreed to tackle the overgrown acres at Eurilla and keep them in order against the day when I might return to Adelaide. He kept us advised of progress in a series of letters which I still treasure. He referred to Eurilla as 'the sleeping giant', and wrote 'Maybe you stop in Sydney with the rat race and my plan for Eurilla stop in the clouds where my mind is suspended right now. I left my soul in Leabrook, my body at Henley Beach, and my mind is above Eurilla—waiting for action.'

When seeking my approval of some new scheme, he wrote 'I am expecting you to bless this life or death project. If not, *ring me next Wednesday at eight o'clock and get rid of me*!'

When at last he knew we would be returning to Adelaide he wrote 'I have a programme for Eurilla. 1978: Friends will ask you if they may visit. 1980: Tourist buses will stop in. 1981: Nicole [my daughter] will get married under giant tree in garden.'

Frank's hard work and good humour were matched by his unfailing courtesy. He always referred to Julie as 'Madam Bonython'. In 1968 the celebrated fibreglass and leather sculpture 'Hat Stand' (otherwise known as 'Miss Jones') by Allen Jones arrived at Eurilla from England. 'Miss Jones', who appears on the jacket of this book, is provocatively formed. She is larger than life and her opulent bosom bursts forth from her jacket. They don't make them like that any more! I placed 'Miss Jones' in the picture window of our living-room, and a little later Frank came past busily raking up the accumulation of leaves and bark from the gum trees. He noticed this near-naked woman gaxing fixedly at him and quickly averted his eyes, unwilling to believe that his 'Madam Bonython' would thus flaunt her charms. This performance was played out week after week until at last he realised that the woman was merely a sculpture and not Julie behaving more boldly than usual.

Frank certainly was right about the 'rat race' of Sydney, and from a domestic point of view Julie and I had many misgivings about the move although it was undoubtedly correct in the business sense. I planned to build a large apartment on top of two sides of the gallery, with French doors and windows looking down into the beautiful courtyard, but the usual bureaucratic delays held up our building permit for sixteen months and we had to find temporary accommodation. We were able to rent a tiny terrace house adjoining the front entrance to the gallery, and the owner allowed us to knock a connecting door in the rear wall. The children lived in this house and we employed its kitchen facilities, while Julie and I lived in the original little apartment I had built above the entrance to the gallery.

Victoria Street, Paddington, was a far cry from Summit Road, Mount Lofty. The filth of Sydney was hard to take after the cleanliness and order of Adelaide, and before long we all developed the 'Paddington stoop' from keeping an eye on the papers, rotting vegetables, broken bottles and assorted dog turds which littered the footpath. Our neighbours were still a trifle troublesome, and one of them made a habit of tossing well-thumbed packages of pornography over onto our roof. Any enjoyment I might have derived from each new offering was spoiled by the fact that it was well marinated in urine from Paddington's multitudinous cats by the time I found it.

Soon after we arrived an evening paper printed a survey listing Sydney's dirtiest suburbs, assessed by the monthly totals of garbage carted away by the various councils. I was staggered to find that Paddington was eighth on the list: in my opinion it should have been on the top. But I soon realised that this was because most of the garbage was not collected but simply left to lie around the streets.

At about the same time the Sydney *Daily Mirror* invited me to contribute a weekly column, on my own choice of subjects, and I launched into print with a scathing indictment of the Paddington garbage and dog turd situation. A little later I was having a big clean-up and reorganisation of the gallery and I cleared a mass of old catalogues, cartons, and other debris from one of the storerooms. The local council promised to send a truck to remove this rubbish from the side lane in which I dumped it, but bureaucracy triumphed again and it did not arrive. During the night a strong wind scattered some of this rubbish amidst the dead cats, broken bottles, and aged excreta of Paddington, and next morning an irate neighbour named Antoinette Marshall slipped a letter under my front door.

She expressed indignation that one who wrote publicly about garbage should so litter the neighbourhood, and remarked that since my name is Bonython I obviously felt that I was not bound by the same rules of conduct that apply to others. She left no doubt that she felt I was the worst form of hypocrite.

I phoned the council and complained bitterly about their broken promise, and they sent a truck the next day. To Ms Antoinette Marshall I wrote a very civil reply, explaining the circumstances and saying that I did not think my name gave me any additional privileges. To conclude, I wrote 'Speaking of names, just because yours happens to be Antoinette does not necessarily mean I think you ought to be guillotined!'

I thought this to be an adequate punchline, but Dave Brubeck later suggested a better one. During one of his tours I told him about the incident and he said I should have written 'Just because your name happens to be Antoinette there's no need to "come on" like Napoleon!'

Despite such problems we began to settle down in Sydney although we had to tackle one recurrent difficulty. This came about because my beautiful gallery was at a lower level than most of the adjoining properties. During the summer thunderstorms which send torrential rain down upon Sydney the water ran down the slope, seeped through the ancient wall that bounded the eastern and southern sides of the gallery site, and ran into the cavity wall of the gallery. If it rained hard enough and long enough the cavity wall acted like a tank until the pressure of water within it had to find release. It began to run under the skirting boards maligned by Harry Seidler, and on one occasion the pressure was so great that water actually squirted in three jets out of the floor-level power points.

Many were the times I had to dash downstairs at dead of night to rescue any free-standing objects, carpets not actually attached to the floor, and paintings stacked against the wall of the stock room. With nature's usual diabolical ingenuity these floods occurred most often on Sundays or Mondays when the gallery was closed, and Julie and I had to cope alone with the task of mopping up the hundreds of gallons of water that flowed relentlessly across the floor. We felt as though we were re-enacting 'The Sorcerer's Apprentice'.

One of these floods descended upon us when the gallery was being used for filming an episode for the A.B.C. series *Certain Women*. The cast had to work barefoot, with the men's trousers rolled up to the knees, while the cameras focused on their bodies above the waist.

The gallery also was used as a location for a sequence in *Age of Consent*, starring James Mason, and for making TV commercials, but fortunately the thunderstorms held off on those occasions.

We soon became used to the big-city atmosphere of Sydney, with police and ambulance sirens wailing along the streets, noisy parties and family arguments erupting from the rows of terrace houses, and our bedroom illuminated by the red glow of the city. Julie enjoyed it more than I did. I still longed for the peace of Adelaide, but at least the gallery was going well. We attracted a constant stream of visitors from many parts of Australia and the world, and I noticed that a remarkable number of purchases, perhaps a quarter of our entire turnover, came from business houses. In Adelaide this was virtually unknown.

Our customers included a handsome young man with excellent taste in both paintings and the opposite sex. He was much taken with Sandy Nunnerley, who worked for me and later made the big time in New York as an interior decorator, and he bought Nolans, Boyds, Tuckers, and Whiteleys. Furthermore he always paid for them in cash, although we noticed on more than one occasion that the notes were slightly scorched. I'm sure that Sandy was just as surprised as the rest of us when we heard that he had been arrested for safe cracking, and to the best of my knowledge he is still doing time. When he was arrested he owed considerable sums to other art galleries, but for some unknown reason he always paid us in full.

Building and maintaining our so-called 'Mecca of the Arts' was an expensive business, and despite the general misconception that I was a millionaire I found it necessary to part with my own art treasures one by one. I sense that this incurred the displeasure of the artists from whom I had bought them, especially Drysdale and Nolan, but I felt I had good reasons for doing so. I could have retained them for my own enjoyment and that of my family, but it was more satisfying to conduct a gallery that set new standards for Australian contemporary art and offered many young artists an opportunity to exhibit their work for the first time.

The painters whose works I sold may have been displeased because I made a very substantial profit. If so, then perhaps they forgot that I bought the paintings when these artists still had to establish their names and when I was one of the few who had faith in them.

Our family always has had dogs, and generally big dogs, but when I decided on the move to Sydney I gave away the two Old English sheepdogs I owned at that time in the belief that the big city was no place for them. Sydney's dog-fouled footpaths reinforced this opinion. However, after we had lived in Sydney for eight months, a silver-grey Alsatian bitch simply walked off the street into the gallery. She was a placid and lovable animal, though very thin, and she bore a number of half-healed scars. She seemed to be looking for someone to take care of her and so, after advertising unsuccessfully for her owner, we decided to keep her. I named her Mischa in memory of the best dog I ever owned, a pure white Alsatian bitch, and she became a favourite with the gallery staff and visitors. I was not to learn the rest of her strange story until I put the gallery up for sale.

21

Spreading the Gospel

THE GREAT success of the Ellington and Basie tours in 1970 and 1971 seemed like a drought-breaker and I was encouraged to launch into a veritable avalanche of jazz promotion. In 1972 I imported two big packages: firstly one which we called 'The History of Jazz' and later the genuine, re-created Glenn Miller Orchestra, operated by the Miller Estate and directed by Buddy de Franco, on a five-State tour.

The 'History of Jazz' tour featured two important bands. One was the seven-piece Preservation Hall Band, comprising a number of courteous elderly gentlemen who despite their ages certainly had lost none of their expertise. The leader was 'Kid' Thomas Valentine, a trumpeter of seventy-five, and the only man younger than seventy was fifty-two. He was the drummer, Alonzo Stewart. The bass player, Joseph Butler, bore the unlikely nickname of 'Twat'.

The other group was 'The Giants of Jazz', assembled by George Wein for his Newport Festival. Giants they were indeed. Dizzy Gillespie played trumpet, Kai Winding trombone, Sonny Stitt saxophone, Thelonious Monk piano, Al McKibbon bass, and we had that most compulsive of drummers, Art Blakey.

By way of a bonus I insisted on throwing in Jaki Byard, one of my particular favourites. He played solo piano in a bewildering variety of styles ranging from 'stride' to the most avant garde.

On a free night in Sydney I took Jaki and a few of my friends to a well-known nightspot in Rose Bay. Normally this watering-hole played only canned music, but a beautiful grand piano stood alongside the small dance floor and eventually we persuaded Jaki to perform. For ten or fifteen minutes he gave a virtuoso jazz recital. I doubt whether Sydney had ever heard anything like it before but it was brought to an abrupt end when a not-so-bright young thing approached the piano and demanded 'Say, can't you play anything we can *dance* to?' Jaki took this with his usual good humour but it broke the spell.

When the Glenn Miller Orchestra arrived I found them to be the exact opposite of the disciplined Ray Charles group. They were great on stage but otherwise they were completely disorganised and kept me running after them like a teacher at a school picnic. (Six years later I was amused by a letter from Ray McKinley, former leader of the band, in which he said that he'd heard my promotional operations were equally disorganised!)

The many problems of the tour included a leading soloist who was hooked on methadone, the allegedly non-addictive compound employed to wean drug-takers off heroin. He carried a supply in his baggage, but it went astray en route to Australia. By the time he reached Perth he was pretty desperate, but I managed to persuade an art-loving medico of my acquaintance to prescribe enough to last him until the baggage was located.

Apart from this, the whole group was totally unprofessional. They missed early morning calls, missed the buses laid on to take them from their hotels to the concert halls and back, and often barely made it on stage in time for the concerts. At the end of the tour one of the young trombonists simply disappeared. The immigration authorities were still looking for him some weeks later and for all I know he is still in Australia.

Like a number of my attractions this tour proved to be just a little too early. The 'nostalgia' boom had yet to reach Australia. The same thing happened some months later when I brought in an exciting blues package comprising Junior Wells and Buddy Guy with the blues singer Big Arthur Crudup.

By 1972 I had learnt from these mistakes, and I brought in 'something for everyone' in the form of guitarist Charlie Byrd and his trio. I teamed them with the Australian group led by Don Burrows and added the young American vibes sensation Gary Burton. The tour did wonderful business. Charlie Byrd, who is one of the pioneers of jazz from South America, proved himself to be not only a fine musician but also a most co-operative personality. In spite of this the tour was not free from problems, although they were not caused by the musicians.

Keeping a group on schedule between one engagement and another was an ulcer-causing operation. Delayed flights, airline strikes, and power strikes frequently loomed on the horizon, and apart from these there was always the possibility of the musicians' instruments going astray between concerts.

Ansett and T.A.A. competed ardently for my business, which was quite considerable when I was flying several groups and their baggage around the country within any given year, but I stuck to T.A.A. until the year of the first Charlie Byrd tour and its sequel. The airline always insisted that all the band instruments and other equipment should be delivered to its freight section immediately after the last concert in any city, to facilitate departure by the inevitable early-morning flight. That was fair enough, but it didn't always work. After Charlie Byrd's Sydney concert we set off for Adelaide, where his appearance was to be a highspot of the 1972 Festival of Arts, and soon after we arrived we found the instruments were missing.

Eventually they were discovered in Alice Springs, 800 miles north of Adelaide. Obviously they had been loaded into the wrong aircraft. We spent an anxious day until the instruments arrived in Adelaide only thirty minutes before the first concert was due to begin.

The airline spokesmen smothered me with anguished apologies and promises that it would never happen again, and so I employed T.A.A. once more, about a month later, when I had the pianist Oscar Peterson and his trio on tour. This time a double bass and a drum kit vanished between Sydney and Melbourne. It was impossible to retrieve them in time for the concert because they had gone to Port Moresby and the airline schedules between Papua New Guinea and Australia did not permit them to be returned for another three days. We were forced to hire alternative instruments, and the result was far from pleasing either to the musicians or their audience. Needless to say I employed Ansett thereafter.

In that year of 1972 *Music Maker* magazine honoured me with the accolade 'The person who has done most for jazz in Australia in 1972.' With all due modesty I believe that I earned it. I followed Oscar Peterson with Erroll Garner, a giant of jazz piano and one of my favourites for more than twenty years. I had interviewed him at Birdland when I was staying with Gene Krupa in New York.

He arrived in Adelaide in the mid-winter month of July. I booked him into the best suite of the best hotel, but Adelaide's 'best' was not so good even as recently as 1972. Soon after his arrival I went into his suite to find him sitting shivering on the huge bed, clad in his overcoat, with clouds of steam billowing into the room through the open door of the bathroom. The hotel heating had broken down and he had turned on the shower full bore in an attempt to warm himself up. He couldn't get out of Adelaide fast enough.

I followed the Erroll Garner tour with an August presentation entitled 'Salute to Louis Armstrong', who had died in the previous year. It was another exciting show, consisting of the veteran pianist Earl Hines and his quintet together with such magnificent trumpeters as Bobby Hackett, Wild Bill Davison, and Clark Terry. Hackett and Davison were among the stars who recorded so many jazz classics for the Commodore label in pre-war years, while Terry, born in that important year of 1920, rose to fame in the Duke Ellington Orchestra. He was acclaimed as one of the most versatile and swinging of jazz instrumentalists.

I always felt that Wild Bill Davison played the cornet in the same way that the Australian artist Stan Rapotec painted canvases—full of exclamation marks and capitals!

These three great trumpeters were backed by a group of some of Australia's best-known musicians, assembled with the help of my old friend Jack Lesberg the bass player. Jack was another product of our great vintage year, and one of his claims to fame is that he survived the horrendous Coconut Grove nightclub fire in Boston in 1942.

Jack was a versatile musician, as adept in classical music as he was on the jazz scene, and even the great conductor Toscanini acknowledged him as 'one of my favourite bass players'. He had plenty of work in America but moved to Australia after the break-up of his marriage, an experience so traumatic that he told me 'I know we Jews were meant to suffer but this is ridiculous!'

To help him find his feet in Australia I gave him a good deal of work, as bass player and leader of some of the Australian groups playing with my 'imports', and also as tour manager. But Jack felt he should be paid a good deal more for his services than his Australian counterparts, on the theory that he was better known. I had good reason to know the fallacy of this assumption because I had long since discovered, in my speedway promotions, that 'big names' from overseas lost all their glamour after the public had seen them two or three times. Perhaps Jack's problem was that he was trying to pay American alimony on Australian wages, although this did not prevent his re-marriage: to a red-headed public relations girl whom he met first in Colorado during a 'jazz bash'. Finally he returned to America.

I rounded off 1972 with the most impressive and expensive attraction for the year: 'Stars of the Newport Festival', featuring the Dave Brubeck–Gerry Mulligan Quintet on one half of the programme followed by the organist Jimmy Smith's Jam Session. Dave Brubeck featured the unique Paul Desmond on alto-saxophone. Jimmy Smith had Joe Newman on trumpet, Art Farmer on flugelhorn, Illinois Jacquet on tenor, James Moody on tenor and flute, Kenny Burrell on guitar, and Roy Haynes on drums. There will never be another package like that one!

Mulligan brought along his actress wife, Sandy Dennis. They were a particularly pleasant couple, although Gerry could be very prickly on occasion, especially when he was assailed with canned music. This was one of his pet peeves. Immediately he boarded an aircraft on an Australian domestic flight he would ask a stewardess to 'Please turn off the Muzak.' She would think he was joking until he turned on his portable tape recorder so loudly that it drowned out the saccharine music, and told her 'I get on an aircraft to be transported, not entertained!' She would never be sure whether he was joking or not, but it made no difference and he would spend the flight writing a letter of complaint to the management. Canned music is still played on domestic flights.

One day we took the Mulligans to a celebrated Sydney restaurant, where Gerry started on a flow of fascinating stories. Unfortunately he became so excited that he gestured broadly just as the waiter was about to serve his main course. He and my artist friend Louis James shared a particularly juicy casserole in their laps.

Once more it seemed that I was making Australia a gift of fine jazz

TOP: At Father's eightieth birthday party, September 1955. Mother has just said 'The guest of honour is like the ice cream—getting a little soft on top!' BOTTOM: June Jacobsen (*left*) with Robin Abel Smith and Jan Chappel (*Author's photos*)

musicians. By the end of the year I had barely broken even, because four of the six tours had lost money. I licked my wounds throughout 1973 and by the end of that year I was feeling optimistic again and I started off 1974 with a bang. I brought in Charlie Byrd for a return visit, which we titled 'The Great Guitars', with the support of Barney Kessel and Herb Ellis. The name stuck and the Charlie Byrd Trio has recorded and travelled under it ever since.

I was living in Sydney in those days and had let Eurilla to my old friends Joe and Jessica Dames and their family. Whenever I was accompanying a tour I tried to fit in a 'rest day' in Adelaide, and the Dames, who will seize any excuse for a party, always enjoyed entertaining the members of various groups. As far as I'm concerned, Joe's only fault is a tendency to 'sing along' with music. Charlie Byrd, Barney Kessel, and Herb Ellis were induced to play a few tunes on an atrocious instrument belonging to one of my children, and as Barney began to play he announced 'Now, as I get into this tune, if anyone has an irresistible urge to sing all I can say is *don't!*'

Joe, who had already started to fill his lungs in joyous anticipation, collapsed like a pricked balloon!

The three guitarists had a wealth of stories about the world of jazz, especially about Joe Venuti who had been the world's greatest jazz violinist for fifty years until he died at over eighty. Joe was an incurable practical joker, who would do such things as telephoning a tuba player and inviting him to a meeting on New York's busiest intersection, complete with instrument. When the player agreed Joe then telephoned twenty-four more of them, one after another, and then took up a vantage point overlooking the intersection as twenty-five tuba players and their massive brass horns milled around in the lunch-hour crowds looking for Joe Venuti.

When Joe went on the road with the one-armed trumpet player Wingy Mannone he found Wingy's artificial arm an irresistible temptation. Before he went to bed Wingy removed the arm, which has a wooden hand in a white glove, and laid it on the table. Joe crept in and shaved a fraction off the forefinger, and repeated the operation each night. As the tour progressed he got a kick out of Wingy's puzzled expression as he examined the ever-increasing floppiness of the glove's forefinger.

On another tour, with a pianist who complained of a bad back and used a walking stick, Joe filed the bottom of the stick each day. The pianist's complaints became more and more heartrending and he became more and more stooped as the tour progressed, until he was walking almost bent double.

At one stage Venuti was a member of a five-piece group engaged to play at a hotel in the Catskill Mountains, New York State. They found that the hotel was occupied almost entirely by retired folk and that it was desperately dull, and so to give it a little ginger they decided on an unusual game of 'Statues'. Naked, they entered the lift and took it down to the

Top: One more time! Dean Hogarth gets a good view as Kym Bonython goes end for end (*David Brock photo*). Bottom: Publisher Rupert Murdoch awards the winner's sash to Harry Neale after a South Australian title event. Kym Bonython watches in his famous checked cap (*David Brock photo*)

ground floor, where it opened onto the community lounge which invariably was crowded with elderly residents. When the door opened the five musicians froze into a pose, held it for a few moments, and then one of them pressed the button and took the lift up again. They repeated the process five times to an ever-increasing audience.

At one stage in Joe's career he was musical director for the Roy Rogers Show. Roy, the singing cowboy who was famous in the 1940s, toured with his equally famous stallion Trigger. Each show opened with a few songs from Roy, and then he would announce dramatically 'And now . . . here's Trigger!'

On this signal the stallion would prance into the arena, rear on its hind legs, and whinny loudly.

One night, while Roy was vocalising, Joe used his violin bow to stimulate the stallion in an area best left alone. When the horse made its appearance it was in a high state of excitement. The audience received an unforgettable sight — and Joe was sacked!

Another of my favourite jazz stories came from the black comedian Willie Lewis. He told of two musicians, wending their way home after a gig, who decided to pause in a local cemetery and smoke a joint. While they were smoking, the two-ton bell in the nearby church belfry let go and fell with a resounding crash. A couple of minutes later one musician asked the other 'What was that, man?'

After some thought, the other replied 'B Flat!'

I doubt whether that one has any foundation in fact but I can vouch for the truth of a story concerning my mother and Sir Malcolm Sargent. I met the noted British conductor in the 1950s when he was staying at Government House, Adelaide. Sir Robert George, the Governor during that era, had been very friendly with me in my farming days when he and Lady George had visited my 'model farm' at Mount Pleasant, and because he knew of my interest in music he invited me to meet Sir Malcolm. I was astonished by the conductor's ignorance of jazz, which he seemed to feel was epitomised by *Rhapsody in Blue*.

At that time my mother was President of the A.B.C. Orchestral Subscribers' Committee and one of her functions was to introduce guests like Sir Malcolm at parties held in their honour. She brought the house down by announcing 'In order to get some background on Sir Malcolm I looked him up in *Who's Who* and was surprised to find he has eight inches!'

The tour of the Charlie Byrd Trio was a resounding success, no doubt because they played classical and popular music as well as jazz and also because it was a time when guitar music was soaring in popularity.

I followed them immediately with another group with the same sort of appeal, led by the flautist Herbie Mann. It comprised some of the top names from New York studios and also was a great success.

These tours elicited some ecstatic reviews in Australian newspapers,

186

although one of them had the musicians rolling around the floor in mild hysteria. It appeared in the *Advertiser* on the morning after 'The Great Guitars' had presented a fantastic concert at Adelaide's Festival Theatre. The writer was the same journalist who acted as speedway correspondent at Rowley Park, and his review included the phrase 'Barney Kessel's steely fingers spun a silver filigreed web of notes'.

Generally speaking, the Australian press is not well served by its musical critics. The level of reporting that followed the press conferences held for visiting jazz personalities often was abysmal. Perhaps the problem is that, like the speedway correspondent seconded as reviewer of the 'Great Guitars' concert, the journalists have to try to cover too many activities and end by knowing a very little about everything. But it must also be said that the Australian press is notorious among visiting entertainers for its brashness and impertinence, and its failure to do its homework. This lack of professionalism is epitomised in the amusing story of the young woman who asked Dave Brubeck 'How many musicians are there in your quartet, Mr Brubeck?'

A more recent example occurred in 1979. I brought the Count Basie Orchestra back to Adelaide, and even though the Count was nearly seventy-five and had survived a severe heart attack his band sounded better than ever. During an A.B.C. interview I was astounded to hear the would-be knowledgeable reporter ask 'And I suppose, Mr Basie, you can remember the famous marching bands of Kansas City?'

The reporter had laid himself wide open to a sardonic put-down by the famous son of Kansas City, who could have enlightened him to the fact that New Orleans is the place famous for those historic and colourful musicians. But the Count is far too much of a gentleman for that. With a wry smile he gently rubbed his cheek, and said in thoughtful tones 'Why no, now that you come to mention it, I can't say that I *do* remember the Kansas City marching bands!'

Similar ignorance was displayed by a reporter who tried to interview Duke Ellington at Melbourne's Essendon airport. After conducting a rather pointless conversation with the maestro the reporter walked back to his camera crew, and as he passed by me I heard him mutter 'Bloody useless!'

I couldn't resist saying 'If you asked intelligent questions you might get intelligent answers.' Not that it made any difference.

The Charlie Byrd and Herbie Mann tours seemed to augur a brighter future but after they had finished I suffered one disaster after another. My next tour should have been the Gary Burton Quartet with the celebrated jazz violinist Stephane Grappelli. George Wein had negotiated the contract for me, and it was complete except for the vital signature on the dotted line, because George took verbal acceptance as a binding agreement. Others did not look on it in the same way and I was staggered to hear that Grappelli would not accompany Burton. He was to come to Australia soon after but for Clifford Hocking, who was another promoter.

Luckily I enjoyed friendly relations with Clifford, who was well aware of the circumstances, and he was generous enough to allow me a share in the venture. In exchange I gave him an equal share in the package 'Two Generations of Brubeck'. This was a tour by Dave Brubeck and his sons, with other musicians, four weeks after Grappelli's visit.

They were successful in Australia but we lost heavily because I had sold the group 'at cost' to a New Zealand promoter for a tour of that country in return for a *pro rata* division of air fares. This character failed to pay his share. Apparently he invested the profits from the Brubeck tour in another package and lost the lot.

I brought out a gifted young guitarist, Ralph Towner, with the Gary Burton group and they produced some memorable music although it failed to appeal to the general public. When they were in Sydney the English comedian Spike Milligan, who also was appearing there at that time, came to the Town Hall to catch the last few minutes of one of the concerts. My tour organiser Patrick O'Neill, who was working for the Milligan show as well, introduced me to him and he said 'You must be the promoter—you're wearing a suit!'

Dave Brubeck brought along his wife Iola with his sons Chris, Dan, and Darius, who were performing in the band, and his youngest son Michael. It was good to renew acquaintance with this gifted family, of whom Darius had an astonishingly high I.Q. When I was staying with them in San Francisco in the 1960s they were playing baseball in the garden, and when Darius failed to hit the ball I heard him give a learned dissertation on the parabolic curve of the ball's trajectory, and comment 'No mass should have that much inertia.' He was then twelve years old.

Dave was extremely proud of the musical accomplishments of his sons and they certainly reciprocated his feelings. They gave me the impression of being one of the happiest and most closely-knit families I've ever encountered.

Dave's longtime partner, of course, was Paul Desmond. They had played together for more than twenty years and become one of the best-known duos in modern music. Like Dave, Paul was extremely intellectual. A versatile saxophone player, with a tone described as being 'like a dry martini', he had a wit to match. On one of his earliest visits to Sydney he took up with a well-known socialite, who took him home after a concert. Next morning he said that she had 'Ten thousand dollars worth of sound equipment . . . and five hundred rock and roll records!'

I think Paul must have had one of those illegal gadgets fitted to his telephone that enabled him to make international phone calls without paying for them. He was addicted to the telephone and for a year or so he called Keith Bruce and me from New York at all hours of the day and night—and sometimes several times a night. He would first announce that he just returned home, that it was five a.m., and that he was 'slightly smashed', and then tell us that he'd just been speaking to friends in London or Hong Kong or other far-flung parts of the world. His habit came in very handy for me because he willingly acted as my go-between on messages to business acquaintances in America and he would phone their replies back to me later in the day.

Paul was a heavy smoker and eventually he contracted lung cancer. He began a course of ray treatment but decided that the cure was worse than the disease and resigned himself to the inevitable. Despite his illness he did not give up occasional stage or recording appearances with Dave Brubeck, although these became progressively more difficult. I still get a lump in my throat whenever I hear his last breathless performance of *You Can't Go Home Again*, with trumpeter Chet Baker.

He died in 1977 and Iola Brubeck wrote me a touching letter describing his end. On the night before his death he had entertained friends from his bed and Iola said he had never been more considerate, outgoing, and amusing. He knew the end was near and specifically requested no service, no memorial, and no flowers, saying that he did not want to be 'one of those monuments on the way to the airport'. He bequeathed his golden saxophone to Michael Brubeck, and asked that no foundation in his name should be endowed for aspiring musicians. 'There are too many bad saxophone players in the world already,' he said.

Eventually his guests left him, and he died during the night. His body was discovered by the cleaning woman next morning.

I followed the Brubeck visit in 1974 with one more tour for that year. It was that of Rahsaan Roland Kirk, who had a formidable reputation as a musician and also as a 'stirrer'. Blind since childhood, he had the unusual faculty of 'circular breathing' which meant that he could hold a note indefinitely by breathing in through the nose while breathing out through the mouth. Harry Carney of the Duke Ellington Orchestra was one of the few other jazz musicians who possessed this ability.

Kirk's main instrument was the tenor saxophone, but he played several other wind instruments—sometimes three at once! Also he could play a whistle with his nose and he used this to stunning effect. It may sound like a gimmick but he did not employ it as such. Despite his affliction he was a whirlwind of activity and full of unbounded vitality and creativity.

Paul Desmond once told me that he toured Europe with Kirk, who was performing on about six different woodwinds. He carried these draped around him in some incredible manner as they moved from city to city, and Paul, reckoning that he would not notice one more instrument, added his own saxophone to the load.

Kirk's tour began in New Zealand and as soon as he arrived I heard that he had been declared *persona non grata* by Pan-American Airways because

189

he had tipped a tray of food over a stewardess on his flight south from America. This seemed an ominous start but he proved most co-operative once he realised that I was not about to 'rip him off'. Apparently he had had some bad experiences with unscrupulous promoters who took advantage of his blindness.

During his visit he added yet another instrument to his repertoire by quickly mastering the didgeridoo. I understand that the Aborigines also use the technique of circular breathing.

Kirk received an enthusiastic welcome by musical *cognoscenti* but the rest of the public stayed away in droves. During three concerts at the Sydney Town Hall, which can hold 2,300 people, the average audience was only 670. In Adelaide he attracted only 274. It was some slight consolation to hear, after he had returned to America, that he had enjoyed the tour. Apparently this was the rarest of compliments from Rahsaan Roland Kirk, who died of a stroke in 1975, but it did not help the financial situation. I lost $18,000 and would have been even worse off but for a grant of $5,000 from the Australian Council for the Arts, for which I was able to apply as a 'guarantee against loss' because I was no longer a member of the Council.

22

'The Bozz'

FROM FAIRLY humble beginnings Rowley Park became known as one of the premier speedways of the world. By the end of the 1950s, competitors from every corner of the globe raced in the big championship nights. Despite Adelaide's comparatively small population, we were attracting some of the biggest crowds to attend any event in Australia. The speedway was an important part of my life through the 1960s into the early 1970s.

In my role as 'the Cecil B. de Mille of Bowden' I sought continually for better and more exciting attractions to keep the public ever more interested in Rowley Park. Our annual fireworks display drew the biggest crowds.

When I first introduced this form of entertainment I used the services of a famous Sydney company, but as the years went by public interest waned because social clubs and department stores used the same firm. The novelty had worn off. In an attempt to obtain some variety I contacted a Japanese firm, Marutamaya Ogatsu Fireworks Company, who put on an annual show for the New York department store of Macy's.

I saw one of these New York displays, tracked down the operator to his hotel, and arranged for a similar show in Adelaide. However it turned out to be something of a disaster. We had to pay for one of the partners of the firm, plus an assistant, to come to Adelaide from Tokyo. On top of this were the freight and duty charges of bringing the fireworks and other gear from Japan, and we ran into some astonishing hassles with the Customs Department. Also we had to argue with the Mines Department, who control explosives and seemed convinced that I intended to blow up half of Adelaide.

Altogether we paid about five times the amount charged by the Sydney firm, but I looked forward to the great night with keen anticipation. In my book, five times the price equals five times the impact, but it worked out precisely the other way round. The show lasted about one-fifth as long as usual, to the great indignation of a crowd accustomed to the spectacular displays provided by the Australian firm.

But, for me, there was an interesting side-effect. When the Japanese

191

were assembling their display I asked the senior man, Rikio Ogatsu, whether he had served in the second World War. He smiled and nodded politely, and further questioning soon elicited the fact that he was in the navy in the Solomon Islands area. From this it was a short step to learning that he was in a cruiser in the vicinity of Buin/Faisi, on the very night when my squadron attacked a number of Japanese warships and freighters. He had in fact been very close to a ship on which I launched a torpedo. An Australian coast-watcher hiding in the jungle later reported that she had beached herself to avoid sinking.

We talked over this coincidence, and after Mr Ogatsu returned to Japan he sent me a letter which I still treasure. He wrote:

Dear Mr Kym Bonython,
We, writer, wish to thank you so much for your many kindness to us, during stay in your City.
It was really much pleasure to have shown our fireworks under your special kind invitation, and at the same time we are very appreciated that our fireworks brought much splendid and successful effect to your this time plan.
Writer have returned home in well on 16th evening directly from Sydney. It is very regret writer did not write soon after returned to Japan is some cold yet for us came from your nice temperature.
There is coming the Cherry Blossom season in Japan and we would expect to visit Japan at your convenience with your family, Mrs Bonython and mother.
We, writer, would like to hear from you about next nice plan of our fireworks as we could display with our special more luxurious set to fit to your nice race fun and all Adelaide citizen.

This letter almost compensated for the disappointing fireworks!

Such displays were still only a sideline to the main business of Rowley Park and I strove continually to keep the speedway events as exciting and up-to-date as possible. In the mid-1950s we followed the trend by introducing 'smash-and-bash' stock car racing. Any old heap that could still run was fitted with heavy bumper bars, sheets of plate steel, and other types of armour to protect their drivers. However this armour made the cars about three times heavier than normal and they were far from stable. Some of these bombs needed only only the slightest nudge in the middle of a turn to make them roll.

For one season I tried my hand at stock car racing in addition to speed car driving. I drove under the *nom de guerre* of 'Bend Hur' in a flamboyantly-decorated car with one of my 'moo horns' under the bonnet and the Swiss cowbells, which once had adorned my gentle Jerseys, strung across the front of the vehicle.

192

We lined the edge of the track with empty 44-gallon drums, and whenever the competitors seemed to be taking things a little too easy the racetrack officials would roll a few out in front of the thundering chariots. This made a lovely noise and caused a few uproarious moments, but the practice became unpopular with competitors who rode over the drums and ripped the sumps off their cars. Eventually the drivers objected to the expense and we dispensed with these hazards.

To attract drivers into these 'smash-and-bash' races we paid £10 to every driver who fielded a car, and publicity-conscious Bill Hambly-Clark, the Adelaide gunsmith who was for some years a race car owner and occasional driver, decided he would beat the system.

He fielded no less than ten stock cars in one race and walked away with £100, which was a nice piece of money in those days. But, by the end of the race, nine of the cars were in ruins and it must have cost him well over £500 to get them back in order . . . always presuming that he bothered to do so.

Hambly-Clark was a colourful character, famed as a marksman and equally famous—or notorious—as a storyteller. One of his typical yarns was about a safari he conducted to central Australia. Bill, who claimed to be able to hit a sixpence at 100 yards, was at the bottom of a hill when a camel suddenly appeared over the brow. Camels were in plague proportions and regarded as fair game, and so Bill took a snap shot and saw the camel disappear. A moment later its head bobbed up again, and Bill fired once more. Once more the camel disappeared, only to bob up yet again. This happened five times in all and Bill thought he must be losing his grip, but he claims that when he went to the top of the hill and looked over he saw five dead camels piled in a heap!

One of the characters I brought to Australia at the time of smash-and-bash stock car racing was Jerzy Wojtowicz, a Pole who won the V.C. when flying with the R.A.F. during the war.

Jerzy agreed to come to Australia only if he could bring his own stock car with him. The standard of equipment used on English tracks at that time was deplorable, but there was no way to tempt Jerzy unless I agreed to this condition.

His car was an incredible heap of junk and looked as though it was held together with baling wire, but nevertheless he was the most successful stock car drive in England. But when this vehicle arrived by sea freight I had to pay a Customs bond of about £300 before it could be landed in Australia.

Jerzy raced with indifferent success against the faster and lighter Australian machines, but he was a great trier and an expert driver. At the end of his Adelaide session, some interstate promoters were anxious to take advantage of his presence in Australia and asked me to release him. They undertook to provide him with a car on their track, and I unwarily agreed to let Jerzy try his luck. The car the promoters provided was an absolute 'bomb' and it seemed almost that they were trying to make Jerzy come off worst. Their local drivers set about demolishing the Polish champion, and poor Jerzy ended with a fractured skull, a broken arm, a broken leg, and other injuries. It seems that this was the end of his racing career because I was never able to trace him again after his injuries healed and he returned to Britain.

For some reason the Americans always tended to be among the most flamboyant of my imports and I brought in a good many of them over the years. They included Leroy Warriner, Johnny Tolan, Sherman Cleveland, Mike McGreevey, Hank Butcher, and Dick Brown.

Warriner was another driver who had been an American Midget Champion. He had behind him a very successful career in all forms of racing, including Indianapolis. One year he competed in the then famous Mexican Road Race, driving a Studebaker with what was known as 'air bag suspension'. A protruding rock punctured one of the air bags and he was almost unable to turn to the left although he could turn like crazy to the right.

Part of the course took drivers over precipitous mountain roads, unfenced and with sheer drops of thousands of feet. Along one of these stretches Warriner was hotly pursued by a Mexican contestant, who kept banging into his rear bumper bar at high speeds. Warriner's navigator became highly apprehensive about these tactics, but Warriner had motored over the whole course just before the event, to get some idea of the layout, and had a trick up his sleeve.

With the Mexican running hard on their heels they came to the crest of a hill, and Warriner looked down the long dusty downhill grade ahead of them. He asked the navigator 'Don't we come to a little village at the bottom of this grade? With a statue of someone-or-another in the middle of the main street? And a sharp ninety-degree turn to the right at the end of the street?'

The navigator consulted his maps, answered 'Yep!' and Warriner said 'Here's where we get rid of that goddam Mexican!'

He began a series of weaving manoeuvres which threw up an impenetrable dust screen behind him, and when he reached the end of the main street he reefed the steering wheel violently to the right and tore round the sharp corner to the squealing of tyres. The Mexican came after him full bore through the blinding clouds of dust, hit the statue, and disintegrated in a great burst of metal and flying machinery.

I asked Warriner whether the Mexican was killed, and he said 'Hell — there's a lot of them goddam Mexicans.'

I believe the Mexican escaped with fairly minor injuries.

By the time Johnny Tolan came to Australia he was past his prime as a driver, and I understand he spent most of his time in America as a professional cardplayer. He was astounded when he was taken to the Sydney Showgrounds to see his first Australian race just before competing himself.

When he saw the mayhem that took place in those days as soon as the starter's flag dropped, with everyone charging for the first corner with the inevitable accidents and numerous re-starts, Tolan said incredulously 'Hell —once the flag drops everything plumb disappears between one ear and the other. Back home our car owners would shoot them bastards!'

A controversial character who graced the Australian tracks for one season was Bus Brosene, a freelance landscape gardener from the American East Coast. At that time an overseas driver was paid on a flat figure, win, lose, or draw. If he won a race, then he was not paid the prize money offered by the promoter to all entrants. In one Rowley Park title race Tattersall came first, I came second, the current American champion Don Meacham was third, and Brosene was fourth. My imports and I had taken all the places for the main event of the night and so I didn't have to pay out any prize money.

One year I was very taken with a promising youngster racing at the Freeport Track on Long Island, and I tried to persuade him to come to Australia. He was keen to do so but his wife had just produced their first child and so he reluctantly decided against the trip. His name was Mario Andretti, and of course he went on to become one of the biggest prizewinners in the motor racing history of the U.S.A. He won the World Championship in 1978. For years after his ascent into the Big League we bumped into each other now and again around the American or European tracks and laughed about the chance that almost brought him to Australia, for what was really peanuts to a driver of his calibre, instead of going on to become the most famous name in motor racing of his day.

Like all performers, speedway stars occasionally tended to be temperamental. Solo rider Ove Fundin was perhaps an example. He came first to Australia as a member of the official Swedish team, but after that I brought him out several times as an individual performer. On his first Adelaide appearance he objected to some rubber markers set two or three feet back inside the inner border of the track. He claimed these were dangerous, but the danger really came from his technique of riding very close to the inner edge. When rounding a corner he leaned his bike over so far that he tended to strike his left wrist against the rubber markers. After his second race he threatened to return home if the markers were not removed, but the officials would not be pressured and the markers were left in place. On the following Tuesday morning I received a letter from Ove, saying 'By the time you read this, I shall be back in Sweden.' He was!

My 'imports' to speedway played a great part in the success of Rowley Park, but the backbone of speedway in this country is of course the Australian drivers. We have produced plenty of fine drivers such as Ray Revel, Jeff Freeman, the Beasley Brothers, Johnnie Stewart, and Jack Brabham, but one who is perhaps not so well known would rank alongside these famous names. He was Harry Neale, popularly known as 'The Black Prince' because

195

he always drove in black trousers, black pullover, and black helmet. He was perhaps one of the first Australian speedway drivers to be able to live off his earnings from the track.

Once I went with him to Sydney to watch the racing there, a week before his first appearance on that track. When he saw their unique method of starting, with the back markers really standing on their accelerators half a lap before the green flag dropped, he rubbed his hands and said 'This is for me!' There was nothing he liked better than gaining a few yards or car lengths before the race even began.

Harry features in one of my favourite speedway stories. When he was reaching his peak there was a German driver named Werner Greve, an earthmoving contractor who seemed to be quite wealthy. He generally appeared in top class equipment and at this particular time he had just taken delivery of an extra powerful new car. Like all speedway drivers he did not fail to let everyone know how good it was, and he buttonholed Harry and said 'Harry, this new car of mine is so powerful that I can use only *half-throttle!*'

Harry looked at him with the humorous sardonic smirk I remember so well, and drawled 'Yeah, I'm only using half-throttle too . . . the *bottom* half!'

Harry's greatest rival at Rowley Park was Arnie Sunstrom. Harry and Arnie probably were the leading competitors of their day and they gave each other no quarter on the track. 'Sunny' had as many people against him as for him and the same could be said of Harry Neale.

On one night in 1959 these two aggressive drivers collided during the feature race, or 'Butchers' Picnic' as it used to be known. It seemed obvious that neither was prepared to give way to the other, but the collision seemed no worse than the accidents which occurred regularly on the track. Unfortunately, however, Sunstrom's car rolled and he received head injuries which were to prove fatal.

Sunstrom supporters blamed Neale, though I did not see that it was his fault. Harry could just as easily have come off worst. Nevertheless the accident caused a lot of bitterness in both camps, as some blamed him and others defended him.

He was very downcast by what had happened and on the next day I was with him in a hotel near the speedway while he tried to decide whether to visit Sunstrom's widow to pay his respects, which he eventually did.

Ironically, Harry died only a few days later in a very similar accident, while competing in the Western Australian State championships held in Perth. The huge crowd that attended his funeral attested to his great popularity as a man and a sportsman. I feel that Harry could have held his own with any race driver in the world. No one since then has equalled his ability and determination. It is a great pity that he did not have the opportunity to compete on American tracks.

196

Probably 'Dangerous' George Tatnell would be nearest to the modern counterpart of Harry Neale. Tatnell is a great showman in the ocker Paul Hogan tradition, yet he is a skilled and versatile driver who appeared in stock cars, super modified cars, and speed cars, and won several National Championships. His trademark, familiar to Sydney racegoers, is a double-decker bus, and in my racing days he could be relied on to stir up the crowds with his sardonic speeches over the public address systems before and/or after the meetings. I stood too close to him during his speech after a race in which we were both placegetters, and he crowned me with a very creamy sponge cake. 'Anything for a laugh' was George's motto, but after that I kept well away from him.

George was always good value for any promoter. He put on a great show with well-prepared equipment, and if he didn't win he invariably featured in the final placings in important events.

An absolute contrast to 'Dangerous' George was Jack Young, a solo bike rider who twice won the World Solo Championship in the 1950s. He had the kind of skills that made everything look terribly easy. Although he was never a spectacular rider, his clashes with Bob Leverenz and later Peter Craven remain the most talked-about races I ever witnessed.

An Adelaide man, he was an unassuming character who, unlike many of his successors, never attempted to capitalise on his international successes. Apparently he preferred an undemanding position as maintenance worker in a brickyard, and going out fishing in his little dinghy, to the pressures of running some kind of business backed by his speedway fame. Who can blame him?

Most Australian motor cycle racing has been handicap rather than scratch, because of our comparative lack of top-class riders. This enables up to seven riders to start in a race, against the maximum of four permitted when they all start from scratch. The public loved to see the stars make up for their handicaps by tearing a path through the slower riders who'd taken off ahead of them, but it was a mighty dangerous procedure. A lot of visiting riders refused to take part in handicap races, or if they did compete they contented themselves by completing the number of laps without trying too hard to pass.

Jack Scott, John Boulger, and Laurie Hodgson were three riders who seemed equally at home in scratch or handicap races. John, who was many times South Australian and Australian champion, was justifiably the idol of the crowd, but poor young Laurie was never able to fulfil his early promise. He had a disastrous accident when passing a slower rider, fractured his spine, and became a paraplegic.

The public is always greedy for thrills and maybe we Australian promoters pandered to them by staging 'mixed programmes' instead of the single-class contests featured overseas. There they will have solo motor bikes one night, stock cars another night, then speed cars, and so on. In

Australia we put on a real Roman Games display with five or six different sections on the programme each night.

I'm often asked whether the races were 'rigged', but with one exception I don't know that this was ever done. Normally, the nearest we'd get to it was on such occasions as when we had Jack Young and Peter Craven riding against each other. I used to tell them 'Win one each and then go for your lives on the third,' but this was done to keep spectator excitement at its peak.

The race that I do believe was rigged was an official Australian Solo Championship. The prize was offered under a new system whereby each promoter put in a lump sum at the start of the season, supplemented by funds from a well-known firm. Each State was to hold a qualifying round and the winners of each of these rounds were to meet in a Grand Final. This was held in a different State capital each year.

When Adelaide's turn came, the current World Champion arrived at the airport on the morning of the big race. He was an overseas competitor of great renown and we greeted him accordingly, but he soon made it plain that he expected a guarantee of $500 in addition to his chance at the night's prize money.

The prize was unprecedentedly high, the riders' transportation from each State was covered by the promoters' contribution to the fund, and the winners of each State final, such as this new arrival, already had pulled down big prizes. This new demand simply was not on, but I was reluctantly obliged to back down on the argument. Big publicity for the meeting had been built around the appearance of the World Champion and I felt he might find some excuse to to pull out.

The Grand Final was staged over a series of heat races, and the highest points scorer for the night was to be named as the new official champion. It was a close-fought contest and the World Champion tied with a notable local competitor, each with an equal number of points. This meant a run-off to settle it.

When the tapes went up, the World Champion shot off to a handy lead but he'd gone no more than fifty yards before he leaned down and fiddled with his carburettor. This gave his opponent the opportunity to shoot past and from then on he was never headed. The World Champion lost.

Soon after that, it became common knowledge that the two riders had arranged a deal. The World Champion took not only the extra guarantee he had extorted from me, but the prize money to boot. His opponent, now officially crowned Australian Champion, was glad to hand it over because the win meant that he could demand extra appearance money every time he raced during the coming season.

To my knowledge this kind of rigging was extremely rare, but it certainly did not reflect well upon the riders involved. Maybe there would have been more rigging on motor cycle racing if betting had been officially allowed, but since it was not, the majority of races were run solely on merit — apart from some moments of minor violence. An occasional lashing out with a steel boot, toe to the shin, or closing a gap, or forcing an opponent out towards the safety fence, were fairly common occurrences, especially on 'Test Match' nights when the Australian Kangaroos met their traditional enemies, the British Lions.

Once each season we ran a charity night, with a Powder Puff Derby as one of its features. My wife Julie and her friend Andy Thorpe, a radio talk-back personality, both tried out for starting berths in one of these races. After Julie's practice run she came in somewhat excited and short of breath, but was rather deflated when I asked why she'd been going so slowly that the car seemed about to stall. Apparently the excitement had made her feel that she was travelling at great speed.

The Powder Puff Derbies were stopped when a car went out of control, hit the fence, and burst into flames. Luckily the driver had enough presence of mind to slip her safety harness and dive out of the window an instant before the car exploded, but the incident was enough to cause the Racing Drivers Association to ban such events in South Australia.

Such novelty events were crowd-pleasers, especially when media personalities competed, but as equipment became more sophisticated and expensive, so the professional drivers became more reluctant to lend their cars to amateurs. Gradually such events disappeared from speedway programmes.

Quite early in my speedway career I took part in one of the 'Crazy Nights' featured by Empire Speedways, who devoted the proceeds to charity. This one was held in Brisbane, where I contested a match race with the local champion and managed to beat him across the line.

Contestants in the Crazy Nights received all kinds of weird and wonderful prizes instead of money, and when I pulled up at the starting line to receive my trophy I was somewhat alarmed to be presented with a twelve-foot carpet snake plus a long narrow box pierced with ventilation holes.

Jack Self, my Rowley Park manager, was towing my speed car back to Adelaide while I headed south in order to collect a ski boat in Sydney. I had arranged to tow it to Melbourne for my old friend Mal Hastie, who had bought the boat from the New South Wales speedboat champion Grace Walker. The snake travelled with me in his box on the back seat.

I reached Mal's Toorak home at about ten p.m. and mooed my horn for him to come out and take over his new plaything. He admired it for a while, then climbed into the cockpit and started the engine. When he descended I produced the snake box in order to show the reptile to Mal and his family, but the moment I opened the lid the snake slithered swiftly over the edge and tried to escape down the road. I managed to grab the end of it and coil it back into the box, with visions of alarmed Toorak-ites phoning the police about cows mooing, speedboats revving, and snakes crawling down the streets of their quiet suburb.

Before I continued the journey to Adelaide I thought the snake must be getting hungry, and went to a pet shop to buy it some white mice. They could provide only a couple of white rats, and in the belief that snakes customarily gulp their dinners alive and whole I put them into the box. But every time I peered through the ventilation holes, I could see only the white rats licking the face of the apparently contented snake.

After that I began to worry about the white rats getting hungry. As soon as I returned to Mount Pleasant I solved the problem by opening the box in the presence of the dairy cat, who made short work of the rats.

Eventually I realised that the snake was in its hibernation period and I stowed it on top of a bag of grain. It slept motionless, accumulating layers of dust, until monthly herd-testing day. This is of vital importance to a stud-breeder because it gives official proof of the productivity of each cow. The government tester measures the quantity of butterfat produced that day, and when this is multiplied by the days of that month a simple formula provides the annual yield.

I never allowed visitors to the dairy on herd-testing days, so that nothing would disturb the normal milking routine. I prepared for that particular day with the usual care, and all went well until four-thirty a.m. when I went out into the dark to bring the herd in for milking. With the cows in the yard I was preparing the milking machines to begin operations when I heard strange disturbances. I peered out into the darkness and saw the cows wheeling fearfully away from the fence.

Closer inspection revealed my friend the snake. It had come out of hibernation, wrapped itself round the top rail of the fence, and was hissing aggressively at cows which came near. With some regrets I fetched my old R.A.A.F. revolver and despatched the snake to that green haven to which all snakes ultimately depart.

This happened around the time when I was thinking of taking over the lease of Rowley Park. On one of my numerous visits I was a trifle disturbed to hear my predecessor, Alf Shields, address the crowd as 'pie eaters' over the public address system when they expressed dissatisfaction with some aspect of the night's programme. Heaven knows the derivation of this ockerism, but it is an expression of supreme contempt and I thought it was no way to speak to paying customers.

Nearly twenty years later I used it myself, with even more feeling than Alf put into his voice. It happened after one evening's feature race, in which I was joint back marker with Bill Wigzell—the man who was passenger in *Bullo-Bee I* during my close shave in that boat. During the race, Bill and I in our separate cars were trying to force our way through into the lead when a slower car spun directly in front of me and stalled diagonally across the track. I took my foot off the throttle to avoid a collision, but Bill Wigzell, with his foot flat to the floor, hit my car a glancing blow, bounced off, and slammed into the safety fence with his car already half rolled over.

Wigzell was far more popular with speedway fans than I was, and his supporters emitted a great outcry of boos and jeers. Apparently they thought I had deliberately caused their champion to crash, in an accident which could have injured him severely and certainly knocked him out of the running for that night.

My blood boiled. I strode to the microphone and said 'Many years ago I was a bit upset to hear the promoter of the day refer to you people as "pie eaters". After tonight, so far as I'm concerned, I think you're *bloody* pie eaters!'

Thereafter 'Pie eater' became my second name. Whenever I passed among the crowds there was an undercurrent of mumbled 'Pie eater' from all sides—I trust not entirely without affection. Sometimes when I pulled up at a city traffic light the driver of the car next to me would mouth 'Pie eater!'

It became as much of a trademark as my checkered cap, which I adopted early in my promotional career. I bought my first in a sporting goods shop in New York, and replenished my supplies on subsequent occasions. But the store vanished and was replaced by a skyscraper, and my cap situation was in dire straits until I had the brainwave of asking one of my gallery artists to silk-screen a checkered pattern onto a piece of satin. I sent this to London's most famous hatters, Herbert Johnson of Bond Street, with an order for six caps to be made up from the material. They complied, although I felt on a subsequent visit to England that they considered it to be somewhat beneath them. Nevertheless I always got a kick from reading 'By Appointment to Her Majesty the Queen' stitched to the lining of the caps they produced for me.

Cap and nickname both played a part in the love-hate relationship between me and the Rowley Park fans. The whole speedway ethos, like that of most spectator sports, was that of enabling the audience to become violent partisans of one contestant or another and relieve their own frustrations by screaming praise or abuse . . . and vicariously living the thrills and terror of the races and the crashes. As an Adelaide man once said about trotting races: 'I don't specially want anybody to have an accident, but if there is one then I like to see it.'

The love-hate relationship was expressed in a poem which once appeared in a speedway journal:

THE BOZZ

Christmas has been and gorn,
The goose ain't what 'e was,
Speedway is on again ya know,
And Kym is still the bozz.

He mightn't drive for quite a while,
Since his latest bit of strife,

Ya sent him up real good that night,
But ya shoulda heard his wife!

Mrs B's been helping ya
To keep him orf the track,
But if speedway's in ya blood
Ya just keep on comin' back.

He's tried real hard to please ya,
The pie-eatin', booing crowd,
He couldn't hear his motor rev
'Cos ya boo's were all too loud.

I'll be glad if he don't come back
In case he hits the fence.
His value as a promoter
Makes a heap lot more o' sense.

So leave the cars to the Maltby's,
The Braendlers, Hogarths and the likes.
If ya gotta ride the Rowley track,
Then get a bloody trike.

As the years at Rowley Park went by I had at least one firm supporter and right-hand man. He was Jack Self, who was secretary of the Racing Drivers Association when I took over the speedway. He had a job in a confectionery factory, but I asked him to become my manager when I took over the lease of the track. He stayed with me until we sold out in 1972, and I must give him a lot of credit for our promotional successes.

Jack had a severe manner but a soft heart which he kept well hidden from the public. Like me, he was something of a perfectionist and he would work astonishingly long hours. When a meeting was scheduled he would water the track at two or three a.m. each morning for several days beforehand, and he looked after track grading, maintenance, running the canteen, making up the prize-money envelopes, and even such tasks as cleaning out the latrines. In fact he took over all heavy toil and left me free for promotional and administrative activities. The phrase 'Jack of all trades' must have been inspired by him.

But not all his efforts were successful. A client of my Adelaide gallery wanted a painting hung in her house, and I asked Jack to look after it for me. Off he went with his tool box to her home in fashionable Medindie. He plugged the wall on which the painting was to be hung and generally made a good job of it—but the client rang me irately to say that plaster from the other side of the wall, in the adjoining room, had broken away and fallen onto her carpet. Suppressing any remarks about the inferior quality of her walls I agreed to re-plaster and re-paint the entire wall, which effectively wiped out any profit from the sale of the painting.

Jack agreed with me in my efforts to keep speedway events running in a streamlined professional manner, and he stood no nonsense. I never tolerated competitors coming out onto the track half-dressed, or imposing unnecessary delays between races, and I insisted that competitors and officials alike should recognise they were employed in 'show business' and that it was up to them to put on a proper face for the crowds.

I had a few bad experiences in this respect, including one involving a group of bike riders led by Ivan Mauger and consisting almost entirely of current and former world champions. Unfortunately, because of an air strike, Ivan wasn't with them when they came to Adelaide and their track attitude was deplorable. I was distressed that riders of such vast experience and success should pay so little attention to the basics of speedway presentation, but perhaps they had become 'big headed' and felt they need not bother about the public which had made them successful.

I engaged Mauger to race in Australia for a whole season soon after I took over Rowley Park. To supplement his then rather modest earnings as a speedway rider I introduced him to a friend, Fred Holyoak, who was joint Managing Director of John Dring, the big Adelaide transport firm. Ivan spent some years in Adelaide, working as a truck driver during the day and a speedway rider at night, and I think it is fair to claim that he developed into a world class competitor by coming up through the ranks of Rowley Park. In fact he gratefully acknowledges the fact in his autobiography, written in the days when, as a rider, he was earning as much in one night as he would have earned in a year as a truck driver.

Among the many spectacular events I staged at Rowley Park was a series of races by Harry Neale against a jet car imported from New Zealand, in the days when jet engines were a novelty. The jet car really was something of a gimmick. There was no doubt that it would wind up to an impressive speed on a long open stretch, but it was unsuited to a limited circumference track. However, it looked great and made an awe-inspiring noise when first fired up. One's abdomen actually vibrated uncomfortably from the impact of the deafening sound waves emitted by the huge exhaust.

On the track, I had Harry come up close on the outside of the jet car, The 'races' undeniably were crowd-pleasers. To the spectators it seemed that Harry was going through a wall of flame, the blast from the jet car's exhaust, to take over the lead.

Noise always was a great problem at Rowley Park. It was situated in a closely-populated area and several attempts were made to close down the operation because of the disturbance to local people. One of these resulted in an inspection of the speedway by the then Chief Justice, Sir Mellis Napier. It remained open, but strict conditions on hours of use and noise levels were imposed. The latter were difficult to enforce because noise is one of the definite attractions of speedway. Spectators love the full-throated roars of

203

open exhausts, especially from the Vincent side-car outfits, the Offenhauser speed cars, and the massive Chevrolet super modified power plants.

When I first visited the Freeport Speedway, near New York, I was surprised by the comparative silence. Obviously promoter Duke Donaldson had had similar restraints put on him by local authorities. As I walked through the entrance the predominant sound was the tyre-squeal on the pavement track. There was hardly any engine noise. The engines were silenced by baffles in the exhausts, and these were checked by speedway officials at the start of each meeting. I felt it took something away from the traditional speedway atmosphere in which the bellow of powerful motors, the heavy aroma of racing fuel, and a haze of dust all blend into an exciting mixture.

Undoubtedly the Rowley Park noise travelled a long way. My brother Jack lived about a mile away, but only a few hundred yards from the public swimming pool complex in the North Adelaide parklands. He complained about the noise from the pool's public address system, and soon after that the lessee of the pool, swimming identity Tom Herraman, called on me. Almost apologetically he explained the situation and said 'I've been taking decibel readings of the noise levels. On a normal pool night the reading is only thirty-four. But last Friday night I took a reading from the same place while there was a speedway meeting at Rowley Park, and the reading went up to ninety!'

Needless to say I was on the telephone as soon as Tom Herraman left my office, to beg Jack to 'call off the dogs'. I had enough worries without my own brother stirring the pot.

One of these was my long-delayed realisation that I was missing out on one of the most profitable of promotional activities: the catering rights. When I took over Rowley Park I unwisely leased these to various organisations, which had been quietly coining money over the years. At last I managed to take them back under my own wing and I found that the profits from selling soft drinks, pies, pasties, and similar items far exceeded those from the gate money. By then attendances had already started to decline because more and more people were staying at home to watch 'the box' instead of thrilling to real adventures.

But my speedway years were good ones. There can be few spectator sports that drew more people than speedway racing, although it received minimal support from the media. The chiefs-of-staff certainly did not understand its popularity. Occasionally I enticed one of the big shots down to the track and we received extra coverage for a little while but it soon declined again.

Gradually my involvement in Rowley Park became more complicated, especially since I had to combine it with my gallery and entrepreneurial activities. A fellow promoter, Frank Arthur, often tried to persuade me to retire from racing and I actually did so—six times! But 'the show must go on' and I still felt some obligation to keep the speedway functioning, even to the extent of putting on numerous stars who did no more than improve the spectacle, although a lesser display would have drawn the same crowds. As so often in my life the inclination to do the right thing has been to the detriment of my bank balance.

At last, in 1973, I decided the time was coming for me to pull out, although I think that year was one of the highspots in South Australian speedway. Our competitors held three out of the five national titles, with John Boulger as Solo Champion, Len Bowes as Side-Car Champion, and Bill Wigzell as the Super Modified Champion.

When I decided to leave Adelaide to live in Sydney we were operating Rowley Park on a three-year lease with a three-year option to renew, and I put my interest on the market by offering the existing lease, which had about eighteen months to run, to any prospective buyer. Almost immediately the Soccer Association which owned the ground advised me that the lease would not be renewed. Apparently they had some plan for the area — possibly to sell it for industrial use. The result, of course, was that I halved my asking price for fixtures such as the boundary fences, grandstands, safety fences, floodlights, sheds, and so on, together with such equipment as trucks and graders.

Whatever plans the Association may have had, they did not carry them through. Instead, they successfully renewed the lease on a year by year basis to two different groups of promoters. This procedure continued for at least six years after I sold the lease and I lost many thousands of dollars in revenue.

But, to quote the famous song, 'I regret nothing.' I have countless memories of those crowded days, both good and bad, and I treasure all of them. Memories of people, such as the aptly-named 'Wild Tim' Hocking with his wooden leg, which got him into trouble more than once. One story about him alleges that he used it literally to browbeat a motorist with whom he argued after some traffic hassle on the Port Road. Probably his most memorable speedway effort was when his wooden leg became stuck in the throttle when he was leading the field. His car spun around and charged directly against those pursuing him, and by some miracle of violent evasive action they all missed him.

And there was Gordon Schubert, who raced under the name of 'Joe Blow' because he didn't want his mother to know about his speedway activities. Probably Joe was the only competitor at Rowley Park to have been 'on his head' more often than I was — a dubious distinction! He had a 'dent knocking shop' and so could fix up his own cars after accidents. They were always a picture, although Laurie Jamieson's would have put them in the shade. Laurie was a member of a renowned speedway family and his career spanned more than forty years. He wisely turned to car racing and owned some of the most beautiful race cars ever seen in this country. Even today he

205

will sometimes pull the covers off his Offenhauser and do battle with the youngsters.

Talking about people, there would be countless stories to tell about my adventures on and off the speedway with my old friend Jack Murray. I've recounted a few of them and I'll round them off with the one about the Boulia Fly Veil.

The flies are bad up Boulia way. It is a one-horse town in south-west Queensland, and at the end of the day the shearers would gather in the local pub for a few beers. Their faces would be black with flies, which clustered round their mouths and got in their ears, noses, and eyes. So they invented the 'Boulia Fly Veil'. All they had to do was cut the seats out of their pants, so that the flies congregated lower down the body and left their faces alone.

At least that's the way Jack tells it — and he swears it's true!

Apart from people, many of my memories involve cars. The most unusual car I bought during twenty-odd years of racing was one built by Frank Kurtis, the American designer. I bought it from Leroy Warriner. The Adelaide press christened it 'The Wonder Car' and if the track suited it then it was unbeatable. But it had been designed for paved track racing, not dirt tracks, and it didn't do so well at Rowley Park.

Its most unusual feature was the position of its four-cylinder Offenhauser engine. It was set to one side, so that the driver's legs were alongside it instead of each side of the engine as is usual in race cars.

The principal problem with the Wonder Car was that you never knew whether it was going to turn to the left as you went into the first corner, or whether it would go straight ahead into the safety fence. This could be quite a disadvantage, not only for myself, but also for those who were close behind me.

On one of the several times I retired I sold it to Bill Goode, a Brisbane promoter and fellow driver. He said gleefully 'I'll get it to handle — no trouble!' but I was rather amused to hear that on its first time out on the Brisbane Showgrounds it went straight into the fence, breaking the driver's arm and doing itself a severe mischief. I understand that it is something of a 'bitser' now, which is a pity because it used to be the prettiest car in Australia.

I suppose my real farewell to racing was in 1976. I was living in Sydney then, and the promoters of the Liverpool Speedway staged a race for 'Golden Oldies'. I was one of ten or eleven veteran drivers, including such people as Frank Brewer, Ray Oram, the Cuneen Brothers, and Len Brock.

We drew for positions, and Len, who gained number eleven, was actually about 100 yards in front of the man on the pole. For ten laps the action was fast and furious, especially since most of us were driving on a paved track for the first time. But by the closing stages we were lapping only half-a-second slower than the current professionals.

Ray Oram and I had a ding-dong battle. We crossed the line in a dead heat, but still some distance behind Len Brock. At the presentation after the event, I grabbed the microphone from the promoter and said 'Nothing's changed! I protest that Brock jumped the start!' That was one of Brock's favourite ploys in days gone by.

We all treated the race as quite a joke but there was some precedent to my experience with Len Brock. About fifteen years earlier I had contracted him to come over to Rowley Park from Perth, where he had been competing. On the night he should have appeared at Rowley Park the meeting was washed out by heavy rain, and Len sought out Jack Self to claim his guaranteed appearance money. However, he did not know that my brother-in-law, then manager of an Adelaide transport firm, had told me that Len's car was still en route from Perth. He could not have competed in any event.

Len did not know the transport manager was related to me, and had told him not to tell me about this situation. It was hard luck for Len, but I vowed never to employ him on my track again and although he was an excellent and spectacular driver I stuck to this resolution.

People often asked me why I had an apparently irresistible urge to risk my neck in speedway racing. I found it hard to answer. Certainly it perturbed my family, and on the single occasion I persuaded my father to come to Rowley Park he turned his back on the track whenever I was racing. I am of a somewhat superstitious nature and always read the horoscope column in any paper I pick up, and one night before entering a big championship event I was slightly alarmed to read that I should 'stay out of heavy traffic late tomorrow night'.

Instantly I envisioned that mad dive into the first corner of a feature race, with fifteen or twenty cars bumping wheels and forcing a hazardous passage through the wall of dirt thrown up by slower cars in front. I've always been very much aware of the risks, but I suppose they enabled me to 'let off steam'—as other people might do through drinking or smoking or some other occupation. Or perhaps I found it necessary somehow to 'prove myself'. I'm no psychoanalyst, but sometimes I feel I may have subconscious guilts about my wartime contribution. Many of my friends, whom I truly believe to have been more worthy than myself, died in thus proving themselves, while I was one of the lesser heroes who was inexplicably spared.

But, whatever the reason may have been, I certainly had a lot of fun.

23

'I Gotta Right to Sing the Blues'

IT SEEMED that my slogan as a promoter of jazz tours of Australia should be 'musically great—financially disastrous'. After the failure of the tour by Rahsaan Roland Kirk I was obliged to cancel a tour by the Charles Mingus group, which was a great pity because Mingus was only slightly less important than Duke Ellington in the jazz world.

Another of my bad guesses for 1974 was the importation of a marvellous white American traditional jazz band led by the trombonist Turk Murphy. On various trips to America I had enjoyed his music in places as far apart as San Francisco, Las Vegas, and Washington, D.C., but I was much mistaken when I thought that Australian audiences would share my enthusiasm even though I tried to boost flagging interest by adding the singer Judith Durham, formerly of The Seekers. Turk played my kind of music, but the tour was yet another disaster . . . which is strange when you recall that the phenomenally successful movie *The Sting* featured exactly the kind of music for which Turk was renowned.

Financially bloody, but still unbowed, I started 1975 with 'The LA 4', a superb quartet of studio musicians from Los Angeles. Bud Shank played saxophone and flute, Laurindo Almeida the guitar, Ray Brown was on bass, and Shelly Manne on drums. Brown and Shank were very businesslike and a trifle uptight, but it would be hard to find two more easy-going and affable personalities than Almeida and Manne. When Joe and Jessica Dames invited them to lunch at Eurilla they gave me one of my highspots of a lifelong involvement with music. Laurindo Almeida played an impromptu guitar recital which held us all spellbound.

But the magic of their music was not powerful enough to cast a spell on Australian audiences and I began to seek a little desperately for 'non-jazz' performers whom I could import in order to raise money to finance further jazz tours. Maybe I should have known better, because I had already experienced a 'bad scene' when I ventured out of the field of jazz.

This was when I brought out Chuck Berry, the black American rock

TOP: A fateful practice run for Swedish riders. Roger Forsberg and Gote Nordin press on regardless while Arne Carlsson lies unconscious on the track in the background (*David Brock photo*). BOTTOM: Sick parade at Rowley Park 1957. Sidecar riders Bruce Kelley, Morrie Hoy, and Bruce Thomas watch the action from the infield with Kym Bonython (*David Brock photo*)

TOP LEFT: Stock car racing at Rowley Park, with 'Bend-Hur' (in lead) executing a favourite manoeuvre. BOTTOM LEFT: Some members of the Australian Council for the Arts, Sydney 1973. *From left* Dr R. Downing, Kym Bonython, Ken Tribe, John Baily, Caroline Jones, Prime Minister Gough Whitlam, Dr H. C. Coombs (Chairman), David Williamson
TOP: The Paddington site as it was in 1967 before the Bonython Gallery was built there.
BOTTOM: A corner inside the Gallery

and roller who had been a big name in the 1950s and was bouncing back into the limelight. Barry Coburn and I combined to bring him to Australia and New Zealand, with Barry handling the latter country. To say that negotiations were horrific would be an understatement.

I had to guarantee him four nights in Australia for a total of $20,000 and pay all his expenses. This was not out of court, but Berry did not believe in banks and apparently did not trust me. I had to pay him the $20,000, in United States banknotes, before he would even leave Los Angeles.

He made this demand only a week before he was due to arrive and it caused real problems. Normally the Reserve Bank insists that performers' fees should be withheld at least until they arrive in Australia, and the usual method of payment is by irrevocable letter of credit. I had to do a lot of fast talking before the bank authorities would waive regulations and allow me to pay Berry in advance, in cash.

But we hadn't finished with him yet. His next demand was that Barry Coburn should meet him in Tahiti with a sack of notes to pay for the New Zealand appearances. If Coburn did not arrive with the cash, then Berry said he would take the next flight from Tahiti back to Los Angeles.

On top of this, he demanded another air ticket from Los Angeles to Australia, for his 'daughter'. His daughter did not arrive and we never saw the ticket again, so I can only presume that Berry cashed it and pocketed the proceeds.

We satisfied all his demands, and after he had made the New Zealand tour he arrived alone in Melbourne late one day. I was prepared for anything by that time and so I hardly flinched when he told me, almost without preliminaries, 'The way I work is this. You tell me what time I'm due to go on stage. I'll play for forty-five minutes after that time. If I can't make it on stage for say thirty minutes after that time, and it's no fault of mine, then I'll play for fifteen minutes and then walk off!'

The next hitch was that the vast battery of amplifiers and speakers that had come with him from New Zealand could not be cleared by Customs. The aircraft was late and the Customs officers finished for the day before it was unloaded . . . and Berry's first Australian concert was scheduled for that night.

More fast talking followed. I telephoned contacts in Canberra and the sound gear ultimately was released, but it was still in the airport, fifteen miles from the concert hall, only twenty minutes before the concert was due to start.

Some people said I should not have scheduled Berry's first concert for the night of his arrival. The facts are that his contract called for 'four concerts in four days' and on the morning of the fifth day he was going to fly back to America.

Eventually the concert got under way ninety minutes late, with technicians frantically assembling the sound equipment while a local group

TOP LEFT: Bob Dickerson with his painting 'The Escalator' Adelaide 1959. TOP RIGHT: Brett Whiteley with his daughter Arkie. This photograph of the artist was taken in London in 1966. BOTTOM: Arthur Boyd with one of his 'Bride' series of paintings, Melbourne 1957 (*Author's photos*)

played the first 'half'. When intermission came I felt that all problems had at last been solved, until Berry coolly demanded an extra $2,000 for the late start. Otherwise, he said, he would not go on.

I had no option but to pay up. There was no way I could go out and tell a huge audience that Berry wouldn't appear because he had demanded more than I was contracted to pay him. They'd have slaughtered me.

By that time, Berry had not even met the three Australian musicians I'd engaged to accompany him. His sole instructions from America had been 'Tell them to listen to my record *The Best of Chuck Berry*,' and when he met them he said only 'Watch my left leg and my right elbow.'

With that he went on stage and knocked everyone dead! Oddball or not, he was a great performer.

Berry's one and only press conference in Australia was scheduled for the following morning. I had told him about this within minutes of his arrival, and handed him a typewritten itinerary on which it was programmed. TV crews from all channels turned up well in advance of time, but Berry did not. I had to cajole him, and pay him some more money, before he condescended to appear. By that time half the reporters had left in disgust. He informed the remainder that the promoter had neglected to tell him about the press conference, and that he was late because he had to do his hair.

The compensation for this kind of behaviour was that he was a fantastic success. He played to an audience of about 14,000 on his two nights in Melbourne and to a capacity audience at Adelaide's Apollo Stadium, where fans were so enthusiastic that they smashed a good many of the seats.

In his Adelaide hotel he spotted an attractive girl and tried to attract her attention by raising a forkload of spaghetti towards his mouth and then, as though hypnotised by her beauty, carrying it on past his shoulder and tipping it down the back of his suit. But he was certainly not crazy when it came to money. During the Adelaide intermission he put the hard word on me again and once more I had to pay up.

I shed no tears when I saw Berry off at Adelaide Airport. The contract enabled me to feature him in another concert but I had been unable to find a suitable indoor site and had 'sold' him to another promoter who took a chance on Sydney's unpredictable weather and put him on outdoors in the Sydney Showgrounds. It turned out to be a perfect night and the entrepreneur did more business in one night than I had in three. But I had no complaints because I did very well out of Chuck Berry . . . at least financially.

I'm told that the Sydney promoter also was hit with the ultimatum for more money during the intermission. But when Chuck was proceeding through departure formalities at Sydney airport, a Customs officer asked to look into his hand bag and found it stuffed with Australian notes, which he promptly confiscated under the currency regulations.

Chuck Berry was my first venture outside jazz, but in March 1975 I arranged a tour by the American pianist Peter Nero and his trio. Nero had been twice to Australia, both times with great success. Technically he was superb, but his music was so mannered and so full of drum rolls and melo-dramatic climaxes—especially when he played selections from that com-mercial warhorse *Jesus Christ—Superstar*—that to me it seemed empty of genuine emotion. Apparently the public was beginning to feel the same way about him because his third visit attracted only mediocre audiences.

Nero was a pleasant enough person, well aware of the power of the press and very ready to make himself available. During his tour I had the temerity to suggest that his public might appreciate a bracket of straight-forward classical pieces, but this did not go down very well.

By 1975 I had had ten losers and the world was in the grip of inflation. All the entrepreneurial costs (air fares, hall hire, advertising and promotion, hotel bills, and of course the performers' fees) were escalating alarmingly. Even I got the message at this point, though I made a last attempt to subsidise future jazz tours by making several phone calls to the management of the British pop group 'The Bay City Rollers'. Perhaps I was rather half-hearted in my efforts but in any case I was convinced that 'there ain't no justice' when their management told me 'We don't know whom we will come to Australia for but whoever it is there must be full houses and a *lot* of noise from the audience. Frankly they're not very good musicians and they mustn't be heard too well!'

I was still tempted to risk another jazz venture and played with the idea of bringing out the trumpeter Miles Davis. To my ageing ears the music he played in the 1950s and 1960s showed him at his peak, but I knew that he had a large following in Australia apart from people of my own age who had admired his earlier recordings.

I was aware that Davis shared a common conviction of musicians and visual artists that the way he presented a piece was the only way it should be done, and that he was even more fanatical than others, to the point of being violently outspoken about other music and musicians, but I was prepared to risk such individuality.

But when I talked it over with Charlie Bourgeois, George Wein's Number One man who had visited Australia several times as road manager for artists I imported, I was given a convincing reason for forgetting the idea. Charlie is an entertaining bachelor whose sense of humour is very much to my taste and we always had a ball together. When I asked him about Davis he took off his hat to reveal his glistening bald pate and said 'See that? I got it that way trying to get through a Miles Davis tour of Europe! Whenever the curtain went up I'd never know whether Miles was even in the same *country* as I was, never mind in the same *theatre*!' So I gave the idea away.

My public participation in the Australian jazz scene seemed to be on the wane in every direction. Early in 1975 I read in the Sydney *Sun* that my A.B.C. jazz broadcasts were to be wound up, as part of budget cuts enforced by the declining economy. This was the first I'd heard of it, and it seemed an odd way to end a programme then in its thirty-ninth year, so I telephoned the Commission to find out what was happening. I was reassured that the newspaper had got its facts wrong. Only forty-eight hours later, the man I contacted rang me in some embarrassment to confirm that my own broadcasting was indeed to be terminated.

Together with Eric Child and Arch McKirdy I was one of three men to whom the A.B.C. had entrusted the spreading of the jazz gospel. No doubt the Assistant General Manager, Dr Clement Semmler, had had something to do with this wide coverage. The other two men both had conducted regular jazz broadcasts for the A.B.C. over a number of years, and I certainly had no reservations about my time being taken over by Eric Child, who has an encyclopaedic knowledge of the subject far superior to my own. But I did not take very kindly to this undercover manner of easing me off the programme.

Eventually I received a letter from the A.B.C. top brass, apologising for the way the situation had been handled and thanking me for my many years of broadcasting service — possibly a world record in my particular subject. The affair left a bad taste in the mouth but I suppose it was fairly typical of bureaucratic organisations.

But, once again, I have no regrets. Jazz has been an integral part of my life and it has brought me countless good friends. Many are world-famous: others are known only to other jazz *aficionados*. They include Les Strand, an organist who made three long-playing records for the American Fantasy label. Probably not more than two or three out of every thousand jazz addicts ever would have heard of Les but I think he should be up there among the greats. I made my first personal contact with him when I had a few minutes to spare while waiting for a flight at Chicago's O'Hare airport. I found his name, listed as 'Musician', in the phone book, and gave him a call. He was delighted to hear from someone from as far away as Australia who liked or even knew about his music, especially since so few Americans recognised his talents.

Two years later he invited me to stay with him and his family in Chicago, and I was touched that he had moved his two teenage girls out of their bedroom so that we could share the room and talk jazz until we fell asleep. We got along famously . . . but he makes better noises at the keyboard than he does during his sleep. I'm told that my performance in that way is pretty good too.

Les is a type that I know only too well: an uncompromising perfectionist. He knows what the public wants, and he knows the kind of music he wants to play. He's not prepared to compromise the latter for the sake of the former, even though it means that he has not had a booking for many years. He makes his living teaching and arranging music while his wife holds down a full-time job in a union office.

Jimmy Smith, the world's most celebrated jazz organist, described Les in *Downbeat* magazine as the 'Art Tatum of the Organ'. In 1971 he won an international contest sponsored by the Yamaha Company for organists from all over the world, culminating with a grand finale in Tokyo. Nevertheless he is still neglected . . . and still he will not lower his standards.

I admire people like that, although it gripes me to see a musician of such virtuosity going to waste. One of my numerous unrealised ambitions is to bring him to Australia, if only for the benefit of that handful of people who would know enough to attend his concerts.

No doubt it would be another loss, and I have to admit that in material terms my dedication to jazz has not been rewarding. Contrary to popular belief, in all my years of conducting jazz radio programmes I did not even receive more than a dozen or so free recordings from distributors. One of the few companies which occasionally sent me a free recording was Swaggie, owned by Nevill Sherburn, and I suspect the reason for this generosity was that I allowed the pianist Earl Hines to record free for this label when he was in Australia in 1972. But things are looking up in this regard. By 1979 I was writing regular jazz reviews for the Adelaide *News* and Australian *Playboy*, and these publications are somewhat more generous with review copies of records.

Often I am asked 'What is jazz?' and I can only answer that, to me, jazz is improvisation. The mark of a true jazz musician is the ability to improvise so that none of his solos are ever quite the same. Louis Armstrong made the classic comment that 'Asking a jazz musician to play something twice in exactly the same way is like going up to a bird in a tree and saying "How's that again?"' Perhaps there's nothing very new about this talent for improvisation. Gene Krupa often admiringly proclaimed that in his opinion Bach was the greatest improviser of them all!

When I listen to jazz musicians who lack this talent the result leaves me cold. For example, take the celebrated French pianist Jacques Loussier. He and his trio are technically superb, but I feel that when they play one of their jazz renditions of Bach it is note-for-note the same as it was the night before — and two years before that. I get the impression that when they break loose and improvise the resulting music is much less coherent.

True jazz has a fragile and elusive quality. Few achieve it consistently and I feel that talented youngsters are not appearing fast enough to replace the vanishing 'innovators'. But maybe this is just another manifestation of advancing age . . . like the time when I learnt to my horror that I was the 'conservative' member of an art-judging panel.

24

A Taste of Paddo

THERE WAS never a dull moment during our life in Sydney and especially in Paddington. The population of that suburb was very mixed, to say the least. A number of the terrace houses were being taken over and modernised by fashionable young couples, but a good many of them still were let to some very temporary tenants. The house right next door to us was occupied in fairly quick succession by a pop guitarist who practised with his amplifier turned up to full volume and swamped every telephone conversation in the gallery; by a man who set the kitchen on fire and had to be rescued by one of my customers, who swarmed over the dividing wall with a fire extinguisher, saturated his suit while putting out the fire, and naturally departed without buying anything; and eventually by an example of 'the eternal triangle'.

This trio consisted of an aggressive bar-tender husband, a slight and attractive brunette wife, and a male lodger. Frequently we heard loud arguments emanating from their kitchen window, from time to time culminating in a punch-up, but all we could do was wonder why the husband did not throw out the lodger or vice versa.

The climax came when we had two Adelaide friends, Fred Thonemann and Pam Cleland, staying in my original apartment. On a Saturday night they dined at a restaurant, returned to the apartment, and as they were preparing for bed heard angry quarrelling and heavy thumps through the bedroom wall. They had been forewarned about our battling neighbours and so did not think much about it. They went to sleep, and next morning I opened the front door to collect the Sunday papers only to see the street swarming with police.

Apparently the husband had returned from his bar-tending job at about midnight and immediately launched into a violent argument with his wife. She concluded it by taking to him with a meat tenderiser and then finishing him off by stabbing him seventeen times with a carving knife in the head, chest, and groin.

Our local publican told me that when she had completed the job of carving up her husband she carried the dripping knife to the lodger's room and exhorted him 'Come quickly — I think I've done him in!'

With admirable aplomb he responded 'Go away. I'll have a look in the morning!'

On that Sunday morning the police seemed to be taking the place apart. Passers-by could see clearly into the blood-spattered living-room, and my daughter Nicole and one of her friends walked along the flat roof of the gallery to gaze into the kitchen. They were just in time to see a police officer placing the bloodstained carving knife into a plastic bag.

At about the same time as this murder I had a slight involvement with the law on my own account. A young woman whom we had known in Adelaide was arrested for possession of stolen Qantas tickets, and it appeared that she had come by them through her friendship with another person whom we had met briefly in Adelaide.

Our young friend was all alone in the big city and naturally she called upon me as a character witness. I thought it better not to tell her that the last time I had appeared in that capacity, for one of my speedway riders, he got eighteen months!

In due course I found myself in the witness box in the Waverley magistrate's court. The accused's lawyer asked me how long I had known her, and where, and I replied that we had been acquainted for six or seven years and that we had met her at the home of an Adelaide identity who frequently entertained artists, musicians, writers, and politicians.

'Even police prosecutors?' he asked.

Thinking of Eb Scarfe, I answered 'Yes, even police prosecutors.'

After a brief cross-examination I was dismissed. I understood that things were looking bad for our friend, and so I was surprised when she phoned me with the jubilant news that her case had been dismissed. She said that my appearance had swung the case in her favour because, it seemed, the magistrate knew me and was favourably impressed by my evidence. Apparently I had flown the magistrate around a number of times during the war, but I have not the slightest recollection of these aerial encounters.

Fortunately our other neighbours in Victoria Street, Paddington, were somewhat more law-abiding. They included Yvonne Holland, a striking and well-endowed blonde who lived with her boyfriend Bob in a dilapidated terrace house only two doors from the gallery. The house also was occupied by sundry cats and birds and two smelly Australian terriers appropriately named Filthy and Silky.

She was a generous and intelligent person with a wide circle of friends, including our son Tim. Whever he 'went missing' we could be fairly sure of finding him in her company. On fine Saturday afternoons she was usually to be found sunning herself in a tattered moquette armchair she had dragged across to the opposite side of the narrow street, clad in a transparent nightie and holding court like a latter-day Queen of Sheba.

Such colourful characters as Yvonne lent a pleasantly Bohemian atmosphere to the neighbourhood of the gallery and it fascinated our visitors. The most astute of these was Benno Schmidt, from the great New York stockbroking firm of J. H. Whitney & Company. Benno was on the board of the American Arts Administration and also of the Chase Manhattan Bank, which had substantial property interests in Australia and was a leading patron of the visual arts in America.

On his first visit to Australia as an emissary of the bank he was so taken by the land around Esperance in Western Australia that he bought a property which he named Orleans Farm. On subsequent visits he filled the unpretentious farmhouse with superb examples of contemporary Australian art, and he was kind enough to say that he obtained the best of his collection from the Bonython Gallery. These included my Drysdales *Margaret Olley* and *The Drover's Wife* as well as paintings by Donald Friend, Clifton Pugh, Godfrey Miller, and John Perceval.

On one of his regular visits to Australia he brought his son Tom with him. Tom was about nineteen: a tall, fair, handsome youngster obviously looking forward to his first visit to Esperance. My daughter Robyn, then the same age as Tom, joined us for a pleasant dinner on the night before they left for Orleans Farm.

The next we heard was that, less than twenty-four hours later, Tom had been killed in a head-on collision between a truck and the farm motor cycle he was riding. One cannot imagine a more desolate journey than that which Benno made on his way back to America, with Tom's body in the baggage compartment of the aircraft.

Another prominent visitor to the Bonython Gallery was the jazz musician Benny Goodman. Despite my friendship with his former drummer, Gene Krupa, I had never met Benny and he was one of the few jazz musicians to visit Australia in the 1960s and early 1970s who did not come out for my organisation. Benny had made several tours of Europe for the English promoter Robert Paterson, who had dealings with another Australian entrepreneur. This link caused Paterson to offer him to the other man, but when Benny came to Australia his road manager was my old bass-playing friend Jack Lesberg, who brought him to an opening at the gallery.

It was intended to be merely a courtesy visit, but he stayed for two-and-a-half hours. He collected modern art and as he viewed the exhibition he told me proudly about his daughter Rachel, whom he claimed to be such a good painter that two of her works hung in his home surrounded by Renoirs, Cézannes, and Monets.

As we shook hands on his departure I said 'Benny, there's only one thing wrong with this tour of yours: you came for the wrong promoter!' He answered 'Kym, I've got to tell you that you've got a better gallery than you've got artists!'

TOP: Kym Bonython with actor Raymond Burr, of *Ironside* and *Perry Mason* fame, in Sydney 1962. BOTTOM: Marlene and Clifton Pugh at Cottles Bridge, with Barry Humphries' 'Fox Riding for a Fall' in foreground (*Author's photo*)

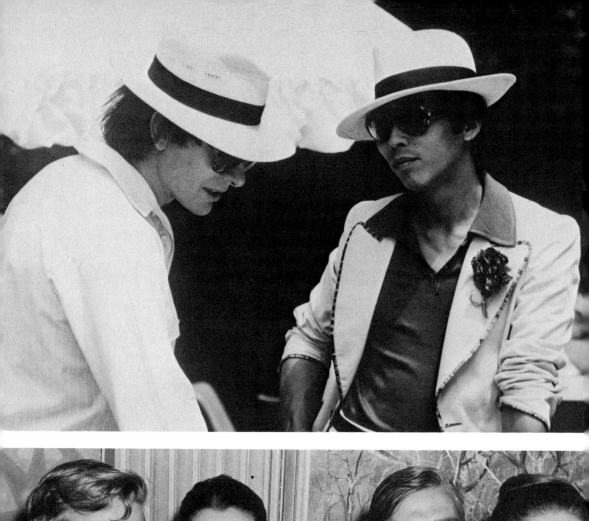

In jazz circles, Benny Goodman is notorious for his frugality and the stories about it are legion. One states that on a bleak Connecticut night his band was rehearsing in a building adjoining his house. It was unheated, and after a while the girl singer said hesitantly 'Benny, it's really cold in here.'

'You think so?' he asked, and left the building. The band thought he had gone to turn on the heat, but after a few minutes he returned wearing a pullover.

One of Benny's sidemen of the 1940s joined his former leader for a date about twenty years afterwards, and later told another ex-Goodman player 'I did a gig with Benny last week. You know, he's changed.'

'I don't believe it!'

'Yes, he's worse!'

But Benny Goodman is not the only man with a keen eye for the value of a dollar. In 1976 the gallery received several letters addressed to artists whose works we had exhibited, and we dutifully sent them on. Some time later, one of the artists concerned showed me a copy of this letter. It was from a very well-known architect, who had been commissioned to design a new Australian Embassy in Europe. The letter I saw, and I can presume only that the others were in similar terms, expressed interest in buying the artist's work for display in the Embassy and asked specifically that any dealings that eventuated should be directly between architect and artist. Apparently the intention was to avoid paying any commission to the gallery which had done so much to help establish the artists' reputations.

Art galleries are of vital importance to artists, especially when they are trying to make a name for themselves. They must have a reputable and attractive venue in which to exhibit their paintings, and an agent to take care of the business dealings. The owner of an art gallery provides them with both these essentials plus many more. I used to receive scores of requests to look at artists' work in a variety of media and I never refused, but eventually I was forced to ask them to bring a few representative pieces of work to the gallery before I viewed the entire range. Otherwise I found I was spending the greater part of my days travelling to and from far distant studios.

Ninety-nine per cent of such contacts were fruitless so far as I was concerned but the one per cent makes up for time wasted. For example, the young Sydney artist Neil Taylor brought me some work at a time when he had never exhibited anywhere. I took to it at once and in the years since then we have sold everything he has produced. He has proved to be one of our more promising younger artists.

Unfortunately one is not infallible and I have sad memories of turning down the work of a young Melbourne artist recommended to me by Charles Bush. The artist sent me a collection of his work painted in England but it did not appeal to me. I thought it was a cross between typical English abstract landscapes and the work of Brett Whiteley, who in turn was

TOP: Film director Peter Weir (*left*) with artist Francis Yin at Mounty Lofty 1978 (*Author's photo*). BOTTOM: At the launching of Kym Bonython's book *Modern Australian Painting and Sculpture* in Adelaide 1960. *From left* Kym·Bonython, Julie Bonython, Laurie Thomas, Josephine Heysen (*News photo*)

influenced by Lloyd Rees. I turned it down and lived to regret it. The artist was Bill Delafield Cook, now one of the best-known contemporary Australian painters. He exhibits regularly in the Redfern Galleries in London and in many European galleries, where his paintings bring high prices. The work he does now is almost unrecognisably different from that he originally submitted to me, but I should have spotted his potential. Pop star Elton John owns six of his paintings.

The pleasures of running an art gallery include the great cross-section of 'types' one encounters and all the odd minor experiences which keep life interesting. These range from the Hong Kong contact who wrote to me as 'Dear Mr Gallery' to the strange inhabitants of the world of art criticism. I have enjoyed meeting many of these, even though I have sometimes found their writings totally incomprehensible, such as those by Dr Donald Brook who wrote the art reviews for the *Sydney Morning Herald* before he took up the Chair of Fine Arts at Flinders University in Adelaide. I really believe that his erudite columns did more to turn people away from enjoyment and appreciation of modern art than they did to help them understand it.

Apart from the artists, sculptors, weavers, and other creative people who have exhibited in my galleries I have been equally lucky in my staff. By the time I closed the Sydney gallery I was working with a fine assembly of people headed by Robin Gibson, who was with me for my whole nine years in the east. Marie de Teliga, wife of the artist Stan de Teliga, and Jennie Bowes looked after the paperwork and doubled as sales assistants, while Jennie Barrett of the brewing family was our receptionist. But perhaps the most colourful was a young Chinese man, Francis Yin, who was with me for several years interrupted by a brief period as actor and set designer with the Nimrod Theatre.

During an exhibition of paintings by Bryan Westwood an obviously Jewish visitor approached Francis and in a conspiratorial whisper offered $2,000 for a painting catalogued at $3,500.

Francis was highly indignant and said 'This isn't a cut-rate department store. We don't indulge in bargaining. The price is three thousand five hundred dollars.'

'But don't you understand—I'm offering you two thousand *cash*. You'd be well advised to consider this offer seriously.'

Francis replied 'Listen—the answer is *no*! We Chinks can be just as tough as you Jews!'

Francis came from Singapore in 1967, and in 1974 he became a naturalised Australian. One of fourteen children, he is a nephew of Leslie Charteris, the author of the world-famous 'Saint' series, who also has Chinese blood. Francis was in charge of my print collection, and he soon proved that one of his greatest attributes was his ability to set up spectacular exhibitions of ceramics, jewellery, and paintings. He himself is an artist of ability who has won several art prizes, and he is a man of great vivacity and humour. One day a friend was driving him along Sydney's busy Oxford Street when they were constantly blocked by a car in front. When at last they drew alongside Francis saw that it was occupied by Chinese, and to their consternation he rolled down the window and yelled 'Bloody Chinks!'

It distressed me when I had to bid farewell to my Sydney staff but there was no help for it. The recession grew worse and although there was still a demand for art our turnover fell away to such a degree that it was no longer economical to pay the running costs of such a large gallery. I put the building on the market and in late 1976 it was purchased by an American advertising agency for their Australian headquarters.

When the news spread that the gallery was for sale one of the papers asked me for a story on why I had decided to leave Sydney. They photographed me standing in the courtyard with our loyal Alsatian, Mischa, by my side, and on the day after the article appeared a woman arrived at the gallery armed with a sheaf of photographs and accompanied by a vet. She took one look at Mischa, burst into tears, and ran to her calling 'Lassie, Lassie!'

It turned out that she had owned Lassie/Mischa since the Alsatian was a pup. During her ownership the dog had rescued two of her children from drowning and saved her from a beating by her husband. The Alsatian heard her screams and crashed through a window to grab her husband by the throat. Apart from these dramatic events the bitch had borne no less than sixty-four pups, as her pendulous belly attested.

But one morning Lassie simply vanished, and her owner gave her up for lost until she saw the photograph in the paper—five years later. It was impossible to say what had happened to her in between.

Luckily the previous owner did not want to take Lassie/Mischa away from us. She simply wanted to ensure that it was her dog and that it had a good home. In 1979, aged more than fifteen, Mischa sleeps contentedly under my mother's grand piano at Eurilla.

In order to close down the gallery with a bang rather than a whimper we mounted a glamorous final exhibition comprising a large show of paintings and drawings by Bryan Westwood, plus a representative display provided by artists whom we had represented during our years in Sydney. We called it our 'Requiem Exhibition' and sent out black-edged invitations to all our friends and patrons.

They responded in like spirit. Roger Meadmore, the Adelaide restaurateur, flyer, and balloonist came dressed as an undertaker. His girlfriend, Genie, was attired in a long black gown with a full black veil. Clive Evatt, an opposition art dealer, arrived with cardboard crocodile tears on his lapel.

Don Burrows and his jazz group performed for us as they had during the opening exhibition, and when it was nearly time for them to pack up I asked Don 'How about closing with something appropriate—like "Wish Me Luck as You Wave Me Goodbye".'

'What about this?' he said, and led the band in 'There'll Never Be Another You'. It was an emotional moment!

Shortly before Christmas 1976 we were busily clearing away and packing up when a sturdily-built grey-haired lady came to my office. Challengingly she said 'Mr Bonython? I've had a bone to pick with you for a long time now!'

Slightly alarmed, I asked her what was on her mind. She said 'In 1943 my husband and I spent our wedding night at Foley's Hotel in Jervis Bay. You and some of your Air Force friends had a jazz band going in the room next to ours and you kept us awake for most of the night.'

For once the perfect answer presented itself. 'Surely you should have been grateful, not annoyed?'

25

'Oh, Didn't He Ramble'

WHERE ELSE but in South Australia would one expect to see Lord Snowdon ordered off private property for taking photographs which included a semi-nude sculpture? I was a fascinated participant in this scenario which I feel nicely exemplifies the mores of my home State.

It happened in November 1977. A Sydney advertising agency had approached me on behalf of their client American Express, and invited me to participate in that company's advertising campaign for 1978. Most people saw the campaign, which consisted of a series of press advertisements featuring such people as the golfer Jack Nicklaus, Gucci the Italian fashion designer, Wayne Reid the tennis player and administrator, and Bruce Gyngell, Chairman of the Australian Broadcasting Tribunal.

Each participant gave a short interview on his attitudes to life and business, with some emphasis on the usefulness of an American Express credit card to men like myself who have to do a lot of travelling.

I agreed to take part in the campaign, and the agency told me that Lord Snowdon would like to photograph me seated on my MV Agusta motor cycle. I queried whether this fitted in with the requisite image of 'serious and successful businessmen' but they still liked the idea and I went along with it.

Snowdon and an agency representative arrived at Eurilla late one November afternoon when the evening shadows were lengthening and Snowdon quickly spotted 'Miss Jones' standing beguilingly in the hallway. He spied a sunny patch in the valley below the house and decided it would be an ideal location for the photographic session—and that 'Miss Jones' must come along too. We quickly set off to make use of the remaining sunlight.

We passed through Piccadilly Valley into Careys Gully, and Snowdon suddenly called a halt alongside a thick forest of pine trees. The agency man went to the nearby homestead to ask permission for us to photograph there, and when this was given we unloaded the sculpture and set to work. A teenage boy with a golf club came from the house to watch us for a while, and then drifted away again.

221

Snowdon exposed a few rolls of film and then we left 'Miss Jones' leaning against a tree and started another series of shots, showing me among the trees and silhouetted against the declining sun. At this point a stern-looking gentleman approached us from the house and observed procedures stonily from about ten yards away, until Snowdon called for 'Miss Jones' to be brought into the picture again.

As soon as the agency man carried her into sight, our observer became quite agitated. He snapped 'I do not want you photographing that object on my property!'

We were rather flabbergasted, but Snowdon most charmingly asked the property owner for his reasons and pointed out that the sculpture was by an artist of world renown, whose works were owned by some of the greatest overseas galleries. It made no difference. The property owner said only 'You have your standards—I have mine. I do not want you photographing that thing on my property!'

He was quite within his rights and there was nothing to do but pack up and call it a day. Snowdon returned to Eurilla next morning and completed his assignment, during which he exposed about fifty rolls of film.

I thought the incident was amusing enough to pass on to one of the local papers but in fact did nothing about it. However, a journalist called me a couple of days later, saying somewhat belatedly that he had heard Snowdon had been in town and asking whether I had any story for him.

I told him about the incident on condition that he read back to me exactly what he intended to print. I expected that a small paragraph would appear in the *Sunday Mail*, but when the reporter rang back the story was a good deal longer than I'd expected. Nevertheless I approved it, but I was not given the opportunity to approve the headlines attached by the newspaper. The story occupied the front page of the *Sunday Mail*, with a massive headline proclaiming 'Banned—because of Her! Hills farmer tells Tony to shove off!'

The story was picked up by the Sydney newspapers and reprinted in abbreviated form, and I'm told that Snowdon was none too happy about it. I wrote to him and explained what had happened, apologised, and remarked that he of all people should be aware of the unpredictability of the press. He did not reply!

By the time of that incident my life had turned in yet another direction. Ironically, I had decided to return to Adelaide partly because it would enable me to be near my aged and very sick mother, but she died less than five months after our return. The end must have been a welcome relief for her as she said often that she longed to be released from suffering. On her last day her doctor told me that she had contracted a touch of pneumonia, but there seemed no need to make more than my usual daily visit on the way home to Eurilla from the gallery. But when I arrived at the hospital I was alarmed by her condition. She was breathing noisily and did not seem to comprehend the presence of my sister Katherine and myself. On the way to the hospital I had called at the North Adelaide nursing home where her old friend Marjorie Bagot was a patient, but when I told her that Marjorie sent her love there was no response. Katherine repeated the message loudly into her ear and she nodded and said 'That's nice.'

I left the hospital and drove home, and soon after that Katherine rang to say it was all over. Twelve weeks later, on 11 September 1977, the family carried out her desire for her ashes to be scattered under the huge cedar tree in the garden at Eurilla. Warren, the eldest of her three children, led the ceremony, which he opened by reading the last two verses of a poem she wrote in 1922 and called 'The Paved Path, Eurilla':

> *To the blue sky a mighty cedar raises*
> *Its sombre boughs where cones like candles cling*
> *And, as of old, I know that God has chosen*
> *The cedar for his temple fashioning.*
>
> *Beneath its spreading shade I reverent stand*
> *And prayers of praise, like breath borne butterflies*
> *Are wafted out to Infinity*
> *To Him who gave me this Paradise.*

We scattered the ashes beneath the tree, and she was back at her beloved Eurilla forever.

When I returned to Adelaide I was not altogether sure how I would re-establish myself, but by a happy coincidence I found my original gallery in Jerningham Street, North Adelaide, was up for sale. By that time, Adelaide real estate prices had caught up with Sydney. The price I paid for the gallery alone was twice as much as I had received from the sale of the gallery and an adjoining house.

The gallery was run-down and neglected and I determined to give it a complete facelift before re-opening. This included the installation of a courtyard like that in our Sydney gallery but much smaller, and the building of a large brick storeroom to replace the little galvanised-iron shed in the nondescript back yard.

I found it very easy to fit back into the Adelaide scene where we had so many friends, and after a few months it was almost as though we had never been away. Naturally I was tempted back to Bowden on a number of occasions to see how the Rowley Park Speedway had been getting on since I abandoned the lease, and for old time's sake I generally wore my notorious checkered cap. Maybe this made for easy recognition by habituees of the speedway, but in any case I was certainly touched when one person after another said 'For Chrissake, Kym, buy the bloody place back!' as I moved through the crowds. But this evidence of continuing support was not enough to tempt me back into the business. Apart from that the future of the site was under a constant cloud.

One of the first things I noticed after returning to Adelaide was the desecration of Frome Road, one of Australia's most beautiful thoroughfares. A series of permanent roadway islands, traffic lights, and parking meters had totally changed the character of this peaceful tree-lined boulevard, and I was impelled to write a letter of protest to the *Advertiser*.

Soon after it was published I was approached by a member of the Adelaide City Council. He pointed out that the atmosphere of the city was changing because there were insufficient 'watchdogs' to check the bureaucrats, and asked whether I had thought of standing for the council.

As the French say, this gave me to think. Throughout my formative years I had been very conscious of Father's involvement in the City Council and his tireless efforts to check the march of vandalism in the name of progress. We lived with his oft-repeated catchcry of 'Hands off the parklands! Restore Adelaide to Colonel Light's Vision!'

Light, of course, was the surveyor who laid out the city of Adelaide with its square mile of residences and commercial buildings surrounded by parklands. His design gave Adelaide its superb green belt, but various councillors have had to fight for more than a century—and are still fighting—to save these parks and gardens from being sequestrated for other purposes.

Nevertheless I was a bit dubious about entering politics, even local politics. Soon after I re-opened the North Adelaide gallery I was visited by an old friend and client, Anne Levy, whose scientist-husband had bought several paintings from me before his untimely death. Anne had been elected as a Labor member in the State government, and we chatted about the current speculation as to the man who might be appointed to the then vacant position of State Governor. I said 'If you have any influence with your Party, I hope you'll try to block at least one of those who are supposed to be in the running.'

When she asked whom I was thinking about I said 'Clyde Cameron. He's made no secret of the fact that he thinks all Bonythons should be lined up and shot!'

But Anne said she hoped Cameron would be appointed because at least he might invite her to Government House, a privilege so far denied her, and said 'I'm sure he would make an exception in your case!'

My knowledge that this kind of feeling did exist made me think hard about entering the political arena, but eventually I plunged in and nominated for the Gawler Ward of the metropolitan area. In May 1978 I joined the City Council, and on the day I took the oath of office Alderman John Chappel made a lighthearted presentation ceremony in the members' room. He handed me the wooden coathanger which he had used for hanging his own council robes, and I found that it had belonged to my father and was still inscribed 'Sir Lav.'.

Top: Christopher Bonython, Australian Amateur Golf Champion, with U.S. golfer Jack Nicklaus (*left*) in Sydney 1975 (*Author's photo*). Bottom: Bonython family group, 1978. *From left* Tim, Nicole, Julie, Michael, and Kym (*Elizabeth Johnswood photo*)

Alderman Walter Bridgland, one of the senior members of Council and a former Lord Mayor, asked me whether I intended to follow in Sir Lavington Bonython's footsteps as a doodler. Apparently Father left his mark in this regard, and I had been told by a member of the South Australian Housing Trust, of which Father was Chairman for some years, that one could always tell where he had been sitting during a meeting by the pencil sketches of ladies' legs on his notepad. Like father, like son!

Returning to Adelaide involved some nostalgic link-ups with the past. One of these was a visit to the former family home, St Corantyn on East Terrace. By that time it had become a mental health outpatients' clinic, and I'm sure my father must have turned in his grave at a 1977 press advertisement inviting female volunteers 'who have failed to achieve sexual orgasm' to join a research programme at St Corantyn! I went to a fundraising event organised by some of my friends, and next morning helped them to clean up. When I said farewell to the old house in 1961 I certainly did not visualise that sixteen years later I would be back there vacuuming its floors!

Just before I returned from Sydney a recently-appointed executive of the Australian Dance Theatre, who was a friend from the past, asked me if I would consider joining its board of management. I had two reasons for declining. The first was that ballet dancing is not one of my consuming passions. The second was that it would have been something of a breach of family loyalty, although my friend could not have known this.

The Australian Dance Theatre actually was founded by my niece Elizabeth, daughter of my half-sister Betty Wilson. A fine dancer and teacher, she left the family nest to dance in the Australian production of *My Fair Lady*, and later went to Europe where she joined the troupe of a black American, Eleo Pomare. His company, then based in Holland, was gaining an international reputation. Betty asked me to visit Liz during one of my trips to Europe, by way of checking that all was well with her. On my return home I was able to reassure Betty, but did not mention that Liz's upstairs apartment was situated in the red-light district of Amsterdam with a brothel doing a thriving trade on the ground floor. I had to run the gauntlet of ladies touting for business before I reached her flat.

Liz returned to Australia, created the Australian Dance Theatre, and became its guiding spirit. Years later she was rather cruelly voted out of office by new members of its board, and this disillusionment caused her to leave Australia to settle in Italy.

Earlier in this book I've touched on my appearance in the TV show *This Is Your Life*. This happened after my return to Adelaide. Viewers of this popular programme will know that its success depends upon surprising the personalities featured, but I thought that I would be too wary a bird to be caught. Friends occasionally told me that I would be a 'natural' for the programme but I always responded 'If I ever am, there's no way I wouldn't know about it before it happened. They won't surprise me.' How wrong I was!

TOP: Barry Humphries creating 'Pus in Boots' for *This Is Your Life*, Sydney 1977 (*Strawberry Photography*). BOTTOM: Julie Bonython with Lord Snowdon at Mount Lofty 1977 (*Author's photo*)

The programme is a miracle of staffwork as they deal simultaneously with about twelve programmes in advance. Anyone who believes a woman can't keep a secret should know about the way that Julie was in repetitive telephone contact with Sydney's Channel 7 for months before the programme, and I hadn't the slightest idea of what was going on.

Everything was very cunningly arranged. In September 1977 I received an invitation from Louis James, the Adelaide artist who had become a firm friend during my gallery days and was then living in Sydney, for Julie and me to attend a 'surprise birthday party' that he was arranging for his wife. Of course I accepted and we travelled over to Sydney.

Louis had made a strong point of the fact that I must arrive at six p.m. to coincide with the arrangements for the 'surprise party' and we turned up on time. I sensed certain mysterious undercurrents but I naturally associated these with the 'surprise party'. Some old friends of mine had a house just across the road and I was strongly tempted to stroll across and have a word with them but everyone persuaded me to stay inside and, again, I thought this was to do with the party arrangements. Certainly I did not guess that everyone was on tenterhooks in case I left the house and saw the Channel 7 crew and their equipment assembling outside in readiness for the invasion.

The surprise was complete, and I was staggered when one of the 'guests' at the party suddenly said 'Kym Bonython . . . This Is Your Life!'

From that moment onwards I was astonished by the steady flow of people, some of whom I had not seen for a good many years, and by the amazing organisation which had brought them all together. I may not have found my eyes overflowing, as has happened to some people who have appeared on the programme, but it was certainly an emotional and nostalgic experience.

The assembled guests were representative of a complete cross-section of my life until then, and when we were talking together it was a kind of two-dimensional experience because my mind was full of more memories than it was possible to put into words . . . or to discuss on a family-type programme that ran for only thirty minutes. Talking with Reg Rechner about R.A.A.F. days made me remember countless personalities from that era, including that hard case Lieutenant Dennis George, R.A.N.R., and his proposed slogan 'Vote for George for Grog and Grummet'. I remembered that people who shared his galvanised-iron living quarters at Nowra claimed that throughout the night he 'emitted noises from every orifice'.

Other memories from those days include the problems of going on leave to Adelaide when I was stationed at Laverton, especially when leave was granted at short notice. Transport was scarce in those wartime years, but on one occasion the Rail Transport Officer at Adelaide took pity on my plight and smuggled me onto a hospital train carrying sick and wounded to the eastern States. I had to go to bed in one of the specially-equipped carriages, and at every stop along the way the train was invaded by

226

sympathetic lovelies who showered the casualties with kisses, praise, commiseration, cakes, and the chocolates which were so scarce in those days. I submerged my guilt feelings without too much trouble.

There were grimmer memories, too, sometimes with that touch of gallows humour so typical of wartime. For example the story of the super-efficient Adjutant at the airfield on Evans Head, which we sometimes used when patrolling against Japanese submarines along the coast of New South Wales. Every day at eleven a.m. sharp this Adjutant gave the fire crew a workout by sounding the alarm. Truck and crew screeched to a halt outside his window, tumbled out with hoses and other gear, and pretended to put out a fire in an imaginary aircraft.

Unfortunately these exercises were literally 'dry runs' and no one ever turned on the hoses. One day the siren blared at its accustomed hour and the fire crew rushed up as usual, but found there had been a genuine crash on another runway. By that time the aircraft was blazing furiously. They sped over to the crash, assembled their gear with accustomed precision, and turned on the valves. But the hoses had been incorrectly fitted, so that they sucked air instead of gushing foam. I don't remember whether the hapless pilot escaped from the blaze.

Reg and I shared memories of Darwin days, and of the time when the Japanese came so close to victory, but fortunately we never had to fly anything as antiquated as the Vildebeest aircraft used by the R.A.F. in a vain attempt to combat the Japanese in Malaya. Allegedly these were so slow that when a pilot released a couple of homing pigeons from one of them, at the extreme limit of his patrol, they beat him back to base.

I could have 'opened the hangar door' with Reg Rechner almost indefinitely but there were others waiting for me — especially Jack Murray. (Incidentally I was one of the guests when he was featured in *This Is Your Life*, so we had two goes at each other!) If time had permitted I would have brought up the story of Jack's D-type Jaguar, one of the first ever seen in Australia. Jack worked out a system which allowed him to take the D-type out for a fast spin down Curlewis Street, along Bondi Esplanade at speeds touching 100 m.p.h. through the lunch-hour crowds, and back to the garage in time to throw a tarpaulin over the car only seconds before the cops caught up with him. When they enquired 'Have you been out in your Jaguar today, Mr Murray?' he said innocently 'What, me? She's been here under the tarpaulin all the time.'

This worked until a suspicious policeman leant against the exhaust pipe and nearly burnt his leg off.

Another person from my speedway days was the widow of 'Two-Gun' Bob Tattersall, whom Channel 7 had brought from America specially to appear on the programme. She too brought back many memories, particularly those of all the other American drivers whom I had brought to Rowley Park over the years, and of Duke Donaldson, the promoter of Long Island's

Freeport Speedway. He had become a long-term acquaintance after I was introduced to him by Don Millager, my friend from schooldays at St Peter's . . . which seems to be some kind of example of life's interweaving strands.

Duke was a great promoter and a fast man with a wisecrack. When I visited America at the time when Harold Mertz had launched his collection of Australian paintings in Washington we were taken to tea at the White House. It was during the presidency of Lyndon B. Johnson, and when Duke heard about this he said sarcastically 'If you want afternoon tea my advice is to go to *Howard* Johnson's . . . at least *they* know what they're doing!' (Howard Johnson's is a chain of restaurants in America.)

Duke had a curious sideline to his speedway activities—he sold velvet linings for coffins. Maybe he thought that the two things went together somehow.

My speedway days were so full of colourful and unusual characters that they could fill a book on their own. Some have fallen by the wayside: others have gone on to international fame. The latter include Ivan Mauger, who by 1979 was able to write his own ticket for speedway appearances. He owns no less than twenty-two racing bikes, each of which is permanently located at one of the world's major speedways on which he appears, and a condition of his contracts with these speedways is that he should be transported everywhere by a chauffeur-driven Rolls Royce!

Another of my speedway mates is Ted Polgreen, who lives near another friend, Dr Dick Burnett, in a seaside suburb of Adelaide. One night Ted appeared at Dick's front door, whitefaced and distraught. He exclaimed 'Doc! Doc! You gotta come quickly! Our dog's been run over and the wife's having hysterics!'

Dick protested he knew nothing about animals but Ted dragged him from his fireside. The badly-injured dog, which had been hit by a motor bike, was in Ted's lounge, where Dick first prescribed a sedative for his wife and then examined the animal. He was insisting that Ted should call a veterinary surgeon when there was a knock at the door. The caller enquired 'Has the doctor arrived yet? He has? Then do you think he could have a look at the motor bike rider who hit the dog? He's still lying unconscious in the gutter!'

One item which could have made a spectacular appearance on *This Is Your Life*, although I'm sure Julie would have forbidden it, is the huge Rick Harvey Memorial Trophy which commemorated a great race driver of the 1950s. Rick was a motor cycle policeman who died after an accident on duty and the trophy was commissioned by admirers in his memory. Aesthetically the trophy is horrific and Julie hated it. I won it in 1960 and she heaved a sigh of relief when I had to return it at the end of the year. But I won it again . . . and yet again. She suffered it for three years in all. Nowadays the winner receives a small replica and the trophy remains on the premises of the Racing Drivers Association.

My jazz and entrepreneurial days were well represented on the TV programme by such personalities as Eric Child, Dick Hughes, and Graeme Bell, who recalled the days when I played with his band in the Tramways Hall, Adelaide. Also there was a film clip of Dave Brubeck, taken in America for the programme.

I wished that many more of my music-making acquaintances could have been present, simply for the pleasure of meeting them again. Men like the great trumpeter Chet Baker, whose unforgettable opening gambit when introduced to Italy's leading jazz pianist Romano Mussolini, son of the late dictator, was 'Sorry to hear about your father!' And that much-neglected organist Les Strand, whom I hope to bring to Adelaide to play on the $450,000 Festival Theatre organ during my time on the Board of Governors of the Adelaide Festival of Arts . . . and of course my old friend Eddie Condon. One of my prized possessions is a tape-recording I made outside his Greenwich Village club, in the early hours of a June morning.

The group chatting there included Eddie's doorman, who was about to take orders in the Roman Catholic Church. Eddie assured us that 'When this guy rings the bells during Mass he'll come on like Hamp'—an allusion to Lionel Hampton, the most famous of vibes players.

Eddie once played at the White House and received a letter of thanks from the President. He wrote back 'Boss—your letter was a surprise. A pleasant one! Don't lose my address. Playing the Bleached House would be my all-time Valentine.'

Thinking of those jazz days reminds me of my drive south from New York to New Orleans. Cruising along the Pennsylvania Turnpike at a comfortable seventy m.p.h. I was startled to be overtaken by a funeral procession headed by a hearse, all belting along at more than eighty. I trust they didn't pass through a township further on, where a signboard welcomed visitors with the warning 'Thirty Days Hath September, April, June, and November—And Anyone Exceeding 50 m.p.h. Through This Town!'

Channel 7 had assembled a formidable team to represent my involvement with modern Australian art, including Sidney Nolan, Pro Hart, Lloyd Rees, John Coburn, Barry Humphries, and John Laws, the Sydney radio personality. John, who was made an O.B.E. for his services to broadcasting, became a close friend during our Sydney years.

I've already written about Barry's 'Pus in Boots' creation which he served up for the programme. By that time he was a household name, but I think it's fair to say that in all his activities he's only 'doing what comes naturally'. I always like the story of his early days, before Mrs Everage became as well-known in Britain as she is in Australia, when he was conducting a Melbourne radio session entitled 'Mrs Everage Selects'. The show was sponsored by a carpet dealer named Kopolov. In the intervals between such well-trodden favourites as *Bluebird of Happiness*, *Laugh, Clown, Laugh*, and *Merry Widow Waltz*, Barry would deliver commercials

229

for Kopolov carpets. One of them ran 'Ladies, have you seen Mr Kopolov's piles lately? You'd be amazed at their length and texture! Feel them for yourselves! And remember, ladies, if you go to Mr Kopolov now you can be made and laid by Christmas!'

By 1977, of course, I had had to leave my Sydney gallery behind me. Meeting my friends again brought back many nostalgic memories of Paddington days, and I could only wish that I had been able to command such fabulous customers as the American collector John Pierpont Morgan, who was so rich that in the 1890s he was able to save the U.S. government from a financial crisis by lending them gold. It is said of him that when he was handed the massive catalogue issued by the London art dealer Agnew's he ticked four items and said 'I'll buy everything except those that I've marked.'

I greatly wished that June Jacobsen could have lived long enough to see the programme. If she could have appeared on it, I'd have reminded her of the likeable youth whom we employed one year to help out in the Christmas rush. He made a great hit with June, and when the staff were exchanging presents just before closing down for Christmas he gave her an unusual pot plant. It turned out to be a 'pot' plant in more ways than one . . . and it had been grown in the gardens of Government House!

Naturally my family was represented on the programme. They were there in person apart from my daughter Robyn Cass who has four times made me a proud grandfather. She was in London, but Channel 7 took a film of her and had it flown out for the occasion.

Warren had plenty to say about my peculiar tastes in food, including the breakfasts of sausages, ice cream, and ginger ale at the Menzies Hotel. I always claim that I'm on a seafood diet. I see food, and I eat it.

Unfortunately this causes a constant Battle of the Bulge, but I try to win this by a little exercise each day. Not too much, of course, because I remember the story of the ninety-year-old who was asked whether he attributed his advanced age to regular exercise. He answered 'The only exercise I do is to act as pallbearer for my friends who do exercises!'

However my conscience occasionally compels me to work out at a health club, and during one of these periods I was 'rowing' alongside an even heftier person than myself. He gasped 'Business is bloody terrible, but after this the rest of the day doesn't seem so bad!'

Warren also mentioned the way I financed my first drum kit by selling my clothes, but I had a comeback. In 1973, Warren had extended his love of bushwalking into a walk across the Simpson Desert. He was accompanied by the artist Charles McCubbin, but they realised they could not backpack all their supplies and equipment across the desert. After many experiments they developed a 'manpowered' trailer, to pull in tandem across deep sand and rocky ridges, and with this in mind I told Warren 'Anyone who pulls a trailer on foot across the Simpson Desert has got to be crazier than I am!'

I wished that more of my family could have been present, including my cousin John Bray. Learned and dignified as a member of the South Australian bar, especially during his term as Chief Justice, he is completely unassuming in private life. He derives constant pleasure from South Australia's splendid beaches and on one occasion some friends took him by boat to Maslins Beach, which had recently been declared open for nude swimmers. John donned his bathing trunks and swam ashore from the boat, and as he waded onto the beach he was greeted by my nephew Andrew Wilson (now Judge Wilson) and his fiancée, both in a state of nature. John chatted to them for a while, and then as he said good-bye he told the girl 'I can't say that I hope to see more of you, but I hope to see you again soon!'

Like every fond father I have a store of childhood anecdotes to trot out on every possible occasion but I'll confine myself to one. It concerns a trip to Vila in New Caledonia which I made with Julie and Michael when the latter was about eleven. Our return flight was delayed and we had to sit around for hours in what was then a somewhat primitive air terminal, devoid even of a fan or refreshment bar despite the heat and humidity. At one point I noticed that Michael had slipped away and when he returned I asked 'Where have you been?'

'Having a drink.'

'A drink? Where did you get it?'

He pointed to the men's room. I didn't remember that there was a drinking fountain there and so I told him to show me just where he had been drinking. He led me into the toilet and pointed to a *pissoire*, an item of French plumbing which he had never seen before.

The incident reminded me of another misinterpretation of French customs, when Julie and I were in Paris soon after our marriage. We decided to lunch at one of the most celebrated of Parisian restaurants, but when we looked at the menu we discovered that it made no provision for ignorant tourists and was written in French. Perhaps in desperation, Julie ordered the only dish she had heard of before. It was Steak Tartare.

With a flourish, the waiter presented her with a delicately prepared mound of raw minced steak topped with a raw egg. She eyed it uncertainly, and then hesitantly asked the waiter if he could take it back to the kitchen and 'Cook it a little more.'

The waiter's shrug and upturned eyes eloquently conveyed his feelings about such barbarians.

If I restrain myself from childhood anecdotes I cannot resist boasting a little about my children's present achievements. Christopher was the amateur golf champion of Australia and of South Australia, and one of the most popular and respected champions in the golfing history of this State, while Michael is following rapidly in his footsteps. Tim became a still and movie photographer and one of his exhibitions of prints drew high praise from Sydney critics in 1978. John Laws wrote for the catalogue of that exhibition

'Tim Bonython is a marvellous example of a product of his environment. He has obviously inherited a great deal of his father's strong sensitivity and understanding of form, and his mother's natural flair and style.'

I think that Nicole also has inherited Julie's 'flair and style'. She has already shown a natural ability to follow in her mother's footsteps as a fashion model.

The TV programme would have gone on for a very long time if it had included all the friends and relations whom I would have liked to be there. As it was, some of it had to be cut out because of time restrictions when it was edited for final viewing. Apart from humans, I would very much like to have included a magpie. The one I have in mind belonged to some neighbours at Tennyson, named Winkler, and they treated their pet magpie rather like a faithful watchdog. Woe betide any unsuspecting trespasser on the Winkler property, because Maggie would race across the lawn like an avenging angel to jab and peck at his legs and ankles.

Maggie was an avid TV fan. Its favourite was Perry Como, and when the singer was performing Maggie perched on the back of the couch watching the screen with unblinking gaze and rocking to and fro in time to the music. If anyone turned off the set Maggie became quite demented.

Like many another TV addict, Maggie would watch the box as long as it was turned on. Occasionally it fell asleep from sheer satiation and dropped like a stone from couch to floor.

This Is Your Life was a useful experience because it brought back so many forgotten memories. I feel that I have led a full and satisfying life, packed full of interest for as long as I can remember. Maybe I've had a little more than my share of good fortune because it would have been so easy for me to end in the wreckage of a Hudson during the war years or in the wreckage of a race car on one of Australia's speedways, but I have had my share of problems and disappointments also. Like every gambler I have won some and lost some, but I always believe that the games have been worth playing.

Maybe I could summarise by quoting a comment which I made when I was living in Paddington. A Sydney newspaper asked me and various other identities how we would like to spend Father's Day, and my answer was 'I'd like to be lying in the sun on a deserted Barrier Reef beach with Faye Dunaway, a plentiful supply of lolly water, unlimited Nudge Bars and no John Valentine's (my gymnasium) tomorrow. Actually I will probably be doing my normal Sunday morning chore—hosing the dog crap off the footpath of Victoria Street, Paddington.'

That's life!

On the night of 6 April 1979 Rowley Park Speedway finally ceased to exist after thirty-one years of operation. It was publicised as a 'nostalgia night' and many celebrated names from the past squeezed into riding leathers or racing clobber for a last appearance on the track where they had earned fame even if not much fortune.

I was one of the old crocks invited to contest one of the car races, in which several drivers even more venerable than myself also faced the starter. Laurie Jamieson bravely loaned me his Offenhauser speed car for the occasion.

TV personality Steve Raymond, who used to be the Sydney Showgrounds speedway commentator, came over to cover the occasion for his national programme and he interviewed me at the wheel of the Offy. He called for a 'typical Rowley Park welcome' for the former promoter, and this evoked an uproar of boos, whistles, and jeers, with a faint sprinkling of cheers. I said into Steve's microphone 'I see the bloody pie eaters are still with us' and this brought on an even louder response. Steve remarked 'I suppose it's not often that a City Councillor has competed at Rowley Park.'

I was uneasily aware that George Tatnell, the former national speed car champion, also was a competitor. I had been on the receiving end of many of his pranks and he did not fail me on this final occasion. He crept up behind me and slapped a massive cream cake across my face. The 'cream' consisted of the contents of a couple of cans of shaving cream. A good deal of this mixture got inside my helmet and I am still trying to scrape its dried remnants out of the lining!

All this went onto Steve's film but the joke was not yet over. When I could see again he asked if I would help his camera crew to take some shots of the Offenhauser before the race started. He asked me to cruise slowly around the track so that the camera car could take a number of shots from various angles and I pushed off accordingly.

I cruised around for several laps at a speed slightly above idling, vainly looking for the camera car. A couple of other drivers whizzed past me but I assumed that they were forming up into position, until the grinning starter suddenly confronted me with the white flag. This signalled that I had only one lap to go! Obviously there had been no camera car, the race was being run, and there was I drifting around with egg (or shaving cream) on my face!

It was too late to make any impression at that stage. I felt bad about it, as my public surely had expected to see me go out in a blaze of glory—or at least with a couple of flips and rolls.

But the crowd enjoyed the joke as I rolled tamely to the end of a speedway career which may not have been very successful but was always spectacular. Maybe I'll have to emerge from retirement for the eighth time just to show that a spark of the old flame still flickers, in the true tradition of 'Per Ardua ad Terra Firma.'

Index

235

237